MOVERS AND SHAKERS
SCALAWAGS AND SUFFRAGETTES

TALES FROM
BELLEFONTAINE
CEMETERY

CAROL FERRING SHEPLEY

Missouri History Museum
St. Louis
Distributed by University of Chicago Press

To Jake and Mimi for their patience,
to Mike Tiemann and Manuel Garcia for sharing their stories,
to Betsy Fordyce for her careful reading,
to Tom Noel for his constant support,
and to Don Streett for getting us started.

© 2008 by the Missouri History Museum
All rights reserved   15   5

Library of Congress Cataloging-in-Publication Data

Shepley, Carol Ferring, 1949-
Movers and Shakers, scalawags and suffragettes : tales from Bellefontaine
Cemetery / Carol Ferring Shepley.
   p. cm.
Includes bibliographical references.
Summary: "The history of Bellefontaine Cemetery in St. Louis is told through
the stories of those who are buried there. Cemetery records and interviews with
insiders inform the research"--Provided by publisher.
ISBN 978-1-883982-86-7 (pbk.)
1. Bellefontaine Cemetery (Saint Louis, Mo.)--History. 2. Saint Louis (Mo.)--
Biography. 3. Saint Louis (Mo.)--History. I. Title.
F474.S262B457 2008
977.8'660099--dc22
              2008046173

Distributed by University of Chicago Press
Printed and bound in the United States by Thomson-Shore, Inc.
Book design by Madonna Gauding
Cover design by Renée Duenow
Color photographs by Robert Pettus

CONTENTS

FOREWORD

AT ONE TIME, THE DEAD were routinely buried in churchyards or unadorned vacant lots set aside for that purpose. When what passed for progress encroached upon the graves, the remains were moved to the next convenient location, or occasionally merely ignored and plowed under. In the early nineteenth century a movement toward more structured burial grounds developed. Cities of the dead, they were called, a rural setting of winding paths, peaceful landscapes, and handsome sculptures that honored both the dead and those they had left behind.

Bellefontaine Cemetery, established in 1849 and dedicated the next year, was an early example of the new kind of graveyard, one meant to be a permanent monument to those who had come and gone before us. In the growing metropolis of St. Louis, the older burial grounds were crowded and deemed unhealthy as well as obstacles to further growth of the city. A group of prominent St. Louisans—"movers and shakers," in common parlance—organized the purchase of a tract of land up on the Bellefontaine Road to be used specifically for a burial park. They hired a landscape architect who immediately developed plans for picturesque pathways and scenic vistas and even reflecting ponds for St. Louis's first garden of the dead. The very year that the work began was the year of a disastrous cholera epidemic that killed more than 10 percent of St. Louis's population. The 4,500 burials would have choked the city's lots while Bellefontaine, far north of the city, would offer a safe and peaceful haven.

Cemeteries became memory places, gardens of remembrance, a tangible reminder of continuity, and affirmation that we are not the first to inhabit this place and will not be the last. A cemetery not far from the small iron mining town where I grew up in Michigan's Upper Peninsula was a backdrop of my youth, a place where I could hear stories of my father's people, where I could feel a connection with those people, most of whom I had never met. I found nothing forlorn or spectral in my visits, not even after my grandmother, whom I loved and knew well, was buried there. I viewed these trips with delighted anticipation because what occurred between the marble stones was a running dialogue, full of marvelous anecdotes and lessons for me to grow on. Here, I realized that I was not alone in the present but that I was connected to the past and to the future. It was in that place that I learned who my people were and learned about myself. Here, I first discovered the ties that extended from me back in time, and here I could imagine that they would also extend beyond my own lifetime into a future inhabited by others.

These are the lessons we can take from cemeteries. They are not places of morbid fascination or the grim lairs of ghouls and ghosts. True, we mourn for the loss of the loved ones we have buried here, but our visits also ensure that their memory remains strong within us and carried on to our children.

Bellefontaine Cemetery is one of the showpieces of St. Louis. As a storied place it has no superior, for here you will come upon some of people who made St. Louis. Some of them, as Carol Ferring Shepley tells us, were well-known movers and shakers, scalawags and suffragettes. Others had names you may not quickly recognize but whose stories will intrigue you. All of them you will surely enjoy.

—Robert R. Archibald, Ph.D.
President, Missouri History Museum

INTRODUCTION

WHEN BELLEFONTAINE CEMETERY was founded in 1849 by a group of St. Louis's leading citizens, railroads were for the most part a progressive dream, and the Mississippi River had not yet been spanned by the majestic arches of the Eads Bridge. Thanks to the confluence of the two great rivers and the energy of its citizenry, St. Louis stood in the first rank of American cities. Until the transcontinental railroad was completed in 1869, all trade with the western United States had to pass through the city. A city as significant as St. Louis demanded a necropolis of suitable magnificence where the city's leading lights could be laid to their eternal rest.

Thus, Bellefontaine became the fourteenth of the great rural cemeteries of the United States, the first west of the Mississippi. Before the nineteenth century, burials took place in churchyards or on family land. As cities became increasingly congested, so did church graveyards—graves were commonly dug two or three deep. Père-Lachaise Cemetery in Paris, founded in 1804, was the first of the new cemeteries to be built in beautiful park-like settings outside of city centers in response to this overcrowding. Rural cemeteries allowed families to honor and visit their dead in an appropriate setting. In the nineteenth century, people were more mindful of their dead because of the high incidence of infant mortality and because average life expectancy did not much exceed forty. Yet the cemetery was placed at a distance from the city center because it was believed that effluvia from corpses was unhealthy.

Almerin Hotchkiss from Green-Wood Cemetery in Brooklyn, New York, was hired by James Yeatman, one of the cemetery founders, to lay out the winding roads and wooded vistas that grace Bellefontaine. Much of the beauty of the site can be attributed to Hotchkiss's careful planning and diligent supervision during the forty-six years he served as superintendent of the cemetery.

Bellefontaine became the final resting place not only for the city's leading citizens, but also for many, such as William Clark, who had died before its establishment and were reinterred among its hills. Thus, a history of Bellefontaine Cemetery becomes a history of St. Louis; the people buried there took the city, the region, and even the country forward.

St. Louis has always capitalized on its location in the center of the United States. The position of its port on the major U.S. waterway led explorers and fur traders who opened up the West to settle there. During the era when steamboats were the most efficient means of conveying goods and people, St. Louisans naturally took to the river. As railroads grew in importance, railroad men found the Gateway to the West the place to settle. Following in the footsteps of these earlier pioneers in transportation, St. Louisans also became leaders in the field of aviation.

The Civil War sent many men to make their peace forever in Bellefontaine. Because of Missouri's status as a border state, some of the cemetery's generals wore blue, others gray. Throughout the cemetery's history, politicians, mayors, senators, and congressmen came to be interred there. They lie among suffragettes who fought for the right to vote them into office. The fields of finance, business, manufacturing, education, and law all produced figures of renown who are buried in Bellefontaine. The arts are also well represented with artists, architects, and authors.

Not all of Bellefontaine's tombstones tell tales of lofty deeds. The cemetery has its share of criminals, scalawags, and notorious women. Murderers, con men, madams, and adulteresses also have stories to tell.

Within the 87,000 graves of Bellefontaine Cemetery are buried men and women who made this country great. Although the selection is by no means complete, this book proposes to tell the stories of the most interesting and noteworthy individuals who lie there. By learning their stories and visiting their graves, we honor their deeds and keep their memories alive. These people shaped our city. As we come to an understanding of their past, we let them into our lives and welcome their influence upon us.

The cemetery is blessed with employees who have made its study their avocation. I have been fortunate to have spent countless hours with superintendent Mike Tiemann and gatekeeper Manuel Garcia, listening and learning from their stories. Both opened their extensive files to me. Together, for three years of Sundays, we explored these sacred spaces and roamed these hallowed hills. Mike Tiemann worked at Bellefontaine for thirty-six years, starting as a boy during school summers and spending the last eleven as superintendent. He retired in 2006. In 1970, Manuel Garcia first visited Bellefontaine in search of the graves of Sara Teasdale and William Clark and lingered long in his pursuit of St. Louis history. In retirement, he returned eleven years ago to serve the gatehouse and share his knowledge with the families who visited. When he passed away in 2006, he also came to rest on a hillside in Bellefontaine close to the characters who fascinated him in life. Tiemann and Garcia's rich remembrances and their files dedicated to the individuals buried here have inspired this history.

PART ONE

MOVERS
AND
SHAKERS

 THE MOVERS AND SHAKERS of St. Louis who are buried in Bellefontaine Cemetery affected not only the city but also the region and the country as a whole. Their stories tell the tales of St. Louis, the settling of the West, the conflicted loyalties of the Civil War, and the struggle for women's suffrage, among others. Most of these people were not born in the city but came to the shores of the Mississippi in search of a better life. They heard St. Louis offered them opportunities to make their mark upon the world, and they used their enormous talents to give shape to a city still raw and unformed. Missouri History Museum president Robert R. Archibald said,

> First settled by Pierre Laclede as a base for trading for furs, St. Louis was founded for commercial reasons, unlike some East Coast or even western cities that were founded for political or religious reasons. This set a tone and character for the city. Because of the tone initially set, St. Louis became a magnet that attracted some of the most entrepreneurial and successful capitalists in the Western Hemisphere, beginning with Laclede himself.[1]

William Greenleaf Eliot, who came to St. Louis in 1834 as a Unitarian minister and later founded Washington University in St. Louis, saw dangers in founding a city so focused on "commercial reasons" and considered it his mission to offer an alternative. Many of St. Louis's leaders sought "religion and learning and morality and education" in their later lives, after they had spent their young years earning money.[2] First and foremost of the movers and shakers is William Clark, who, along with Meriwether Lewis, used the city as the port of exit for his explorations of the West and would stay to govern and set policies for the treatment of Native Americans.

Integral to commerce was geography, which made St. Louis what it is, with both its position near the joining of the Mississippi and Missouri rivers and its location in the center of the nation. The Mississippi River ferried the first settlers up from New Orleans. Before the era of the railroads, rivers provided the swiftest means of conveying people and goods over vast distances. Later, as other modes of transportation surpassed river traffic, St. Louis's central location proved advantageous to such entrepreneurs as brewer Adolphus Busch and aviation pioneer James S. McDonnell Jr. Even though the St. Louis of 2008 almost turns its back on the river, the city never would have existed without the Mississippi. For bridge builder James Buchanan Eads, the Mississippi River was "the stream which . . . holds in its watery embrace the destinies of the American people."[3]

Hearing stories of St. Louis, the mecca of the West, settlers came there on foot or by the inland waterways and then used the Missouri River as a conduit to take them farther west. In the city itself, fur traders and explorers bought their supplies, guns, and maps, and they heard tales of the perils ahead of them. Later, businessmen such as Robert S. Brookings bought manufactured goods there to sell throughout the western part of the country. Because so much of the city's trade was oriented to the West, St. Louis became the last eastern city, a combination of both the last of the old ways and the jumping off place for the new.

St. Louis combines cultural elements of the four regions of the country (North, South, East, and West), as well as many nationalities, principally French, German, English, and Scotch Irish. Unlike the other groups, the Germans came seeking political freedom, fleeing from their disappointment in the failed revolutions of 1848.

Because of its industry, wealth, and strategic location, and because it was such a microcosm of the split between Northern and Southern loyalties during the Civil War, Abraham Lincoln attached great significance to St. Louis. Banker-philanthropist James Yeatman served on a commission advising the president as to the situation in the city. Important generals from St. Louis served both sides of the conflict. General Sterling Price led the Confederate troops on the field of battle, while General John Pope fought for the Union, exemplifying the claim of the 1994 book *The Civil War in St. Louis* that "it would almost be possible to retell the history of the Civil War in Missouri simply by moving from gravesite to gravesite within [the] Cemetery."[4]

St. Louis produced men who led the nation in industry, medical research, journalism, and finance. Industrialists, such as Edgar Queeny of Monsanto Chemical Works and Edward Mallinckrodt of Mallinckrodt Chemical Works, used their fortunes to improve their city. Others, like William K. Bixby and Robert Brookings, retired relatively young from the world of commerce to devote themselves entirely to philanthropy. With the Washington University Medical School and notable researchers such as Nobel Prize winners Gerty and Carl Cori, St. Louis became a great medical center. When St. Louis was still just a small town of one thousand souls, the city's first newspaper was published, setting the tone for an emphasis on journalism. Many of the city's successful businessmen eventually became bankers and were thus able to finance other people's dreams. St. Louisan William McChesney Martin Jr. led the Federal Reserve System for nineteen years, setting monetary policy for the entire country.

Many of St. Louis's movers and shakers exhibited a similar pattern in their lives. Coming from relatively humble origins, they were adventurous and did not take the easy way in life. Believing in themselves, they persisted despite failures. The best—men like Eads, Brookings, and Yeatman—believed the purpose of their labors was not to enrich themselves, but to improve the lot of humankind.

As for the women, their stories followed a different path. They were first wives and mothers. With their families established, women such as Virginia Minor and Edna Fischel Gellhorn set out to achieve their mission in life, securing the vote for women and fostering better social welfare for all. Unmarried and without children, Eliza Haycraft became one of the town's wealthiest businesspeople. Widowed and with her children grown, Irma Rombauer wrote the country's best-selling cookbook.

To read the stories of the city's movers and shakers is to understand the lifeblood of St. Louis. They took the region forward and made the country great. They were critical to American democracy.

---

1. Robert R. Archibald (president, Missouri History Museum), interview with the author, March 26, 2008.
2. Charlotte Eliot, *William Greenleaf Eliot* (Boston: Houghton, Mifflin, 1904), 35.
3. Howard S. Miller, *The Eads Bridge* (St. Louis: Missouri Historical Society Press, 1999), 69.
4. William C. Winter, *The Civil War in St. Louis* (St. Louis: Missouri Historical Society, 1994), 110.

GEORGE INGHAM BARNETT
1815–1898

AFTER ARRIVING IN New York City from his native England in 1839, George Ingham Barnett set off three months later for St. Louis in the belief that the ambitious and growing city offered opportunity for a young architect. He found abundant work as the first European-trained architect in the city.[1] The 2,500 buildings he designed put a lasting stamp on Missouri. Examples of his favored Italianate style, among his best-known buildings still in existence are the Missouri Governor's Mansion and Henry Shaw's two homes at the Missouri Botanical Garden. Barnett's great friendship and collaboration with Shaw inspired some of the architect's best work. All found him "very warm in his friendships, exceedingly hospitable, and . . . noted for his straightforward dealings. He took a deep interest in the city's welfare, and was very active in all public enterprises."[2]

Barnett left school early to learn carpentry before he embarked upon an apprenticeship to Sir Thomas Hine, one of the leading architects in England. He came to St. Louis at the age of twenty-four and began almost immediately doing perspective drawings for Henry Singleton. Singleton had won the competition to design the city's courthouse, later completed by William Rumbold, but was untrained to do perspective renderings. Barnett next worked for Meriwether Lewis Clark, a West Point–trained engineer who was the son of William Clark, designing the Church of St. Vincent de Paul, which was consecrated in 1845 and is the only building still standing from Barnett's first decade of practice.

After completion of the church, Barnett formed his own firm. Through the years, he had many partners, including Charles Peck, Henry Garcia Isaacs, and Isaac Taylor, who would become the chief architect for the Louisiana Purchase Exposition of 1904. Among Barnett's early commissions was St. Louis's first skyscraper, the six-story Barnum's City

Hotel, built in 1854 (no longer in existence). He designed and supervised construction for other St. Louis landmark hotels, including the Lindell and the Southern. The Southern, the first fireproof building in the West, was in the planning stages when the Civil War broke out and delayed its construction. Fur trader Robert Campbell (see Part 4) backed Barnett in completing this downtown hotel in 1881. Barnett also designed Nashville's Maxwell Hotel, still standing, where Maxwell House coffee was first served. Other St. Louis commercial buildings Barnett designed include the Main Street Merchants' Exchange, the Third and Olive post office, and Barr's Dry Goods Store. Sadly, not one stands today. Perhaps the reason so many of Barnett's commercial buildings have been razed was that conveniences standard to the twentieth century did not exist then, chief among them bathrooms and electric elevators.

Many of Barnett's house projects have survived. The Missouri Governor's Mansion, considered one of Barnett's masterpieces,[3] cost $75,000 to build in 1872 ($1,277,000 in 2006 dollars), boasted thirteen bedrooms, and had every luxury except closets and bathrooms. While Barnett primarily designed in the Italianate style, the Governor's Mansion sports a mansard roof, a French detail perhaps contributed by his partner at the time, Alfred Piquenard. Thousands visit the mansion every year. Yet architectural historian John Albury Bryan considers "the finest of all the homes built in Missouri in ante-bellum days"[4] to be Barnett's Kennett's Castle. This Italianate estate set on 2,700 acres was built by Ferdinand Kennett, brother of Luther Kennett, who served on the original Bellefontaine Cemetery Board of Trustees. According to Bryan, "This famous home was completed in 1854, and even at that remote date, with all the common labor performed by the owner's slaves, and the limestone for the walls quarried from his own ground, the cost amounted to more than $125,000."[5] Washington University in St. Louis's former president Robert Brookings later owned the estate (see page 46). Besides Brookings, and Kennett, Barnett had social and business ties to most of the merchant princes of the St. Louis of his day, as evidenced in the palatial private residences he designed and built for them. Today, several are still used as residences on Lafayette Square. The best known of these is the Blair-Huse house at 2043 Park Avenue. First designed in 1870 by Barnett for Lincoln's postmaster general, Montgomery Blair, who was politician Frank Blair's brother, it was enlarged considerably in 1877 by Barnett for fuel and ice magnate William Huse. Starting in 1969, this house, more elaborate in its interior detail than the Governor's Mansion, underwent a thirteen-year renovation project that sparked the regeneration of Lafayette Square.

Of all the city's merchant princes, Henry Shaw, benefactor of the Missouri Botanical Garden and the adjoining Tower Grove Park, proved most loyal to Barnett, so loyal that today the garden and the park present a veritable encyclopedia of the architect's work. Like Barnett, Henry Shaw came to St. Louis from England to make his fortune. Shaw had so much success selling hardware that he was able to retire twenty years later in 1839, the very year Barnett first set foot on the western bank of the Mississippi. The two Englishmen became the best of friends. When bachelor Shaw left the business world at the age of forty, his intentions were to travel and to devote himself to the creation of beauty. In 1849, Shaw commissioned his friend Barnett to design both his country and his city mansions. Today, both stand side by side in the garden. The country house, which pays tribute to the Italian Renaissance style, gave the neighborhood its name because its tower could be seen above a grove of sassafras trees. The city house, built at the busy corner of Seventh and Locust, survived St. Louis's relentless growth only because Shaw designated in his will that it be moved to his garden. Barnett also designed such Botanical Garden landmarks as the Linnaean House and the Cleveland Avenue Gatehouse. In Tower Grove Park, his work remains in the Palm House and the Grand Avenue entrance. Yet perhaps the most beautiful of all Barnett's works in Shaw's garden and park is the owner's mausoleum. An octagonal structure with a jaunty green copper roof sits in a grove close to Shaw's country house. The benefactor worked closely with the architect to create it. Its life-size statue of a recumbent Shaw holding a rose was stored in the basement until Shaw's death. The importance Shaw attached to his final resting place can be inferred from the fact that he spent $13,265 for his mausoleum in 1889—almost a third of the $40,000 he had spent on his country house thirty-one years earlier. Windows on seven sides of the tomb look out onto the garden that Shaw loved.

Barnett also designed three mausoleums for Bellefontaine Cemetery. The tomb of Dr. D. S. Brock was built of yellow limestone in 1874 (see page 8 of insert). George R. Taylor was married to a descendant of Auguste

Chouteau and had commissioned commercial buildings from Barnett. Thus, when Taylor died in 1880, Barnett was selected to design his tomb; made of pink granite, it has a pediment that frames two female figures representing death and resurrection.[6] The Ulrici mausoleum unfortunately no longer stands.

Despite all the grand mansions he created, Barnett lived simply in a small house at Jefferson and Chestnut. He also marked his own grave simply, with a tombstone bearing a shrouded urn symbolizing the end of life. Lying between his two wives is the man who earned "the first rank among all the early architects of Missouri and the West."[7]

1. Carolyn Hewes Toft, Esley Hamilton, and Mary Henderson Gass, *The Way We Came: A Century of the AIA in St. Louis* (St Louis: Patrice Press, 1991), facing page 1.

2. William Hyde and Howard Conard, *Encyclopedia of the History St. Louis* (New York: Southern History Company, 1899), 98.

3. Governor B. Gratz Brown, Manuel Garcia files, Bellefontaine Cemetery.

4. John Albury Bryan, *Missouri's Contribution to American Architecture* (St. Louis: St. Louis Architectural Club, 1928), 13.

5. Ibid.

6. David J. Simmons, "Three Tombs Designed by George I. Barnett," *The Society of Architectural Historians, Missouri Valley Chapter Newsletter* 3, no. 3 (fall 1997).

7. Bryan, *Missouri's Contribution*, 11.

EDWARD BATES
1793–1869

WHEN ABRAHAM LINCOLN appointed Edward Bates attorney general of the United States, Bates told the president he would have turned him down in times of peace, as he had previously turned down a cabinet appointment during the administration of Millard Fillmore. Having seventeen children to support made public service a financial sacrifice this St. Louis statesman and lawyer could ill afford. But because the country was in "trouble and danger," he felt it was "his duty"[1] to do what he could to restore peace and preserve the Union. Thus, he became the first cabinet member from west of the Mississippi.

Throughout his forty-seven years of public service, Bates represented what is best about St. Louis and the Mississippi Valley. He so loved St. Louis that during his whole life he celebrated the anniversary of his arrival in the River City on April 29. He expected St. Louis to be "the greatest city upon the continent."[2]

Edward Bates stood five feet seven and always wore the modest, old-fashioned garb of his Quaker heritage. The hair on his head remained black his whole life, though his flowing beard turned white. Lincoln quipped that this was because Bates "used his chin more than his head."[3] Most of his life, he lived with his children at a farm in Florissant known as Grape Hill, of which he said, "It took all the money Lawyer Bates could make to support Farmer Bates."[4] When he died in 1869, he was originally buried at his beloved Grape Hill, though his wife, Julia Coalter, was to be laid to rest beside her parents in Bellefontaine when she died in 1880. In 1906, Edward Bates was reinterred beside Julia in the Coalter lot. Consistent with the humility with which he lived his life, his simple headstone bears only his name and the words: "Lawyer, statesman, 1793 to 1869, son of Thomas Fleming Bates."

Born in Goochland, Virginia, the youngest son of the twelve children of Thomas and Caroline Bates, his keen moral sense was tempered by adversity. When his father died in 1805, the eleven-year-old Edward was sent to live first with a brother, then with a cousin, because his mother could not provide for her large family. He showed an early aptitude for study, especially poetry, and was educated at home until he entered a private academy in Maryland at the age of fourteen. He intended to attend Princeton, but those plans fell through. He enlisted in the army in the War of 1812 and then followed his older brother Frederick to St. Louis in 1814.

The twenty-one-year-old Bates picked a propitious moment to join the movement westward, for St. Louis was soon to become a boomtown. He came well connected: Frederick had recently been appointed secretary of the Missouri Territory and was soon to be elected the state's second governor. With Frederick's help, Edward set about reading law in the office of

Rufus Easton, a distinguished frontier attorney, and was admitted to the bar in the winter of 1816. With lawyers in great demand in the frontier town, Edward Bates's career took off. The ambitious young attorney built a lucrative private practice until he was appointed district attorney for the territory in 1818. After two years, he was elected delegate, the second youngest at age twenty-seven, to the Missouri Constitutional Convention after the territory was admitted to statehood with the Missouri Compromise of 1820. He was considered one of the principal authors of the state constitution and was elected Missouri's first attorney general. He seemed headed for a life in politics when he was elected to the state legislature in 1822, appointed U.S. attorney for the Missouri District in 1824, and elected congressman in 1827. Although he lost his campaign for re-election to the House of Representatives, he served in the Missouri legislature from 1830 to 1836. He spent the next seventeen years achieving prominence in private practice until 1853 when he was elected judge.

In 1823, an event occurred "that altered Bates' life and forever shifted his focus—he fell in love with and married Julia Coalter."[5] Julia came from a wealthy and politically well-connected family. One of her four sisters married Hamilton Gamble, who was to be governor of Missouri during the Civil War. Bates had initially courted this sister, Caroline. Herein lies a tale that illustrates the excellent character of Edward Bates. Although she refused his suit, they remained friends, and she trusted him enough to confide that it was Gamble she loved but could not marry because he was a drinking man. Magnanimously, Bates took this information to Gamble and induced him to swear off drinking so he could win Caroline as his bride. Despite the fact that Julia was not his first choice, she was the light of his life and provided him with seventeen children.

Although he spent the major part of his career as a Whig and was president of the Whig national convention in 1856, he took a strong stand against the abandonment of the Missouri Compromise and the admission of Kansas as a slave state. He had freed his own slaves, including one Richard Anderson who became an important black pastor and the founder of Central Baptist Church. This position drew him closer to the Republican Party, and he became the Missouri delegation's presidential nominee to the 1860 convention. Although he received forty-eight votes on the first ballot, the nomination went to Lincoln on the third ballot. Bates gave the Lincoln campaign his wholehearted support and was rewarded with a cabinet post.

Bates's influence in the cabinet waned as more radical members took control. Weary of being away from home, he resigned his post of attorney general in November 1864, shortly after his commander in chief had been re-elected. He sought nomination for chief justice of the Supreme Court, but was disappointed in his suit.

Bates spent his last five years in St. Louis. His savings had been depleted by his years in Washington, D.C., and he was forced to borrow money from his son Barton to buy a home in the city of St. Louis. Eventually, he had to sell Grape Hill for $8,000 to pay off his debts. His health deteriorated, and he died peacefully surrounded by his family.

Upon the dedication of Forest Park on June 25, 1876, the ceremony ended with the unveiling of a statue of Bates. He stands, larger than life, with his arm extended as if in greeting or to make a point. The granite pedestal is adorned with medallions of other important St. Louisans who were his colleagues: James B. Eads, Hamilton Gamble, attorney Charles Gibson, and Senator Henry Geyer. Yet Bates, in his simplicity and purposefulness, stands atop them all.

---

1. Doris Kearns Goodwin, *Team of Rivals: The Political Genius of Abraham Lincoln* (New York: Simon & Schuster, 2005), 286.

2. Edward Bates speech, July 4, 1851, quoted in *Bulletin of the Missouri Historical Society* (July 1960): 315.

3. Goodwin, *Team of Rivals*, 22–23.

4. J. Thomas Scharf, *History of St. Louis City and County* (Philadelphia: L. H. Everts, 1883), 1464.

5. Goodwin, *Team of Rivals*, 63.

WILLIAM BEAUMONT
1785–1853

WILLIAM BEAUMONT, a Connecticut farm boy who never attended medical school, is remembered for research that changed the understanding of the human digestive process. Beaumont accomplished this feat in an age when medicine was more philosophy than science. He is considered "the first great American physiologist,"[1] according to Sir William Osler, regius professor of medicine, Oxford University. However, Dr. Steven LeFrak, chairman of the Barnes-Jewish Hospital Bioethics Committee, believes it is Beaumont's code of ethics for human research that is his greatest accomplishment.[2] In this code, Beaumont lists six principles for using humans as research subjects. Among them are: "The voluntary consent of the subject is necessary" and "The experiment is to be discontinued when it causes distress to the subject."[3]

Beaumont came to St. Louis in 1834 to serve as the military doctor at Jefferson Barracks. His name lives on in three St. Louis institutions, Beaumont High School, Beaumont Street, and the Beaumont Medical Building, as well as several hospitals in Michigan and one army hospital in Texas. For fifty-five years, ending in 1990, the St. Louis Medical Society laid a wreath on his grave on his birthday in a celebration often accompanied by the Beaumont High School choir.

The second of nine children, William Beaumont left his birthplace of Lebanon, Connecticut, to make his way in the world as a schoolteacher in Champlain, New York, near the Canadian border. There, he commenced a lifelong habit of keeping a diary and decided to better his lot by reading medical books for three years under the guidance of Dr. Pomeroy of Burlington, Vermont. In 1810, he apprenticed himself to Dr. Benjamin Chandler of St. Albans, Vermont. At a time when bloodletting and the application of leeches were considered treatment, and opium and whiskey medicine, Beaumont's route to mastering the profession was acceptable since there were few medical schools in the United States.

In June 1812, the Third Medical Society of Vermont licensed Beaumont to practice medicine, and three months later he was commissioned a surgeon's mate in the army. In April 1813, he saw action when the retreating British blew up a powder magazine. During the war, he was fortunate to win the admiration of surgeon Joseph Lovell, who later became surgeon general of the United States and Beaumont's greatest ally in his research.

Following an unsuccessful foray into private practice in Plattsburgh, New York, where he met his future wife, Deborah Green Platt, Beaumont returned to the military in 1820 and was posted to Fort Mackinac, an island in Lake Michigan near the Canadian border. He married Deborah in 1821 and brought her back to Fort Mackinac along with the eleven-year-old stepson of her widowed sister. On June 8, 1822, their first child was born, their daughter Sarah.

Two days before the birth, an event occurred that gave Beaumont the chance of his lifetime. In the crowded American Fur Company store, someone fired a shotgun at a young half-Indian, half-French fur trader named Alexis St. Martin. Within minutes, Beaumont arrived to tend to the wound. He described a hole "the size of a palm of a man's hand; blowing off and fracturing the sixth rib. . . . Found a portion of the lung as large as a turkey's egg protruding through the external wound . . . and below this another protrusion resembling a portion of the stomach. . . . I considered any attempt to save his life entirely useless."[4] Although Beaumont's wife was about to go into labor with his first child and he did not think St. Martin could "survive twenty minutes,"[5] Beaumont cleaned the wound and returned twice a day for a year to dress it. At the end of the year, the army decided it was too expensive to keep St. Martin and ordered him sent as a pauper by open boat to Montreal. Beaumont, believing the difficult journey would surely kill his patient, pleaded with the authorities not to do so. When the military refused, the good doctor took St. Martin into his own home, where he managed to care for him along with his wife, infant daughter, and stepson on his salary of $40 a month.

Despite the fact that the wound would never close and sometimes had to be covered manually to prevent food from spilling out, St. Martin returned to health and vigor. Three years after the accident, at noon on August 1, 1825, Beaumont took advantage of the possibilities inherent in the situation and began his studies by putting small bits of food tied with silk string into the hole—known as a fistula. At one, two, and three o'clock, Beaumont pulled out the strings to observe the rate at which the food was digesting. Later he would extract gastric juices from the stomach and use them to digest food outside the body.

He continued these experiments until 1834. Surgeon General Lovell immediately recognized the importance of the experiments and supported Beaumont with funding, medical literature, and leaves of absence to work in conjunction with researchers at the University of Virginia and Yale.

In 1833, Beaumont put forth his findings in a volume titled *Experiments and Observations on the Gastric Juice and the Physiology of Digestion*. Beaumont dedicated it to his patron Lovell and introduced the work by saying, "if I may be permitted to cast my mite into the treasury of knowledge, and to be the means, either directly or indirectly, of subserving the cause of truth, and ameliorating the condition of human suffering."[6] He published it himself in an edition of 1,000 in Plattsburgh with the help of his cousin Dr. Samuel Beaumont. It went into a second edition of 1,500 in 1847. The world recognized its significance, and German and British editions followed. Even so, when Beaumont attempted to procure some remuneration from Congress for experiments that had been conducted largely at his own expense, a bill to appropriate $10,000 for him was defeated.

The year following the book's publication, Beaumont was posted to Jefferson Barracks in St. Louis, where he was to spend the rest of his life, respected and prosperous. Because his responsibilities at the fort were light, he was able to live close to town, where he established a private practice and engaged in real estate speculation. In 1839, during a depressed economy, Beaumont earned $10,000, a generous income at the time.

In 1836, Beaumont's patron, Joseph Lovell, died and was succeeded as surgeon general by Thomas Lawson, who proved no friend to Beaumont. He attempted to transfer Beaumont back to live at Jefferson Barracks, where it would be impossible for him to continue his private practice. Beaumont's good friends, Officers Ethan Allen Hitchcock and Robert E. Lee, interceded for him, as did the two Missouri senators, Thomas Hart Benton (see page 19) and Lewis F. Linn, who had great respect for his work. Unfortunately, Beaumont lacked tact in all of his dealings, and his letters angered the surgeon general who, therefore, sought an opportunity to humiliate him. He did so by ordering Beaumont to Florida to serve as medic in the Seminole Wars. Since Lawson rejected all further attempts at intercession by Hitchcock and Lee, Beaumont resigned his commission rather than leave St. Louis.

His remaining fourteen years were spent in great happiness surrounded by his wife and three children, Sarah, Israel, and Lucretia, and many distinguished friends. Major Hitchcock often visited to play the flute to the accompaniment of Sarah at the piano. Her devoted father grew increasingly deaf and was reported to grasp the piano with his teeth to have a sense of what she was playing. In 1836, Saint Louis University established its medical school, and Dr. William Greenleaf Eliot (see page 72) invited Beaumont to be its first chair of surgery. He gave great service to rich and poor alike during the cholera epidemic of 1849.

Beaumont died April 25, 1853, after having slipped on an icy step a month earlier while visiting a patient. Dr. Eliot attended his deathbed, helped him make a will, and became executor of the will.

Beaumont pursued St. Martin his whole life, but the fur trader with a window to his stomach refused further experimentation after 1834. He lived fifty-eight years after his accident, twenty-seven years longer than the doctor who saved his life and used it to further medical science. When St. Martin died in 1880 in Canada, his family deliberately let his body decompose for four days and then buried it eight feet deep in an unmarked grave. They put heavy rocks on his coffin to give his bodily remains peace from the curious.

Although untrained as a scientific researcher, Beaumont did precise, methodical experiments that established fundamental truths about the process of human digestion. According to the *Dictionary of American Biography*, "Every physician who prescribes for digestive disorders and every patient who is benefited by such prescription owes gratitude to the memory of William Beaumont for the benefit of mankind."[7]

---

1. Jesse Shire Myer, *The Life and Letters of Dr. William Beaumont* (St. Louis: Mosby, 1912), xxiii.

2. Steven LeFrak, conversation with the author, October 2006.

3. H. Beecher, *Research and the Individual Human Subject* (Boston: Little, Brown, 1970).

4. *Dictionary of American Biography* (New York: Charles Scribner's Sons, 1936), 106.

5. Ibid.

6. William Beaumont, *Experiments and Observations on the Gastric Juice and the Physiology of Digestion* (Birmingham, AL: Classics of Medicine Library, 1980), 5.

7. *American Biography*, 109.

THOMAS HART BENTON
1782–1858

THOMAS HART BENTON served Missouri faithfully as its first senator. Elected to five terms, he was also the first U.S. senator to serve as long as thirty years. Having migrated west from North Carolina to Tennessee and then to St. Louis, he always considered himself a Western man and championed the causes of his region accordingly. But in 1850 the issue of slavery forced him to put the interests of his country before those of his state, and thus he lost a bid for re-election. Although a slave owner himself, he believed that the extension of slavery would tear the Union apart. Unfortunately for Benton, the majority in Missouri felt otherwise. Two later presidents, Theodore Roosevelt and John F. Kennedy, admired his integrity and dedication to what he perceived as the just cause, no matter the personal consequences. Both wrote historical studies of Benton.

During his long Senate term, Benton wielded enormous power. According to cemetery superintendent Michael Tiemann, "He was the great senator, a great compromiser. There were four giants in the United States Senate from 1820 to 1850: John C. Calhoun, Daniel Webster, Thomas Hart Benton, and Henry Clay from Kentucky. . . . These four senators basically ran the Senate."[1]

Although Benton had been cruelly thrown out of office as senator and as representative, and he had lost a gubernatorial bid, Missourians revised their feelings about him and accorded him a hero's funeral when he died in Washington, D.C., of throat cancer at age seventy-six. In the words of Roosevelt:

> As soon as the news reached Missouri, . . . all classes of the people
> united to do honor to the memory of the dead statesman, realizing
> that they had lost a man who towered head and shoulders above

both friends and foes. The body was taken to St. Louis and, after lying in state, was buried in Bellefontaine Cemetery, with more than forty thousand people witnessing the funeral. All of the public buildings were draped in mourning; all places of business were closed, and the flags everywhere were at half-mast. Thus, at the very end the great city of the West at last again paid a fitting homage to the West's mightiest son. [2]

In Washington, D.C.,'s Capitol Building, each U.S. state is represented by two statues of native sons in Statuary Hall. Thomas Hart Benton and Frank Blair Jr. represent Missouri. In St. Louis, Benton's name is honored in Benton Park, and his statue presides over Lafayette Park. A crowd of forty thousand gathered for its dedication in 1868, ten years after his death. Thirty cannons fired to honor his years in the Senate. The statue of Benton by sculptor Harriet Hosmer wears a Roman toga and faces west.

Thomas Hart Benton was born in North Carolina in 1782 to Jesse and Ann Benton. He was only eight years old when his father died, leaving him head of the family. With five of his seven brothers and sisters dying of tuberculosis, he would always remain close to his mother. After a short course of study at the University of North Carolina, he joined his mother in Tennessee to farm the three thousand acres that his father had left her. Failure at cotton farming led him to the law and a lifelong sympathy for the struggles of settlers. With little money, he was able to pass the bar thanks to the patronage of such leaders as Andrew Jackson.

Benton served as state senator in Tennessee and as the commander of a corps of volunteers that he raised during the War of 1812. His brother Jesse quarreled with Andrew Jackson. Thomas seconded him in a duel against Jackson, in which Jackson was wounded in the arm and his brother took a bullet in the derriere. In the aftermath of that debacle, Thomas left the state for St. Louis in 1815, where he practiced law and edited a newspaper, the *Missouri Enquirer*. His travels as aide-de-camp to General Jackson during the War of 1812 had revealed to him the significance of the Mississippi River in the expansion and commerce of the United States. For his whole life, he always referred to it as "the King of Floods" and "the Father of Waters." A man of vision, he soon realized the manifest destiny of the country was to expand across the continent to the Pacific Ocean.

Benton's duel on Bloody Island was the most notorious incident in his career. While he was a perfect gentleman with the ladies and a fond father, Benton had a violent temper that he exercised fatally in 1817. He and Charles Lucas had represented adversaries in a court case, and while their differences in the course of the trial did not appear anything out of the ordinary for lawyers, Benton's words festered in Lucas's mind. On election day, August 4, he insulted Benton by asking if he had paid his taxes in time to entitle him to vote. Benton responded by calling him a "puppy," considered a horrendous insult at the time because it meant the son of a female dog. Lucas demanded retribution. When they fought a first duel with pistols at thirty feet on August 12, Benton shot Lucas in the neck. Lucas survived to demand a second contest. On September 27, they fought at a mere ten feet, a lethal distance, and Lucas was killed. Even though he forgave Benton before he died, his father, J. B. C. Lucas, spent the rest of his life defaming Benton.

Elected one of Missouri's first pair of senators in 1820, Benton soon established himself as a congressional leader who championed the interests of the West. Prominent among these were the reform of government land sales and the establishment of a transcontinental railroad. Author William M. Meigs said that Benton "became convinced that sales of land by a government to the highest bidder among its own citizens was a false policy, and that the true course was to be found in 'gratuitous grants to actual settlers,' whose labor would then extract wealth from the soil and add to the strength of the nation."[3] He introduced legislation to this effect yearly until it was finally adopted during the Jackson administration. He did not live to see the apotheosis of his ideal through the Homestead Act of 1862, which granted every settler 160 acres after five years of farming the acreage.

He came to understand the power of the rail. He introduced bills four times for a transcontinental railroad uniting the East Coast with San Francisco through St. Louis. Although again he did not live to see his dream realized, in 1869 it occurred when the last spike was driven into the railroad that linked the coasts. Unfortunately, its route passed through Chicago rather than St. Louis.

It was the incendiary issue of slavery that led to Benton's defeat in the 1850 senatorial election. Although a Southerner and slave owner himself, he believed that the issue threatened the Union, and he always put the Union above all other interests.

In 1849, the Missouri legislature passed resolutions that, according to President Kennedy, "expressed Missouri's desire to cooperate with other slaveholding states, and instructed her Senators to vote accordingly. Outraged at this setback, Benton charged that the resolutions had been inspired in Washington and falsified real opinion in Missouri."[4] Knowing that he was committing political suicide, Benton defied these strictures and voted his conscience to strengthen the Union and defeat the interests of the slaveholding states by opposing the nullification acts. For this courageous deed, Kennedy included him in *Profiles in Courage* and Theodore Roosevelt praised his towering morality, calling him "heroic."[5]

Benton's loyalty to his wife was equally intense, admirable, and at times challenging. In 1820, he married Elizabeth McDowell, daughter of a prominent Virginia family. Together they had six children, four daughters and two sons, both of whom predeceased them. His affection for his wife was palpable, especially after she was afflicted by a stroke in 1844 that led to her slow decline. "From that point till her death in 1854, he never went out to a public place of amusement, spending all his time not occupied with public duties in writing by her bedside."[6] Before her mind failed utterly, he would sometimes carry her down to visit with company. Once, after she had deteriorated, she appeared at the door of the salon wearing very little clothing while Benton was entertaining a party of distinguished men. Benton took her by the hand and introduced her to the company with great dignity. Meigs said, "He then placed her beside him and went on with the conversation, precisely as if everything was as might be wanted while the others took no notice of the occurrence but were deeply moved at the tenderness shown by him."[7]

Thomas Hart Benton was a man of great vision, a statesman, not a politician. His moral courage earned not only the admiration of Presidents Roosevelt and Kennedy but also the honor of posterity.

---

1. Tiemann, *Oral History*, tape VII, 138.
2. Theodore Roosevelt, *Thomas Hart Benton, Gouverneur Morris* (New York: Charles Scribner's Sons, 1926), 227.
3. William M. Meigs, *The Life of Thomas Hart Benton* (Philadelphia: J. B. Lippincott, 1904), 164.
4. John F. Kennedy, *Profiles in Courage* (New York: Harper and Brothers, 1961), 90.
5. Roosevelt, *Benton, Morris*, 204.
6. Theodore Roosevelt, "Thomas Hart Benton," in *The Works of Theodore Roosevelt* (New York: Scribner's, 1903), 343.
7. Meigs, *The Life of Benton*, 515.

WILLIAM K. BIXBY

1857–1931

WILLIAM K. BIXBY started out as a baggage handler at age sixteen in Palestine, Texas.[1] Soon his intelligence and charm caught the eye of the company president, who took Bixby with him to St. Louis. There, success led to success until he retired at the age of forty-nine to collect art and rare books and to serve as a civic leader. Though he had only a high school education, his appetite for learning was prodigious, and he received honorary degrees of a master of arts from Amherst College and a bachelor of laws from the University of Missouri as well as an honorary membership in Phi Beta Kappa. "W. K. Bixby was simultaneously an imposing figure (he was quite tall and rotund with piercing, dark eyes), and a quiet, cultivated reader of Thoreau's *Walden*."[2] For all his honors and successes, he made his greatest mark as a philanthropist. His name lives on in St. Louis in William K. Bixby Hall at Washington University and in the William K. Bixby Trust for Asian Art at the Saint Louis Art Museum.

Throughout his life, Bixby was devoted to his family. He and his wife, Lillian Tuttle Bixby, had seven children whom they raised in a mansion they built at 13 Portland Place in 1896. One way they kept children and grandchildren close was to summer together every year at the house they built on Mohican Point on Lake George in Upstate New York, Lillian Bixby's birthplace. There, both Lillian and William died three months apart, in August and October of 1931, surrounded by their children. The Missouri Historical Society, the Saint Louis Art Museum, and Washington University's School of Fine Art closed on the day of his funeral. Both Bixbys are buried in the family mausoleum in Bellefontaine Cemetery along with many of their children and grandchildren. Only Stella Fresh Bixby, wife of Bixby's son William H. Bixby, is buried outside the mausoleum on the family plot because, according to family legend, she did not want to be shut up inside.[3]

Called "precocious and driven,"[4] Bixby started in a humble position in railroads and became a multimillionaire railcar industrialist by the time he retired in the highest position of the company. During his years working for the railroad, three towns along the routes were named for him: Bixby, Illinois; Bixby, Missouri; and Bixby, Texas.[5]

In St. Louis, Bixby switched from railway management to railroad car manufacturing, where he would make his fortune. Starting out in 1883 as lumber agent for Missouri Car and Foundry, by 1887 Bixby had become vice president and general manager of the company.

In 1899, Bixby worked to consolidate eighteen companies into the American Car and Foundry Company. The company owned all aspects of railroad car production, from ore deposits and timber tracts to furnaces and mills to the car-building shops. From plants around the country, the company shipped passenger and freight cars all over the world for an annual gross of $75 million. In 1905, having accumulated a fortune, Bixby stepped down from the company to devote himself to his family, philanthropies, and collections.

Bixby later served as president of Laclede Gas and director of several St. Louis banks. He applied himself as diligently to his collections as he had to his businesses and received equal if not greater results. Literature intrigued him as well as art. "His library of original manuscripts was among the finest in the country, second only to that of J. P. Morgan. . . . In 1921, he sold his library to the Huntington Library of San Marino, Cal. for $2 million."[6] Keeping his treasures in a fireproof library, he generously shared manuscripts and paid as much as $35,000 for Charles Dickens's original love letters that inspired *David Copperfield*.[7] Founder of the Burns Club of St. Louis, he admired Robert Burns and became such an expert that he could recognize a fake Burns letter by an inappropriate capital letter *T*.[8]

Bixby's discerning eye, thanks to his photographic memory,[9] led him to amass a major collection of fine art. His estate included works by such masters as Rembrandt, Frans Hals, and Camille Corot. Saint Louis Art Museum curator of Asian art Steven Owyoung called Bixby's Song dynasty scroll "one of the great works in the museum."[10] Bixby brought it back from an extended tour he took of East Asia in 1919 to purchase art for himself and the new museum.

The Saint Louis Art Museum was not the only recipient of Bixby's largesse: His philanthropies touched art, education, and social welfare. A 1925 *Post-Dispatch* editorial commented:

> Mr. Bixby has contributed liberally in work and money to this city's art life. He has been generous in a material way, as his great wealth enabled him to be, and he has been equally generous of his time and enthusiasm. St. Louis has seen pictures it never would have seen except for Mr. Bixby, and his princely gift to Washington

University, the Bixby Hall of Fine Arts, will be a permanent, inspirational influence.[11]

Even so, a 1939 biography claims that he gave the Missouri Historical Society around 50,000 manuscripts, "including one of the largest collections of Thomas Jefferson letters in America, the original Burr-Hamilton correspondence, extensive Civil War data, letters, autographs and portraits of every President of the United States, and personalia of Eugene Field, Andrew Jackson, Sam Houston and other distinguished Americans."[12]

He served twice as president of the board for the Missouri Historical Society, from 1907 to 1913 and from 1925 to 1930. During his first term, he was instrumental along with David R. Francis in securing the society's present site and building for its headquarters. In 1928, he was elected president of Washington University but was too ill to serve except in name.[13]

Never limited in his youth by lack of money or education, William K. Bixby recognized no boundaries to his enthusiasms as he matured. The great wealth he accumulated became the touchstone for great collections and magnanimous benevolence to the city of St. Louis. Sixty-eight years after his death, the *Post-Dispatch* named him one of the most influential St. Louisans of the twentieth century.[14] Yet he never lost sight of the importance of family and friends. As curator Owyoung so aptly expressed it, "Mr. Bixby was an extraordinary man, larger than life, but down to earth."[15]

---

1. Robert R. Archibald, "From Baggage Handler to Philanthropist: William Bixby," *St. Louis Business Journal*, October 2–8, 1995, 25A.
2. Catherine Schaefer Frankel, "Mohican Cottage on Lake George" (master's thesis, University of Pennsylvania, 1990), 12.
3. Carolyn Bixby Fordyce (William K. Bixby's granddaughter), conversation with the author, 2007.
4. Brent Benjamin, *Handbook of the Collection of the Saint Louis Art Museum* (St. Louis: Saint Louis Art Museum, 2004), 11.
5. W. H. Samson, *Sketch of W. K. Bixby*, Bixby Family Papers, Lake George, NY, 3.
6. Landmarks Association, *Tombstone Talks* (St. Louis: Author, 1975), 18.
7. Manuel Garcia files, Bellefontaine Cemetery.
8. Ibid.

9. Carolyn Bixby Fordyce, conversation with the author.

10. David Bonetti, "Spotlight on Asian Arts," *St. Louis Post-Dispatch*, March 13, 2005, F3.

11. *Mr. William K. Bixby,* Manuel Garcia files, Bellefontaine Cemetery, 231.

12. "William Keeney Bixby," *The National Cyclopedia of American Biography* (New York: James T. White & Co., 1984).

13. "Influential St. Louisans of the 1900s," *St. Louis Post-Dispatch*, November 8, 1999, A2.

14. Archibald, "Baggage Handler."

15. Bonetti, "Asian Arts."

FRANK BLAIR JR.
1821–1875

IN THE DOME of the Capitol Building in Washington, D.C., every state has two statues to represent its greatest sons: Francis Preston "Frank" Blair Jr. and Thomas Hart Benton honor Missouri. Blair earned his monument as congressman, senator, general, and Lincoln's hatchet man. Born into a prominent family with great political influence, Frank was the favorite son of a father who was a presidential confidant and who believed his son could one day become president. He was sought after as one of the finest orators of his day. Prone to fistfights, he cared only for principle and lived out his convictions to the point of changing political parties twice.

Blair stood six feet tall, with flaming red hair, piercing gray eyes, and an enormous, droopy mustache, the very image of a cavalier. When he gave one of his four-hour-long speeches, he brandished a pistol on the podium, should his words provoke a fight. He neglected his finances in the heat of his quixotic devotion to his causes and died nearly impoverished. One biographer said, "His generosity and magnanimity led to his absolute financial ruin."[1] His impecuniousness embarrassed his wife, Apolline Alexander Blair, who regretted having to borrow money from Frank's parents. One of his nieces refused to speak to him because of his financial dependence on his parents. He was both widely loved and deeply hated. Senator George Graham Vest, a contemporary, said, "He had more personal friends than any public man who ever lived in Missouri. He had bitter enemies like all men of positive convictions will always have, but even his enemies never doubted Frank Blair's sincerity, and always respected him because he was open, fair, fearless, honest and true to his convictions."[2]

Blair died at fifty-four, the father of eight children, with the youngest just three years old. He wore himself out with hard living, deep drinking, and smoking thirty cigars a day. Although his constituents had voted him out of Congress, all of Missouri grieved over his passing on July 9, 1875. The city of St. Louis was draped in mourning, and flags flew at half-mast. Hundreds paid their last respects as he lay in state in his home on Chestnut Street. The survivors of his First Regiment, Missouri Volunteers, escorted their commander's casket when he was laid to rest in Bellefontaine Cemetery beneath a Celtic cross. Ten years later, a crowd of fifteen thousand again honored Blair with the dedication of a statue at the Lindell and Kingshighway entrance to Forest Park. Among the speakers was William Tecumseh Sherman, who had privately called Blair "noble and intelligent as a soldier, but as a politician . . . erratic and unstable."[3]

Frank Blair Jr. was born in Kentucky on February 19, 1821, the year that Missouri entered the Union as a state. His family made up a distinguished political dynasty, with his maternal grandfather governor of Kentucky, his father the confidant of presidents from Andrew Jackson to Lincoln, and his brother Montgomery a member of Lincoln's cabinet. Washington's Blair House, next to the White House, was once the family mansion. President Jackson brought the family to Washington so Blair's father, Francis Preston Blair Sr., could edit the administration's newspaper. After college and law school, his father's friend, Senator Thomas Hart Benton, encouraged Frank to come to St. Louis as he had encouraged his brother Montgomery before him. Frank went into practice with his brother, who was to represent Dred Scott in his case before the Supreme Court. Drained physically by three years of hard work, Frank went west to recover his health. He was visiting a distant cousin, Charles Bent, at Fort Bent on the Santa Fe Trail, when the Mexican War broke out. General Stephen Watts Kearny asked him to serve as attorney general for the new territory of New Mexico. There, Frank assisted in drafting a constitution and code of laws, based on Mexican law and the Missouri code.

When he returned to St. Louis in 1847, he married his distant cousin Apolline. He resumed his law practice and started the first of three newspapers (the other two were the precursors of the *Globe-Democrat* and the *Post-Dispatch*). Thus, he launched his career in politics. After serving two terms in the Missouri legislature, he was elected to Congress in 1856. As a Free-Soil candidate, he freed his own slaves by 1860, boldly championing the emancipation of slaves. Although he also advocated that the freedmen be shipped off to a colony in Africa, his position was largely pragmatic: Slavery robbed white laborers of jobs.

This stand against slavery inspired Blair to switch to the new Republican Party in 1857. He had lost his campaign to be re-elected to the House in 1858 but was returned to Congress in 1860, where he held the crucial post of chairman of the Committee of Military Affairs. At the Republican convention of 1860, he first supported Edward Bates of Missouri but changed his support to Abraham Lincoln, who trusted him implicitly for the next four years, a trust that was never disappointed.

Seeing war as inevitable even before the election, Blair organized a uniformed campaign club known as the Wide Awakes, made up largely of German immigrants who wholeheartedly believed in emancipation. Blair heard rumblings of a plot by the secessionist governor of Missouri, Claiborne Fox Jackson, to capture the U.S. arsenal in St. Louis. To find out the facts, Captain Nathaniel Lyon dressed in Blair's mother-in-law's ample dress and packed pistols under the skirt. Because Mrs. Alexander was well known to be blind, this disguise allowed Lyon to ride her coach through the Confederate encampment and do his own spying to determine if there was indeed cause for alarm. The next day, Captain Lyon, aided by Captain Blair, led the Home Guard from the arsenal to encircle Camp Jackson and force the Rebels to surrender.

While Blair is credited with keeping Missouri in the Union with the Camp Jackson campaign, soon after, he was thrown in jail for vociferously opposing the military command of General John Frémont. The Blairs, father and son, had proposed Frémont as commander to Lincoln, for they were well acquainted with him as the son-in-law of Thomas Hart Benton. Frank Blair became disillusioned with Frémont's extravagant lifestyle and reluctance to fight. The Blairs were able to secure the general's recall. Jessie Benton Frémont, Senator Benton's daughter, never forgave Blair.

Blair would prove a great general, one of the best of those not trained at West Point. He started out by raising and training volunteers for the Union army. When these companies united to form a regiment, he was unanimously elected colonel of the First Regiment of Missouri Volunteers. He was made brigadier general in 1861 and rose to major general in 1862. At a critical ebb in Union fortunes, he raised seven more regiments from Missouri.

He led an advance through blistering Confederate cross fire in the campaign against Vicksburg, Mississippi, and commanded divisions in the battles of Lookout Mountain and Missionary Ridge in Tennessee. As the head of the Seventeenth Corps, he joined Sherman's campaigns, including the March to the Sea.

Frank Blair fought courageously not only on the battlefront but also on the floor of the House of Representatives, where he championed the interests of his commander in chief. He served simultaneously in the army and Congress until he resigned his seat in the House in 1863.

At the close of the war, he came home to both a hero's welcome and financial ruin. He attempted to restore his fortunes with a cotton plantation in Mississippi, but the enterprise failed. Blair returned to Missouri, left the Republican Party over his opposition to Reconstruction, and was nominated as the Democrats' vice presidential candidate in 1868 along with Horatio Seymour, who ran for president. Seymour and Blair suffered a resounding defeat, carrying just eight states to Ulysses S. Grant's twenty-six.

Blair was given another opportunity to serve his country three years later when Senator Charles Drake, author of Missouri's harsh Reconstruction policies, saw that his plans had fallen from favor. In 1871, when President Grant appointed Drake chief justice of the U.S. Court of Claims, a lifetime post, Drake resigned his Senate seat. The Missouri legislature responded by appointing Blair to serve out the last two years of Drake's term. Blair lost his next race for the Senate in 1872 and suffered a stroke the following year. The Missouri governor named him state commissioner of insurance; this job brought Blair the much-needed salary of $5,000.

Frank Blair threw himself into every fight, never taking the easy answer or the popular position. Powerfully ambitious, he never let his ambitions blind him to the honorable course of action. In the course of doing what he saw as right and just, he switched careers and parties, thrashing between the military and the political, Republicans and Democrats. Hotheaded, impulsive, and fierce, Blair was the right man at the most difficult time in U.S. history to keep Missouri in the Union. By putting two Missourians in his cabinet and by heeding the counsel of the Blairs, Lincoln recognized the strategic importance of this border state and of the Blair family. Although Frank Blair never achieved his ultimate presidential ambitions, he served his country admirably and nobly, even to his personal detriment.

---

1. William Ernest Smith, *The Francis Preston Blair Family in Politics* (New York: MacMillan, 1933), 112.
2. William E. Parrish, *Frank Blair: Lincoln's Conservative* (Columbia: University of Missouri, 1998), xi.
3. Lloyd Lewis, *Sherman, Fighting Prophet* (Lincoln: University of Nebraska, 1993), 636.

HENRY TAYLOR BLOW
1817–1875

HENRY TAYLOR BLOW committed himself to St. Louis's progress in business, government, race relations, international trade, education, and the arts. Ironically, he is perhaps best known for his role in the Dred Scott case and as the father of the famous Susan Blow, who started the first all-district kindergarten in the nation. Yet he founded successful manufacturing and mining companies, and he was president of a railroad, state representative, congressman, and ambassador as well. Today, both a school and a street bear his name.

Henry Taylor Blow was born eighth of the ten children of Peter and Elizabeth Taylor Blow in Southampton County, Virginia. Mrs. Blow must have been very proud of her family of origin, for three of her children bear the middle name of Taylor, and Henry Taylor's next younger brother was named Taylor Blow. The Blows moved first to Alabama and then, in 1830, to St. Louis, where they kept a boardinghouse. Mrs. Blow died the next year. Peter Blow did not have a large estate to leave his children, but he was able to educate his sons. Henry graduated from the Jesuit academy that would later be known as Saint Louis University, and he entered a law office with the intention of becoming a lawyer. His father's death in 1832 put an end to Henry's legal studies. Peter left all he had to his two unmarried daughters and to his two youngest sons, Taylor and William. At fifteen, Henry was considered enough of a man to take care of himself. The year before, his sister Charlotte Taylor Blow had married Joseph Charless Jr., whose father had founded the first newspaper west of the Mississippi (see Part 7).

The Charlesses would help Henry find his way in life. Charless hired Henry as a clerk in his wholesale drug and paint company, which he owned with his father. When Joseph Charless Sr. retired in 1836, Charless

Jr. made Henry a partner. According to James Neal Primm in the *Lion of the Valley*, as a businessman Blow was "hawkish, hard-driving and ambitious."[1] Two years after Blow became partner, the company's name was changed to Charless, Blow and Company. As the business prospered, the manufacturing of white lead grew increasingly important. In 1844, the partnership was dissolved, leaving Charless with the drugstore and Blow with the manufacturing firm, now called Collier White Lead and Oil Company, which would grow to be one of the largest factories in the city. Henry took the helm of many businesses. He and his brother Peter organized the Granby Mining and Smelting Company. He served as president of the Iron Mountain Railroad. He was also instrumental in establishing a furnace for the iron industry in Carondelet.

Henry's business successes freed him from the day-to-day drudgery of earning a living and allowed him to focus on his family and friends. He married Minerva, daughter of saddle manufacturer Thornton Grimsley, in

1840. They had nine children. He was a man ahead of his time, encouraging the education of his daughters. In 1849, because their house in St. Louis had burned to the ground and a cholera epidemic was raging, he moved his family to the then-separate city of Carondelet to escape. There, his father-in-law had gifted them with seventeen choice acres. They built a Victorian mansion that included a library with elaborate paneling and stained glass windows that would later be reassembled in the Missouri History Museum.[2] The family hosted many guests, for Blow was courteous and gracious, as befitted a southern gentleman.

His southern upbringing, however, did not influence his politics. He believed in the abolition of slavery, calling the institution "an incubus upon [Missouri's] prosperity and that of her citizens."[3] To this end, he and his family participated in a legal case that tested the limits of slavery and whether a slave was considered a citizen. Peter and Elizabeth Blow had owned a slave who would later come to be known as Dred Scott. He was sold to a Dr. Emerson, who took him to live in the free state of Illinois and the free territory of Wisconsin. When Scott returned to St. Louis, Henry and Taylor Blow encouraged him to sue for his freedom based upon the fact that he had lived in free states.[4] Henry and his brother-in-law put up bonds to finance the case, allowing it to work through the legal system all the way to the Supreme Court. There, Scott lost his bid to be a free man on a ruling based on the principle that a slave is property and not a citizen. Emerson's widow then gave Scott to Taylor, who gave him his freedom.

Politically, Blow's influence spread beyond the Mississippi Valley to the nation as a whole. Henry joined the Republican Party, the party that sought to do away with slavery, in 1854, a time when it took courage of conviction to do so. He was elected to the Missouri State Senate the same year. In 1860, he represented Missouri as a delegate to the Chicago convention that nominated Abraham Lincoln. In 1861, Lincoln appointed him U.S. ambassador to Venezuela. In this capacity, he worked to improve trade between that country and the Mississippi Valley, but he soon resigned to return to the States to put his talents to work for the Union cause. During the Civil War, he was elected to the U.S. House of Representatives, in 1862 and again in 1864. At the end of his second term in 1867, he refused to run again so that he could go back to his many business interests in St. Louis. He did return to public service in 1869, when he accepted President Ulysses S. Grant's appointment as ambassador to Brazil. In 1874, he again reluctantly accepted a public service position, an appointment to the board of commissioners assigned to reorganize the government of the District of Columbia.

Blow died suddenly while on holiday in Saratoga Springs, New York, in 1875, just three months after the death of his wife of thirty-five years. His body was brought back to St. Louis for an extravagant funeral. In an article long enough to fill two full columns, the *Republican* described the rosewood and silver casket in a parlor of the family mansion "and over it, supported by six pillars, was a beautiful floral canopy, composed of the rarest and sweetest flowers."[5] The service lasted two hours, and a special train took mourners from St. Louis to his Carondelet home. The mile-long funeral procession traveled nearly twenty-five miles to Blow's final resting place in Bellefontaine Cemetery.

Blow left his greatest legacy to the city of St. Louis in religious, cultural, and educational endeavors. He enriched the city's life by helping found and fund many establishments including a Presbyterian church, the Philosophical Society, the St. Louis Philharmonic Society, the Twentieth Century Club, the Western Academy of Art, and a Carondelet public school. Students still attend Blow School (named after him, not his daughter) in Carondelet, which is now a part of St. Louis.

---

1. James Neal Primm, *Lion of the Valley* (St. Louis: Missouri Historical Society, 1998), 225.

2. The stained glass windows are currently in storage.

3. *St. Louis Daily Missouri Democrat*, July 2, 1853.

4. John A. Bryan, "The Blow Family and Their Slave Dred Scott," *Bulletin of the Missouri Historical Society* IV (October 1948–July 1949): 231.

5. Obituary, *St. Louis Republican*.

SUSAN BLOW
1843-1916

TODAY, IT IS TAKEN for granted that elementary school starts with kindergarten. In 1873, Susan Blow fought to bring this concept into the St. Louis Public Schools, making St. Louis the first school district in the nation to offer kindergarten. By the time of her death in 1916, more than four hundred cities had kindergartens in the public schools.[1] Before the St. Louis experiment, children started their schooling at age seven and often ended it by age ten. Blow's work was considered so important that her portrait hangs in the governor's reception room in the State Capitol in Jefferson City along with three other prominent Missourians, Mark Twain among them; and the school that housed the first citywide, public school kindergarten in the nation was named to the National Register of Historic Places in 1982. Although her own education was spotty, she wrote learned articles on Dante and educational theory, lectured around the country, and held a teaching position at Columbia University.

When Susan Blow died in New York City on March 26, 1916, her body was brought home to St. Louis to be buried at Bellefontaine Cemetery. The next month, St. Louis celebrated her spirit with a special meeting of the Susan E. Blow Froebel League. Shortly thereafter, a Susan E. Blow Memorial Fund was established to sponsor lectures. Unfortunately, the organization died out the next year, after the United States entered World War I, because the ideas that inspired Blow were German in origin.

Blow was born to wealth and privilege as the first of nine children of Henry Taylor Blow and Minerva Grimsley Blow. Her father had made a fortune in lead manufacturing, among other businesses. The family was very religious: Henry Taylor Blow had founded a Presbyterian church. Her parents placed a high priority on education: Her father had contributed the funds to build the Blow School, a public school still in existence.

Henry Blow served as U.S. congressman and ambassador to Venezuela and Brazil. In 1849, when Susan was six, their house was destroyed during the Great Fire that raged during the Great Cholera Epidemic. Henry Blow took his family out of the city of St. Louis to settle in the relatively safe and separate city of Carondelet.

Although Victorian families placed little emphasis upon educating their daughters, the Blows did put Susan in and out of school several times. At age six, she spent several months in a French school. She then stayed home until she was sent at age eight for a short stint to a school in St. Louis. A governess guided her studies until she was fourteen, when her father brought in a teacher to start a classroom for Susan and a few friends in Carondelet. At sixteen, she and a sister were sent to New York to attend a finishing school known as Miss Haines's, which was not a "thorough one."[2] Fortunately, her father had a fine library where she read extensively such authors as Hegel, Kant, and the Concord school of transcendentalism. Further demonstrating her remarkable intelligence, she taught herself Portuguese so she could serve as her father's secretary when he was ambassador to Brazil.

Attentive parents, the Blows worried about "her aversion to everything except study."[3] Indeed, she never married and was considered a member of the St. Louis School, a literary, philosophical, and educational movement. In 1871, the family made the grand tour of Europe, and Susan became acquainted with the work of Friedrich Froebel, a Swiss educator who believed education should begin in early childhood when a child's intelligence and aptitude for learning could be trained through play. She observed the Froebel-inspired kindergartens that had spread throughout western Europe, Germany in particular, and resolved to bring them back to her hometown. Her father was willing to set up her kindergarten as a private school, but she felt that her mission lay with the children of the public school system.

Her beliefs dovetailed with those of William Torrey Harris, St. Louis superintendent of schools and then U.S. commissioner of education and the man for whom Harris-Stowe Teachers College was named. Faced with a city that had grown in population from 30,000 in 1840 to 300,000 in 1870, the new superintendent wisely undertook a study of the distribution of children throughout the city. What he learned was that many children attended school for only three years, particularly those living along the levee and in the factory districts. Many children were roaming the streets by the age of three. Harris gave Blow his full support with her kindergarten mission, for he believed it would take slum children off the streets and teach them habits of cleanliness and give them a taste for learning they would not otherwise receive. Later, he came to believe that the children of the wealthy also needed kindergarten because they might be neglected and left with servants.

With Harris's blessing, Blow went to New York for a year to study Froebel's methods with his disciple, Maria Kraus-Boelte. Upon her return in 1873, the school board of St. Louis accepted Blow's offer to direct the city's first public school kindergarten in room four of the Des Peres School in Carondelet, with a paid assistant, Mary A. Timberlake, working under her direction. In an article in the *Missouri Historical Review*, Selwyn K. Troen wrote:

They designed a program which bridged the "nurture" of the family and the established program of the district school. Much of their effort was devoted to teaching the young child a complex of virtues and values that were necessary for his integration into the manner and discipline of community life. Thus, great emphasis was placed upon "moral discipline" and he was taught to be neat and clean. . . . He was also trained in those . . . habits of regularity, punctuality, silence, obedience and self-control.[4]

The children learned everything they needed to know in kindergarten through carefully scripted games and songs, which Susan translated from Froebel's German week to week. In addition, in order to learn concepts of space and numbers, the children were given what Froebel called the gifts: blocks, balls, cylinders, and cubes. They worked with paper and clay, weaving and modeling to learn manual dexterity. They planted seeds in a garden outside the classroom and observed their growth. Susan Blow also fought to acquaint the children with great literature through telling stories from the Bible or myths and legends. Compared to the grim and regimented upper grades, kindergarten classrooms were bright and cheerful with children sitting around tables instead of in rows.

The program was so successful that each of the city schools came to start its own kindergarten until the sixty-eight pupils of the Des Peres School in 1873 had grown to nearly nine thousand in schools throughout the city in the eleven years that Blow directed the program. In 1875 when the school board attempted to end the program in a cost-cutting measure, 1,500 people signed a petition that successfully urged them not to do so. In his annual report of 1875–1876, Harris devoted forty pages to the kindergarten. The next year, the United States Centennial Commission in Philadelphia recognized Blow's exhibit with an award to St. Louis for the excellence of kindergarten within the public school system. Her students took her methods all over the country. Not only did she accept no remuneration for her efforts, but she also donated her own money to buy supplies for the kindergartens. Many young women, 150 in 1876–1877 alone, volunteered as assistants in her kindergartens as well.

All of her hard work exhausted her. In 1884, she stopped working because her doctors had diagnosed her with a thyroid condition known as Graves' disease. She stayed in St. Louis for four more years until she moved to Boston in 1884 along with Laura Fischer, who went to direct the kindergarten program of the Boston Public Schools. Blow wrote a book on Dante that was published in 1890. In 1893, after an operation, her health improved and she began the first of five books on Froebel's theories. She helped found the International Kindergarten Union. In 1910, her address to this organization in a meeting held at St. Louis's Soldan High School was met with a standing ovation. Despite the fact that she had no high school education, she was given a three-year appointment to the Teachers College of Columbia University.

In 1895, she moved to Cazenovia, New York, to be near one of her sisters. She began lecturing about early childhood education across the country, quitting just a month before her death. Susan Blow was a woman with a mission that she accomplished by drawing upon her personal wealth and her remarkable intelligence.

---

1. Obituary, *St. Louis Globe-Democrat*, March 28, 1916.
2. Patricia Rice, "She Put Kindergarten in Public Education," *St. Louis Post-Dispatch*, September 12, 1974.
3. Ibid.
4. Selwyn K. Troen, "Operation Headstart: The Beginning of the Public School Kindergarten Movement," *Missouri Historical Review* (July 1953): 218.

ROBERT S. BROOKINGS
1850–1932

ROBERT BROOKINGS excelled in everything he undertook: business, philanthropy, and public service. Undeterred by convention, he became a partner in a corporation at twenty-one and married for the first time at seventy-seven. Although his formal education consisted only of elementary school and one year of high school, he became an educator and economic theorist. His work laid the foundation for Washington University in St. Louis's present strength and for the Brookings Institution, a Washington, D.C., government think tank that would not exist without his efforts. By the time his ashes returned to St. Louis to rest eternally at Bellefontaine Cemetery, the universities of Yale, Harvard, Washington, and Missouri had granted him honorary degrees, and the governments of the United States, France, and Italy had awarded him the Distinguished Service Medal, the Legion of Honor, and the Commander of the Crown, respectively.

Born in Maryland, Brookings left high school after one year and set out for St. Louis, the bustling gateway city where opportunity lay. Because his physician father had died when Brookings was two, money was scarce in the family. Brookings arrived in St. Louis in 1867 as a handsome boy of seventeen, following in his brother's footsteps to work as a clerk. Room and board ate up his entire $25-a-month salary, so he moonlighted as a bookkeeper for an additional $10. He joined the same firm as his brother, the Cupples and Marston Company, which sold woodenware. Coming into work early to practice sales techniques, he soon persuaded Samuel Cupples to give him a job as a salesman, known as a drummer. Using hard-nosed tactics and gifted salesmanship, he and his brother proved tremendous successes and decided to start their own firm four years after he began working for Cupples. "It was said later of Samuel Cupples that he was an able man; but that he displayed genius only once in his life,"[1] when he told Robert Brookings that he would make him a partner rather than lose the young man. Brookings spent ten years on the road, and by the end of that period the Cupples Company dominated the woodenware trade in the whole country.[2] By the time he was thirty, Brookings was a millionaire, and although his title was only vice president, he was practically the sole power at Cupples.[3]

Perhaps the greatest triumph of his business career for both himself and his city was Cupples Station, completed in 1895. Casting a shrewd eye over the company balance sheet, he saw opportunity in an alarming increase in drayage rates for conveying freight from railroads in the heart of the city to warehouses along the river. He came up with the original idea of locating the warehouses for all city merchants directly on the railroad so trains could load or unload inside the warehouses themselves, eliminating drayage altogether. It was an idea "worth more to the commercial interests of the city than any other institution,"[4] according to the 1899 *Encyclopedia of the History of St. Louis*. A model of efficiency, the eighteen warehouses of Cupples Station designed by William Eames and Thomas Young would be operated as a separate corporation that "revolutionized the distribution of goods in St. Louis and served as a model for other cities."[5] Near the south end of the Eads Bridge Tunnel, Cupples Station had its own complex of ten tracks running directly beneath the seven-story warehouses. But the effort to buy up the equivalent of eight blocks from many different owners and then build the warehouses brought Brookings to near exhaustion when loans came due during a business crash. Faced with bankruptcy when no U.S. bank would advance the money, Brookings's innovation was saved by a $3 million loan from a British bank.

The success and also perhaps the emotional aftermath of developing Cupples Station provoked a turning point in Brookings's life. He retired from business at the age of forty-six to devote himself to public welfare. Because he had attempted to compensate for his own limitations with a program of reading directed by a Washington University dean, Brookings decided to devote himself to education as the means of helping others improve themselves. Casting about for a worthy institution, he at first considered founding his own university but instead fixed upon the struggling Washington University because it continued to provide a good education for its one hundred students even though it operated under dire financial strain.

In November 1895, Brookings took over the presidency of the school's Board of Trustees and began the process of transforming the small city school into one of the leading universities in the Midwest, thus putting it on the path to national prominence. Within three months, he had secured the funds—largely by soliciting his friends—for the purchase of the one-hundred-acre parcel that would become the Hilltop Campus. By 1899, the school's endowment rested secure, built upon the rock-solid foundation of Cupples Station representing a $3 million donation by Brookings and Cupples. Eminent industrialists and friends such as William K. Bixby, Adolphus Busch, and Edward Mallinckrodt proved some of his best lieutenants in the building campaign. Ever resourceful, Brookings found much-needed capital by renting out the new buildings to the 1904 World's Fair. Brookings gave his greatest service to the university by developing its medical school into "one of the finest medical centers in the country."[6]

A 1917 appointment to the War Industries Board put Brookings on course for a third career. President Woodrow Wilson was well aware that modern war was total war, and he formed the War Industries Board to make sure that U.S. companies were united in the effort to supply and distribute all of the goods and food the army and navy needed. In 1918, Wilson appointed Brookings chairman of a board in charge of price fixing. If an industry was making three times more profit during the war than before the war, Brookings made sure the industry accepted price controls.

In the course of his war experience, Brookings recognized the nation's need for young men and women trained as statesmen, a perception that was realized in the Brookings Institution. Moving to Washington, D.C., he settled in a small suburban cottage to simplify his life from the grand style of St. Louis and to devote all of his financial resources to his new endeavor. In 1916, he had been appointed the first board chairman of the Institute for Government Research. Six years later, he persuaded the Carnegie Corporation to provide funds to establish the Institute of Economics. Two years after that, he gave his own money to start a graduate school of economics and government. These three institutes combined to form the Brookings Institution in 1928. Called the "oldest and most ambitious of the many 'think tanks,'"[7] research from the Brookings Institution centered on intricate problems of finance and economics. Brookings Institution reports "left an indelible mark on federal government, from the creation of the federal budget process in the early 1920s to the triumph of its tax proposals in the 1986 Tax Reform Act."[8] By 1973, the institution had such power that the Nixon administration plotted to burn it down.[9] Brookings involved himself heavily in the operation of the institution. Economics fascinated him to the point that he published three books espousing theories about how management, capital, and labor could work together for the good of humankind.

Until Brookings was seventy-seven, he lived as a bachelor in great style. He built three mansions in St. Louis and purchased a vast country estate, filling them with elaborate furniture and paintings. In 1927, he surprised all his friends by eloping with fifty-one-year-old Isabel January. She had long been his confidante, contributing a building to the Washington University Law School and another as headquarters for the Brookings Institution.

A cutthroat businessman, yet a pursuer of the arts, Robert Brookings approached all endeavors with single-minded focus, taking an original viewpoint of every proposition. Deficient in formal schooling, he built Washington University and founded the Brookings Institution so that others might have the education he lacked.

---

1. Hermann Hagedorn, *Brookings: A Biography* (New York: MacMillan, 1936), 53.
2. Ibid., 55.
3. Ibid., 74.
4. Hyde and Conard, *Encyclopedia of St. Louis*, 245.
5. *American Biography*, 122.
6. Ibid., 123.
7. Jon Sawyer, "The Granddaddy of All Think Tanks," *St. Louis Post-Dispatch*, March 17, 1991, 1F.
8. Ibid.
9. Ibid.

ADOLPHUS BUSCH
1839–1913

LILLY ANHEUSER BUSCH
1844–1928

EVERYTHING ABOUT HIM was grand. President William Howard Taft called him "Prince." He and his wife had thirteen children and four houses. His estate was the largest that was probated in Missouri at the time. He earned $2 million a year. The headline about his death led the front page of the *Globe-Democrat* on October 11, 1913: "Adolphus Busch, St. Louis's best known citizen and philanthropist, died last night in his castle on the Rhine."[1]

His funeral reflected the opulence of his life. An estimated thirty thousand people viewed the body when it lay in state in the family mansion. Among them were the U.S. secretary of agriculture and the presidents of Harvard and the University of California. Twenty-five trucks took floral arrangements to the cemetery while a 250-piece band led the solemn parade. The procession stretched twenty miles along Broadway from No. 1 Busch Place, across from the brewery, to Bellefontaine Cemetery. The street was lined with as many as 100,000 mourners. During the burial, Mayor Henry W. Kiel asked that the city observe five minutes of respect. Lights went off at the Jefferson and Planter's House hotels, and the streetcars stopped. Former U.S. secretary of labor and commerce Charles Nagel gave the eulogy, calling Busch "a giant among men."[2]

Two years after his burial, his grieving widow, Lilly Anheuser Busch, decided that the mausoleum her parents had erected at Bellefontaine was not suitable for her prince. She had it torn down and the other family members, including her parents, reinterred outside. The new Bavarian

Gothic structure designed by Thomas Barnett was completed in 1921. It cost $250,000, a sum worth about $10 million in 2005,[3] according to Bellefontaine Cemetery superintendent Michael Tiemann. The walls are Missouri red granite, pink in color. Tiemann said, "It was quarried in Missouri. When it was finally all cut up, they assembled all the pieces at the quarry to make sure everything fit. Then supposedly they took it apart, and as they took it apart they numbered every piece. Then they brought it all out here. It was like putting a giant erector set back together again."[4] The roof is gray slate and has bronze ribs, lacy towers, and gargoyles. The inside is lit by radiant stained glass; statues of a knight and his lady over the portal guard the tombs of Lilly and Adolphus. Grapevines, representing Adolphus's birthplace in German wine country as well as his favorite beverage (he called beer "dot schlop"),[5] climb the bronze gate. Above them, Bavarian forest creatures and hop flowers decorate the lintel, which bears the apt motto "Veni, Vidi, Vici"—Julius Caesar's immortal words meaning, "I came, I saw, I conquered."

Adolphus Busch followed two of his older brothers to the United States in 1857. Although he was wealthy and well educated, as the twenty-first of twenty-two children, he did not expect a large share of his father Ulrich's estate. St. Louis's location on the continent's greatest waterway drew the Busch family like a magnet because, having been raised along the Rhine, they were skilled in river trade. After a brief stint as a mud clerk assessing the cargo of riverboats, he entered into a partnership with Ernst Battenberg to found the first of many businesses, a company that sold brewing supplies. The three dozen–odd breweries in the city created a booming market for his business. According to James Neal Primm, author of *Lion of the Valley*, over one-seventh of the inhabitants of the city at that time were German immigrants or descendants with a thirst for beer.[6] In addition to being a great market for beer, St. Louis was blessed with the two natural resources necessary for manufacturing and storing it in the days before refrigeration—an ample water supply and caves for keeping it cool.

In 1861, Adolphus married Elise "Lilly" Anheuser, the daughter of one of his customers, Eberhard Anheuser. Eberhard was a wealthy soap manufacturer who had lent money to the Bavarian Brewery, which he renamed Anheuser when the small company went bankrupt. Eberhard bought out the other creditors rather than lose his investment.

Following a six-month stint in the army during the Civil War, Busch returned to St. Louis and entered the business. He bought out the stake of Anheuser's partner, William D'Oench. Busch devoted his considerable energy and business acumen to making and distributing beer, although he did not actually become president of the company until Eberhard died in 1880. The year before, his success had been recognized when the brewery again changed names. This time the name stuck: Anheuser-Busch.

Busch's immediate use of two technical innovations, pasteurization and refrigeration, catapulted the company to national prominence. According to William J. Vollmer, corporate historian of the Anheuser-Busch Company, Adolphus probably learned of Louis Pasteur's experiments during one of his trips to Europe to study brewing techniques.[7] Busch tested pasteurization and became the first American brewer to bottle pasteurized beer, four years before Pasteur published his studies in 1876. Busch immediately saw the implications for creating a national market for his product. Before pasteurization, all beer had to be manufactured locally because it spoiled in two weeks. Busch also recognized the significance of another innovation: Manufactured refrigeration freed brewers from having to use caves to cool beer. While the Lemp Brewery (see Part 2) was the first to use refrigeration locally, "Busch was the first to use it on a massive scale,"[8] said Vollmer. Busch soon used refrigerated railroad cars to ship his product around the country.

Further demonstrating his business acumen, Busch was an early practitioner of what is now called vertical integration, buying all components of the business, from raw materials to distribution. He owned bottling factories, ice-manufacturing plants, stave makers, timberland, coal mines, and a refrigeration company. He organized the Manufacturer's Railway and bought other railways. In Europe, he bought the rights from Rudolf Diesel to assemble diesel engines in America.

Busch went to work to improve the flavor of his beer. Carl Conrad, an importer of wines and champagnes, first registered the name Budweiser and had the Anheuser Company manufacture it for him. He and Busch traveled to Europe, where Busch studied the pilsner process used in brewing Budweiser. According to Peter Hernon and Terry Ganey in *Under the Influence*, "Adolphus got the rights to Budweiser from C. Conrad and Company in October 1882 when Conrad went bankrupt."[9]

After Busch's death, "[Lilly] lived her life peacefully, but her remaining years [were] clouded by scandal."[10] Lilly remained at her castle in Germany for three years after the outbreak of World War I. There, according to Tiemann, "She was the houseguest of the kaiser."[11] In 1917, President Woodrow Wilson established the office of Alien Property Custodian. Lilly's children were told that she had to get back to the United States or this newly founded office would confiscate her property. Upon her return, the seventy-four-year-old Lilly was submitted to forty hours of detention and a humiliating physical examination because of widespread anti-German sentiment. To offset this bad publicity, she opened the gardens of her home in Pasadena, California, to the public and donated the ticket revenue to disabled veterans. She had another skirmish with the law in 1927; Lilly and two of her daughters were fined $57,000 by the collector of the Port of New York upon their return from a European tour. This unusually large fine was levied against the Busch ladies for not declaring jewelry bought abroad. Her son August said that the jewels in question came from a knee-length diamond necklace, purchased in the United States, that Lilly had brought to the Continent to have remade into bracelets. Authorities refused to listen to him.

According to Hernon and Ganey, "The smuggling affair darkened Lilly's last days."[12] A few months later, she had a heart attack and developed pneumonia. The four children who lived in the United States were summoned to her bedside in Pasadena, and a week later, on February 17, 1928, she died. A train bore her body back to St. Louis, where she lay in state to be buried beside her husband. Thus, the lady once more took her place beside her knight in the beautiful Bavarian Gothic chapel that she built for them.

---

1. *St. Louis Globe-Democrat*, October 11, 1913, 1.
2. Peter Hernon and Terry Ganey, *Under the Influence: The Unauthorized Story of the Anheuser-Busch Dynasty* (New York: Simon & Schuster, 1991), 86.
3. "How Much Is That?," *Economic History Services*, http://eh.net.
4. Michael Tiemann, *Oral History*, tape XII, 209.
5. Hernon and Ganey, *Under the Influence*, photo caption facing 194.
6. Primm, *Lion of the Valley*, 196, 314.
7. Gregory Cancelada, "Adolphus Busch's Vision Created Brewing Giant." *St. Louis Post-Dispatch*, n.d., 9.
8. Ibid., 11.
9. Hernon and Ganey, *Under the Influence*, 37.
10. Ibid., 136.
11. Tiemann, *Oral History*, 208.
12. Hernon and Ganey, *Under the Influence*, 138.

WILLIAM CHAUVENET
1820–1870

WILLIAM CHAUVENET exhibited an unusual combination of leadership and academic excellence. He was imbued with a personal mission to use his gifts where they could do the most good.

Chauvenet was born in 1820 in Milford, Pennsylvania. He entered Yale at age sixteen. There, he was a frequent contributor to the school paper and a pianist with the Beethoven Society. Despite his scholarly attainments, he did not neglect the social side of life; he was one of the eight founders of the prestigious Skull and Bones Society.[1] He graduated in 1840 with highest honors in mathematics and classics.

An 1841 appointment as professor of mathematics to the navy led Chauvenet to see the necessity of a United States naval academy. While not the first to propose a naval academy, he was the one to see the concept through to completion. When Chauvenet first taught midshipmen, naval officers were trained during active service aboard ship. He first instructed in math onboard the USS *Mississippi*. He became head of the Naval Asylum in 1842, where prospective officers took an eight-month course on land. Not satisfied with the course, Chauvenet drew up a tentative plan for a two-year course and presented it to several succeeding secretaries of the navy until it was finally accepted in 1845. When the Naval Academy was formed at Annapolis, Maryland, Chauvenet became president of the academic board. In 1851, Chauvenet sat on the board that recommended the course of study be extended to four years. He served at various times as professor of mathematics, surveying, astronomy, and navigation. At his insistence, an astronomical observatory was established. At an 1890 Annapolis alumni dinner, Admiral S. R. Franklin proclaimed Chauvenet the "Father of the Naval Academy."[2] In 1916, Congress placed a bronze plaque to this effect in the library at Annapolis.

At Washington University in St. Louis, Chauvenet once again saw an opportunity to assist in organizing a great educational institution. Although he had previously turned down a chair in mathematics at Yale in 1855 to continue his work at Annapolis, Chauvenet accepted a position at Washington University in 1859. He refused a second offer from Yale, this time a professorship of astronomy and natural philosophy. With the death of Washington University's first chancellor, Joseph Hoyt, who had been Chauvenet's classmate at Yale, Chauvenet was selected to lead the new institution in 1861. He served as chancellor until his death in 1870, when William Greenleaf Eliot, the university's founder, succeeded him at the helm.

Chauvenet wrote many treatises and textbooks that continued to be used well into the twentieth century.[3] His greatest work was *A Manual of Spherical and Practical Astronomy*. His *Theory of the Ribbed Arch* introduced James Buchanan Eads to the mathematical formulas necessary to design his great bridge.

William Chauvenet conferred great distinction on the educational institutions he helped form: the U.S. Naval Academy and Washington University. He was conscious at every step of the implications of an education. With enthusiasm, energy, and vision, he laid the paths that others would successfully follow.

---

1. "Tardy Honors at Last Given to St. Louisan 'Father of the Naval Academy,'" *St. Louis Post-Dispatch Sunday Magazine,* January 20, 1918, 12.

2. Ibid.

3. "William Chauvenet," Manuel Garcia files, Bellefontaine Cemetery.

AT THE HIGHEST POINT of the cemetery, beneath a simple but elegant granite obelisk graced with his bronze likeness, lies William Clark. It is appropriate that his grave commands a view of the Mississippi River close to the point where it joins the Missouri River, for the Missouri bore Clark, Meriwether Lewis, and their comrades west on their Voyage of Discovery.

Clark was originally buried in 1838 on the property of his prosperous nephew John O'Fallon (the property is now known as O'Fallon Park). It was the grandest funeral of the day. Cannons fired a military salute, and the funeral procession stretched out more than a mile. The entire city of St. Louis mourned him.

Clark and six other members of his family were reinterred in Bellefontaine Cemetery on October 23, 1860. The monument, the most-visited site in the cemetery, was dedicated in 1904 to mark the centennial of the Louisiana Purchase. Clark's son, Jefferson Kearny Clark, paid $25,000 (equivalent to approximately $425,000 in 2005) for it and drew up the plans, but his wife, Mary Susan Glasgow Clark, had to complete them after he died in 1900. The Clark monument was restored and rededicated May 21, 2004, on the bicentennial of the day that the Corps of Discovery set out from St. Charles, Missouri. At this event, representatives of the Shoshone, Osage, and Mandan tribes spoke, reflecting Clark's service to their nations as superintendent of Indians[1] during the final three decades of his life.

Clark's greatest adventure began as part of President Thomas Jefferson's vision for finding a passage by water to the Pacific Ocean. Jefferson had already commissioned the expedition to find the Northwest Passage to the Pacific in 1803 when he brought about the Louisiana Purchase. Jefferson thus gave the mission the added objective of finding out just what it was he had purchased from Napoléon. Jefferson hired and trained his secretary, Meriwether Lewis, to lead what would prove to be one of the greatest explorations of all times.

Soon afterward, Lewis was given the opportunity to add another officer to the Corps of Discovery. He chose Clark, the man under whom he had served in the army of General "Mad Anthony" Wayne in the Northwest Indian Wars in 1795. While they had only served together six months, it was time enough for Lewis and Clark to form a close relationship. They each brought different and necessary strengths to the expedition they were to lead. While both possessed superior intellectual and athletic abilities, Lewis and Clark needed each other's skills. Lewis was trained to make observations of plants and animals, which he carefully documented. Clark had the skills to handle boats and to find paths through the wilderness. Both kept careful journals, though Clark was embarrassed about his lack of education and deferred to Lewis when something needed to be formally written.[2] Lewis made celestial observations to plot the longitude and latitude of their trail. Using these, his own notes, and information garnered from fur traders and military explorers, Clark made a map in 1810 that he deemed "much more Correct than any which has been before published."[3] In fact, in 2004, Clark scholar Landon Y. Jones called this map "a cartographic masterpiece, a remarkably accurate rendering of the inner continent of North America."[4]

While Clark began his career as an Indian fighter in the mold of his older brother George Rogers Clark, the Voyage of Discovery changed his attitude toward Indians. The Corps of Discovery would never have survived without the Indians they met along the way. The Mandan and Clatsop provided them with food over the long winters, the Shoshones gave them the horses they needed to cross the mountains, the Nez Perce told the expedition important information, and a Shoshone known as "Old Toby" guided them through the Rockies. Having thought of Indians as their enemies in the past, Clark and Lewis made a great effort to treat them with respect along the trail. They had been specifically told to do so in the president's letter of instruction to Lewis.

Mindful of the importance of the territory that the expedition covered and the resistance of both Indians and British traders to U.S. claims of sovereignty, Clark spent winters on the trail drawing up a plan for a series of forts and trading posts. When the expedition approached the Pacific, the ordinarily prosaic Clark wrote what has become one of the best-remembered phrases from both captains' journals: "Ocian in view! O! the joy!"[5]

Cheering crowds greeted their return to St. Louis on September 23, 1806. While they were unable to find the Northwest Passage, their expedition was in every other way a success, and all good things seemed to be coming their way. Congress granted the captains double pay and 1,600 acres of land west of the Mississippi. (Throughout his life, Clark would remain land rich but cash poor.) Lewis was appointed territorial governor of Louisiana, a region that included Missouri and was based in St. Louis, while federal officials named Clark agent of Indian affairs and brigadier general of the militia. Happily, Clark began courting Julia Hancock, who was only fifteen years to his thirty-six.[6] They married in 1808 and in the next ten years had five children, the first of whom they named Meriwether Lewis Clark.

Fortune, however, soon turned its back on both of the explorers. Along with Manuel Lisa, Clark made a significant investment in the Missouri Fur Company, and Lewis came on board as a silent partner. Its failure along with other debts put them in financial peril.

After Lewis's death, Clark took over the editing of their journals, which were published in 1814. Sales were disappointing, and he never earned a penny for these labors. Today they are considered classics.

In 1813, Clark was appointed territorial governor for seven years, the post that Lewis had formerly held, and continued to act as Indian agent. When Missouri became a state in 1820, he ran for governor. Despite his popularity in the territory, he lost the election. Although he had spent his entire adult life in government, he had never held an elective office and did not understand campaigning. Moreover, his beloved wife Julia was seriously ill, and in a sentimental gesture, he left midcampaign and took her to visit her family in Virginia, where she died.

Widowed and defeated, he returned to St. Louis to raise his five young children. The next year, he married Julia's cousin and friend Harriet Kennerly Radford, a widow with three young children of her own. She bore Clark two more children. Though eighteen years his junior, she died in 1831, leaving him a widower for the last seven years of his life.

After his defeat in the gubernatorial election, Clark was appointed U.S. superintendent of Indian affairs at St. Louis and served in this post until he died in 1838. During his career, he signed thirty-seven separate treaties with the Indians. These resulted in absorbing Indian territories to feed the insatiable land hunger of white settlers. He must have been a masterful negotiator in implementing federal policy: The treaties Clark signed gave the United States title to 419 million acres of Indian land, sending more than 80,000 natives from their homelands to the west. In 1808, he persuaded the peaceful, assimilated Osage tribe of Missouri to surrender 50,000 acres of its fertile lands for a blacksmith, a mill, plows, two log houses, gunpowder, $1,800, and the promise of U.S. Army protection against their enemies. While he hailed the treaty as a triumph at the time, in later years he lamented his role in the taking of rich Osage lands for such a pittance. According to Major Ethan Allen Hitchcock, his aide in the St. Louis Indian Office, Clark said shortly before he died "that it was the hardest treaty on the Indians he ever made, and that if he was to be damned hereafter it would be for the making of that treaty. It really seemed to weigh upon his conscience, and he was the kindest man in the world to any Osages who might visit St. Louis, but then he was kind to everybody."[7]

Therein lies the moral ambiguity of his position; Clark was kinder to the Indians than most, yet his policies took away their ancestral lands. Clark had a vision of Indians turning away from hunting to become peaceful citizen-farmers: "Notwithstanding his long years of association with native people, the thought that they might prefer to retain their traditional ways never seems to have seriously entered his mind."[8] Clark was convinced that the only way to prevent deadly conflicts between Indians and white settlers was to remove the Indians from potential confrontation with the settlers. In other words, he thought he was saving them even though he took them away from their homes and livelihoods and turned them into refugees.

Clark's name is known to every school child in this country for his role in the Lewis and Clark expedition, but it is his tenures as Indian agent, territorial governor, and superintendent of Indians that created his most enduring legacy. Despite the fact that Clark is responsible for claiming more land from the Indians than any other person,[9] this part of his life has seldom been written about.[10] The fact remains that the treaties he negotiated not only began to change the complexion of the West from red to white but also from wilderness to farmland. His work formed the basis of future Indian policy, thus molding the face of the United States.

---

1. This position was later known as superintendent of Indian affairs.
2. Landon Y. Jones (author of *William Clark and the Shaping of the West*), e-mail to the author, October 8, 2007.
3. Landon Y. Jones, *William Clark and the Shaping of the West* (New York: Hill and Wang, 2004), 192.
4. Ibid.

5. Ibid., 114.

6. Carolyn Gilman, *Lewis and Clark: Across the Divide* (Washington, D.C.: Smithsonian Books, 2003), 130. Clark family legend has it that Clark decided Julia Hancock was the one he would marry when he first saw her at her family's Virginia plantation five years earlier. "If so, he was prescient because she was only ten years old."

7. William E. Foley, *Wilderness Journey* (Columbia: University of Missouri Press, 2004), 174.

8. Ibid., 236.

9. Jay Buckley, *William Clark, Indian Diplomat* (Norman: University of Oklahoma, 2008), xiii.

10. Ibid., x.

CARL CORI
1896–1984
GERTY CORI
1896–1957

WHEN GERTY CORI shared the Nobel Prize in Medicine with Carl Cori in 1947, she became the first American woman to take the prize, the third woman in history. The Coris' work was so intertwined that it is impossible to distinguish their efforts. In his half of their Nobel acceptance speech Carl said, "Our efforts have been largely complementary, and one without the other would not have gone as far as in combination."[1] Yet such was the prejudice against women at the time that he had to qualify his remarks by saying, "That the award . . . included my wife as well has been a source of deep satisfaction to me."[2] In 1931, when the equally qualified Coris came to Washington University in St. Louis, Carl became chairman of the department and Gerty became a research assistant. At a 2008 symposium honoring Gerty, it was revealed: "This was one of the few places that offered her a position. . . . She was happy to have it."[3] Ironically, today Gerty is the more celebrated of the pair for she is considered a pioneer as a woman of science. A March 2008 U.S. postage stamp issue of four great American scientists paid tribute to Gerty with a stamp bearing her portrait.

Both were born in 1896 in a part of Austria that later became Czechoslovakia, but they didn't meet until medical school. When Gerty (Gerty was not her nickname; she was named after an Austrian warship)[4] decided she wanted to study science, she discovered she lacked the prerequisites in Latin, physics, chemistry, and mathematics. Within one year, she attained the equivalent of eight years of Latin and five of science and math[5] and was admitted to medical school at the University of Prague, an unusual achievement for a woman at that time. Gerty and Carl both entered at age eighteen and earned their medical degrees four years later in 1920, at which time they married. They collaborated on a research project on the immune bodies of blood that led to their first joint publication.[6] Carl was drafted into the Austrian army during World War I. The couple immigrated to the United States in 1922 because of what Carl called "indelible impressions" from the war as well as fears over rising anti-Semitism since Gerty was Jewish.[7] They were naturalized as U.S. citizens in 1928.

In the United States, the Coris met resistance to their collaboration, stemming from prejudice against women in science. The director of the Institute for the Study of Malignant Disease, their first U.S. post, threatened to dismiss Gerty if she did not cease pursuing research with her husband.[8] She did not do so, nor was she dismissed. When Carl was offered a position at the University of Buffalo, Gerty was told that she was "interfering with her husband's career and that doing this was un-American."[9] Carl refused the position because the University of Buffalo would not allow him to work with his wife. Thus, Washington University's offer of positions for both Gerty and Carl seemed fortuitous, even though her rank and salary were much lower than his. Even to achieve this uneven status, Chancellor Arthur Holley Compton had to make a special allowance overruling university nepotism rules. It would be thirteen years before Gerty would achieve the same rank of full professor as her husband, just months before they were awarded the Nobel Prize.

A small, plain room only twenty-five feet square,[10] the Cori laboratory at Washington University was designated a National Historic Landmark by the American Chemical Society.[11] The lab became legendary both for the Coris' groundbreaking biochemical research and for the scientists they mentored. Of these, six went on to become Nobel Prize winners, a distinction that has been "unmatched in science."[12]

Gerty spent as much time as possible in the lab, continuing her research until the last moment before their only son, Thomas, was born.[13] When she contracted a serious illness, she took breaks on a cot in her office when she felt too weak to work. A month before she died, Carl carried her from room to room at the lab, so fervent was her desire to work. "In spite of her illness, Gerty completed some of her most important work during the final years of her life."[14]

The Nobel committee called the discovery for which the Coris were awarded the prize "one of the most brilliant achievements of modern history."[15] They unraveled one of the basic secrets of body chemistry, the way in which the body stores energy and converts it to fuel. In 1935, the Coris first announced their discovery of the metabolic pathway by which the body uses sugar in the form of glucose for fuel. Today, that process is known as the Cori cycle. In the Cori cycle, the liver takes glycogen and converts it to glucose. This sugar is sent to the muscles where it is expended as energy, sent back to the liver as lactic acid, and then recycled. Taught today in seventh-grade biology, it was unknown until the Coris "not only came up with the cycle but demonstrated the recycling,"[16] said

David Kipnis, M.D., chairman of the department of medicine of Washington University. The couple's research also found that the breakdown of glycogen to glucose required an enzyme that the Coris isolated in 1936. This enzyme came to be known as the Cori ester.[17] While these discoveries did not offer cures for metabolic ills, they paved the way for research that could do so.

Although she learned that she had a rare, fatal disease of the bone marrow only months before she accepted the Nobel Prize, Gerty Cori fought until the end to work and to live fully. In her years at the Institute for the Study of Malignant Disease, she had studied the effects of X-rays on the human body, which "may have brought about her illness later in life."[18]

When she died, her ashes were scattered, but her son later erected a cenotaph (a memorial without the person's physical remains) to the memories of Gerty and Carl Cori in Bellefontaine Cemetery.

In 1960, Carl married again. His new wife, Anne Fitzgerald-Jones, shared his extrascientific interests in archaeology, art, and literature. "Carl Cori's wit and grace flourished during this last period of his life in the warm atmosphere of his and Anne Cori's home."[19] At the age of seventy, Carl moved with Anne to Boston, where he took a position at the Harvard Medical School. There, just as Gerty had done before him, he continued with his research until he died at the age of eighty-eight.

Gerty and Carl Cori were fortunate to enjoy what Shakespeare termed "the marriage of true minds." Together, they rejoiced in discovering fundamental truths about the human body.

---

1. Mary Dains, ed., *Show Me Missouri Women* (Kirksville, MO: Thomas Jefferson University, 1989), 206.

2. Ibid.

3. Courtney Lehew, introductory remarks presented at "Gerty Cori, M.D.: A Celebration of Her Work," Washington University Medical School, St. Louis, March 17, 2008.

4. Obituary, *St. Louis Globe-Democrat*, October, 27, 1957.

5. Marilyn Bailey Ogilvie and Joy Dorothy Harvey, *The Biographical Dictionary of Women in Science* (New York: Taylor and Francis, 2000), 293.

6. Dains, *Missouri Women*.

7. David Kipnis, M.D. (chairman of the department of medicine, Washington University in St. Louis), interview with the author, March 25, 2008. Gerty had converted to Catholicism hoping to be more acceptable to Carl's parents. "Both she and Carl were irreligious."

8. Ogilvie and Harvey, *Women in Science*.

9. Ibid.

10. George McCue, "Cori + Cori = Nobel Prize," *Science Illustrated*, 1947, Missouri Historical Society files, 24.

11. Larry Shapiro, M.D. (vice chancellor for medical affairs of Washington University), remarks presented at "Gerty Cori, M.D.: A Celebration of Her Work," Washington University Medical School, March 17, 2008.

12. Ibid.

13. Ogilvie and Harvey, *Women in Science*.

14. Shaun Hunter, *Leaders in Medicine* (New York: Weigl Educational Publishers, 1998), 11.

15. Hunter, *Leaders*, 10.

16. Kipnis, interview. Kipnis himself is internationally known as a pioneer in diabetes research.

17. The Cori ester is pictured in the background of the Gerty Cori postage stamp. "There is an error in the structure of the molecule. By the time it was noticed, 20 million had been printed," said Carl Frieden, Ph.D., at the 2008 Gerty Cori symposium.

18. Hunter, *Leaders*, 9.

19. National Council Staff, *Biographical Memoirs* (Washington, DC: National Academies Press, 1992), 96.

JAMES BUCHANAN EADS
1820–1887

KNOWLEDGE OF THE name James Buchanan Eads has almost disappeared except for two of his greatest accomplishments. First, the Eads Bridge that spans the Mississippi at St. Louis is the only bridge to be named for its engineer.[1] Second, his name is commemorated in both the town of Port Eads along the Louisiana jetties and in Eads Square in New Orleans for his building of the jetties that turned New Orleans into the world's largest port. In 1927, a vote by the deans of America's engineering colleges included Eads among the top five engineers of all time, along with Leonardo da Vinci, James Watts, Ferdinand de Lesseps, and Thomas A. Edison.[2]

Eads was a kind and generous man. During the Civil War, he sent a check for $1,000 to the War Department to help homeless Confederates as well as Union sympathizers because the war was "an accursed contest between brothers."[3] After the war was over, he held a fair to raise money to help feed and house the thousands of homeless refugees who swarmed into St. Louis.[4] Moreover, he believed the purpose of his engineering feats was not to enrich himself but to improve the lot of humankind.

Eads began life as a near pauper, selling apples on the streets of St. Louis to help support his sisters and mother, who ran a boardinghouse. Yet he ended life with such wealth and renown that *Scientific American* proposed that he run for president of the United States. He died while on vacation in the Bahamas. Even though he and his second wife, Eunice, had moved to New York four years earlier, his funeral was celebrated in St. Louis, and he was buried in the family vault beneath a marble sepulcher. A newspaper account of the time read, "The funeral will be a very quiet and unostentatious one, and none but the intimate friends of the family will be allowed to view the remains at the church."[5] More than his genius, orators spoke of his kindness and generosity.[6] Flags flew at half-mast in Port Eads.

Born in Lawrenceburg, Indiana, Eads moved several times because his father, Thomas C. Eads, was a ne'er-do-well pursuing his fortune. The family lost all its possessions in a steamboat fire that broke out as they landed in St. Louis in 1833. When his Missouri business venture failed, Thomas Eads moved upriver, leaving his wife and children behind. Thirteen-year-old James had to leave school to clerk for dry goods merchant Barrett Williams, who, appreciating the boy's spirit and intelligence, gave him free range of his library. In Williams's library, Eads began the self-education that would continue throughout his life. In later years, when Williams suffered a reversal of fortune, Eads would reciprocate his former employer's generosity by giving him enough money to provide comfortably for Williams's old age.

At twenty-two, Eads presented drawings of a salvage boat of his own design to two shipbuilders, Calvin Case and William Nelson. Although Eads had no capital and no previous experience in ship design, his drawings were so good and his confidence so inspiring that the two men went into partnership with him. At the time, salvaging river wrecks was nearly impossible because of the strong Mississippi currents. Eads invented a diving bell using a forty-gallon wine barrel. Since the work was so perilous, he did much of the diving himself. Not only did salvaging make Eads wealthy, but it also gave him an intimate knowledge of the river, for he walked its turbulent depths from the Gulf of Mexico to Iowa.

Eads rose to national prominence during the Civil War. He was a great advocate of the importance of the Mississippi in national defense, and his schemes fed into the strategy of blockading the South. In 1861, Eads was called out of retirement to design for the navy the ironclad gunboats that enabled General Ulysses S. Grant to take Vicksburg, Mississippi. He was given ninety days to build them, and within two weeks he had four thousand men working night and day at his shipyards in Carondelet. By the time the Union ironclads had won their crucial victories at Fort Henry and Fort Donelson in Tennessee and Kentucky, the government still had not paid Eads. When he was finally paid, he sent his first earnings to aid the Confederate victims.

In 1866, a small bridge company was formed in St. Louis with the objective of spanning the Mississippi. Bridges had already crossed the Mississippi north of the city near Chicago, where the riverbed was less deep and the current less swift. City fathers feared this link to the West would cause Chicago to surpass St. Louis as a railroad center, which indeed did come to pass. Eads was chosen chief engineer even though he had no prior experience in bridge building.

Eads proposed a bridge that was elegant in its simplicity, but the public considered it impossible to realize because of its many innovations. These included the first significant use of steel—a material so new as to be considered exotic; the ribbed arch structure; a sand pump; a refinement of the pneumatic caisson method of construction; the cantilevered method of construction; and the bridge's size, making it the largest bridge of its time with the longest spans (five hundred feet). Many of Eads's forty-seven patents were taken out for aspects of the bridge's structure and for devices for its construction.

The difficulties in constructing this bridge would have been insurmountable for a lesser man. Piers had to be sunk almost one hundred feet below the surface of the river. All the while, the builders had to fight a current that ran twelve and a half feet per second and filled with ice floes in the winter. Understanding the shifting sands of the river bottom, Eads knew the bridge's piers had to rest on bedrock. This meant building masonry piers as high as 120 feet (the height of a ten-story building) with as much as seventy-eight feet of that height descending through the sandy riverbed until it hit bedrock. Eads perfected a method of building that he had seen in Europe: Masonry was built atop a caisson, or a metal chamber filled with compressed air. As more stone was added, the increased weight caused the caisson to sink deeper. Workers descended into this chamber to shovel sand into a pump that shot it out into the air, allowing the masonry to descend into the riverbed. Thirteen men died in the process, and two more were paralyzed because at that time no one was aware of the condition now known as the bends. "Even today, this is the deepest pneumatic caisson ever constructed."[7]

President Grant highlighted the program of the dedication of the bridge on July 4, 1874.[8] General William T. Sherman drove the gold spike of completion. Two days earlier, fourteen locomotives had crossed the bridge together to prove it would hold. At the ceremony, Eads promised, "The bridge will exist just as long as it continues to be useful to the people who come after us, even if its years should number those of the Pyramids."[9]

Still, his monumental construction was not impervious to the wiles of man. The railroads boycotted the bridge, thus eliminating their tolls as a source of revenue and forcing the bridge company into bankruptcy. Four years after its completion, the Eads Bridge was sold at auction for 20 cents on the dollar. The sale caused the failure of the National Bank of the State of Missouri. It was the largest bank failure the United States had experienced up to that time. Eads, however, did not suffer financially.[10] Although many involved in the financing of the bridge were indicted, he managed to avoid prosecution.

Eads Bridge has withstood the test of time. Examinations of the bridge's strength through the years have proven Eads correct in his estimation of its endurance. In 1949, electromagnetic strain gauges indicated that the original allowable load of three thousand pounds per lineal foot could be raised to five thousand pounds. Indeed, it is still considered one of the greatest bridges ever built and was designated a National Historic Landmark in 1964. In 1879, poet Walt Whitman wrote, "I have haunted the river every night lately, where I could get a look at the bridge by moon-light. It is indeed a structure of perfection and beauty unsurpassable, and I never tire of it."[11] It continued to inspire praise upon its hundredth anniversary when the *New York Times* architectural critic Ada Louise Huxtable called it "among the most beautiful works of man."[12]

Though unparalleled, the bridge was not Eads's final project. In 1873, even before the bridge was completed, Eads undertook a new venture, reshaping the river. At this time, the pass from the Mississippi to the Gulf of Mexico at New Orleans was so narrow and shallow that on any given day as many as fifty ships waited because only one or two could pass through at a time. While the Army Corps of Engineers proposed to dredge a channel, Eads put forth the novel and far less expensive idea of building jetties to restrict the river, using the currents' own energy to carve a channel. He had such confidence about his plan that he offered to build it at his own risk. If the channel succeeded, the government would pay him $10 million. If it did not, he would get nothing. Needless to say, the government paid. When he died, Eads was working on yet another grand scheme: a railroad capable of carrying ships across Mexico from the Gulf to the Pacific.

The Mississippi River almost ran in the veins of James Buchanan Eads. His accomplishments all drew their inspiration and purpose from the river that he called "the stream which . . . holds in its watery embrace the destinies of the American people."[13] All his accomplishments drew their inspiration and purpose from the river.

---

1. John A. Kouwehnhoven, "Eads Bridge: The Celebration," *Missouri Historical Society Bulletin* (April 1974): 161.

2. Florence Dorsey, *Road to the Sea: The Story of James B. Eads and the Mississippi River* (New York: Rhinehart, 1947), 307.

3. Ibid., 83.

4. Father M. Walasin, S.J., *A Tribute to James Buchanan Eads, Patriot, Engineer, Bridge-Builder*, Saint Louis University, 1974, Manuel Garcia files, Bellefontaine Cemetery, 3.

5. "A Quiet Funeral," obituary, 1887, Manuel Garcia files, Bellefontaine Cemetery.

6. Dorsey, *Road to the Sea*, 297.

7. *The Eads Bridge*. Exhibit catalog for an exhibition at the Art Museum (Princeton, NJ: Princeton University, 1974), 44.

8. Due to his involvement in the Whiskey Scandal, Grant decided it would be wiser not to appear.

9. Walter B. Stevens, *St. Louis: The Fourth City* (Chicago: Clarke, 1909), 581.

10. Because Eads had negotiated the company's loans without being paid for his services, he asked for and was granted the right to use his stock in the bridge company to pay back his indebtedness to the same company. According to Robert W. Jackson, in *Rails across the Mississippi: A History of the St. Louis Bridge* (Urbana: University of Illinois Press, 2001), 212, Eads "had a sweet deal . . . because he would lose little if the bridge company went bankrupt, but if at any point in the future the company started making money he could pay for the stock at that point and reap the rewards."

11. *The Eads Bridge* exhibit catalog, 6.

12. Ada Louise Huxtable, "Eads Bridge: A Momentous Event in Engineering and Art," *New York Times*, 1974, Manuel Garcia files, Bellefontaine Cemetery.

13. Howard S. Miller, *The Eads Bridge* (St. Louis: Missouri Historical Society, 1999), 69.

WILLIAM GREENLEAF ELIOT
1811–1887

"IF I COME, I come to remain, and to lay my ashes down in the valley of the Mississippi,"[1] the twenty-three-year-old William Greenleaf Eliot wrote in 1834 upon leaving Boston to take the pulpit in a Unitarian church in St. Louis. True to his word, Eliot's body was laid to rest in Bellefontaine Cemetery fifty-three years later. Two of his sons, who were also Unitarian ministers, led the simple funeral at the Church of the Messiah, where their father served as pastor for thirty-nine years. According to newspaper accounts, "The multitude that thronged the Church . . . testified to the esteem and affection with which the deceased was held."[2] The casket was carried by eight pallbearers, none a family member, yet each named Eliot in his honor. His famous grandson, poet T. S. Eliot, said, "My father gave a good part of his life, and my grandfather the greater part, to the service of St. Louis and the State; and my mother took a leading part in Juvenile Court Reform there; and they all lie in Bellefontaine now."[3]

It is not primarily as a Unitarian minister but as an educator that Eliot's memory lives. He founded Washington University in St. Louis and Mary Institute, now known as Mary Institute Country Day School. Serving as president of the public school board of St. Louis, he discovered that five thousand children were not in school and determined to remedy this situation. In 1849, despite a cholera epidemic and the Great Fire, Eliot inspired the citizens to vote for a tax for public education that enabled the city to have some of the best schools in the nation at that time.

Eliot believed in the powers of education to create a moral citizenry and saw the West as a region needing civilizing. In 1847, he refused at great personal sacrifice to return to a prestigious ministry in Boston because he felt his duty lay in St. Louis. He felt that in the West as opposed to the East, men put moneymaking before all other goals.

Eliot was born in New Bedford, Massachusetts, the third of eight children, to a family of New England political and moral leaders. After his father's shipping business failed due to the War of 1812, the family moved to Washington, D.C., where his father worked for the postal department. William Greenleaf Eliot Jr. earned his undergraduate degree at Columbian College in Washington. In 1834, he graduated from Harvard Divinity School, which would award him an honorary doctor of divinity in 1854 in recognition of his work in the West. His first and only congregation would be the St. Louis Unitarian church.

In 1827, he returned to Washington, D.C., to marry his first cousin Abby Cranch Eliot, daughter of a judge. They had fourteen children, only five of whom survived him. His first born, Mary Rhodes Eliot, died tragically at sixteen in 1855. In her honor, the girls' school he founded in 1859 was named Mary Institute.

In 1853, the Missouri legislature granted a charter to the Eliot Seminary without Eliot's knowledge thanks to the efforts of Eliot's friend and parishioner Wayman Crow. The next year, at the first meeting of the incorporators of the Eliot Seminary, Eliot was elected president. A very humble man, he insisted that the name be changed to Washington University due to the coincidence that both the charter and the incorporation had occurred on February 22, Washington's birthday. Moreover, he wanted the institution to be a university, not a seminary, because he felt it should be nonsectarian.

According to Eliot's design, the university operated with three departments: the Academic, the Collegiate, and the Practical. The Academic Department consisted of two college preparatory schools, Smith Academy for boys (which closed in 1917) and Mary Institute for girls. In conceiving of his ideal of the university as coeducational and by founding a secondary school so that women could prepare for higher education, Eliot proved himself a feminist. As to the college, Eliot said in the inaugural address, "Our assigned task is to make for St. Louis what Harvard College is to Boston, or Yale to the city of its abode."[4] Eliot felt the Practical Department was uniquely important for a Western university. There, part-time students took evening classes pursuing "practical and scientific education of those who are preparing for the mechanical, agricultural and other industrial pursuits."[5] It was known as O'Fallon Polytechnic Institute after Colonel John O'Fallon, its primary donor. Part of the polytechnic was eventually spun off to the St. Louis Public Schools, and the rest became the university's Department of Engineering.

Never drawing a salary from the university, Eliot served as the president of its Board of Directors for life and became the third chancellor in 1870, following Joseph Hoyt and William Chauvenet. He resigned as pastor of the Church of the Messiah upon becoming chancellor.

Eliot's idealism led him to create a vehicle to care for the sick and wounded during the Civil War. He also raised the money to fund it. Because the government was wholly unprepared to do so, a civilian organization called the U.S. Sanitary Commission was created. Based in Washington, the commission's reach did not extend to the Mississippi Valley. Eliot, therefore, proposed to Major General John C. Frémont, commander of the Western Department, the creation of the Western Sanitary Commission based in St. Louis. Eliot asked that he and four friends make up the board, with James Yeatman as president (see page 144 for more on the commission).

Eliot was convinced of Missouri's strategic significance to the Union and used all of his considerable powers of persuasion to keep the border state from seceding. He believed in the gradual emancipation of slaves, except in the cases in which individuals had lived a long life as a slave and were unsuited to freedom. Although he kept no slaves himself, Eliot argued against outright abolition because he believed "sudden changes of institutions [were] never as good as gradual changes."[6] Once the Civil War broke out, he dropped this stance and advocated an immediate end to slavery. He wrote a book called *Life of Archer Alexander* that read like fiction; it told the story of a slave he helped achieve freedom.

Eliot, for all his New England character, came to love the wild place of St. Louis. In 1836, after two years there, he said: "For myself, I would not leave the corner that I now occupy for the best pulpit in Boston. To one who enters into the western spirit and realizes the truth as to the future greatness of this valley, there is much to fascinate, and compensate for privations and loneliness."[7]

1. Earl K. Holt III, *William Greenleaf Eliot: Conservative Radical* (St. Louis: First Unitarian Church, 1985), 21.

2. "Death of Dr. W.G. Eliot," *St. Louis Globe-Democrat*, January 28, 1887.

3. T. S. Eliot, letter to Marquise Childs, quoted in William H. Gass, "Literary Landmarks: The *St. Louis Post-Dispatch* Letter of T. S. Eliot," *Gateway Heritage* 20, no. 2 (Fall 1999): 74.

4. Eliot, *William Greenleaf Eliot*, 102.

5. Mayor John How, quoted in Alexander Langsdorf, *History of Washington University: 1853–1953*, Washington University Archives, unpublished manuscript.

6. Holt, *William Greenleaf Eliot*, 41.

7. William A. Deiss, *William Greenleaf Eliot: The Formative Years (1811–1834)*, Smithsonian Institution Archives, 32.

SAMUEL FORDYCE
1840–1919

THANKS TO SAMUEL FORDYCE, ten thousand miles of railroad opened the Southwest to the rest of the country. Much of the construction he supervised in person. His keen financial dealings also paved the way for many miles of rails. He was a wheeler-dealer not above an opportune lie when he thought it was in everyone's best interest. His deep and patriotic vision led him to reach out to heal the wounds of war, reconciling the South with the North.

Fordyce built an empire starting with little capital other than his own good character. As a boy, he slept on a lean-to porch. When he died in 1919 at age seventy-nine, he was a multimillionaire.[1] His oldest son, John Rison Fordyce, described him: "He was six feet tall, of heavy build, displaying something of brawn in his make-up. His hair was silvery and his twinkling eyes were of steel blue. Of kindly countenance, a friend once said that his most striking quality was that of being thoroughly alert."[2] As evidenced by the stories in his autobiography dictated the year before he died, he had a wry sense of humor and was aggressive, charming, clever, and loyal.

During the Civil War, Fordyce threw himself into the thick of action. From second lieutenant, he rose to the rank of captain and was named inspector general of cavalry in the Army of the Ohio. However, when Fordyce contracted a severe case of malaria in 1863, he was forced to resign his commission.

Seeking a mild climate because of his malarial condition, Fordyce settled in Huntsville, Alabama. There, he claims, "I set out systematically to 'heal the breach' which war had made."[3] He met and married Susan Chadick, his wife of fifty-four years. Susan was a Confederate colonel's daughter whose friends told her that "her marriage to a '——— Yankee' cut her off from Southern society."[4] So the couple determined "to make them like us."[5] This he accomplished both with his ability to make friends and with the influential dealings of the private banking house, Fordyce and Rison, that he had founded. He was asked to address the Southern Industrial Congress in 1911. He said: "The war is over, . . . and we are again one people, all moving harmoniously together to the music of the Union, and worshipping at the shrine of the Stars and Stripes."[6]

In 1873, his health was in such precarious condition that he sold his interest in the bank, packed up his wife and three young children, and moved to Hot Springs, Arkansas, to be near the mineral baths. After resolving a complicated land title situation, he built the Arlington Hotel and later a theater and the Fordyce Bath House. He lobbied Congress to pass legislation that made the springs government property, essentially the beginning of what would become the National Park Service. He commented, "I have always considered that if I had done nothing else in life except having had this Hot Springs bill passed reserving the hot water mountain . . . for the use of the public that this act of mine alone was a great benefaction."[7]

In 1881, restless after his success in Arkansas, Fordyce was looking for other opportunities when J. W. Paramore, with whom he had served in the army, offered him the position of vice president and treasurer of the St. Louis, Arkansas and Texas Railroad, better known as the Cotton Belt System. When the Cotton Belt went bankrupt in 1885, Fordyce was named receiver and then president after he saved the system from its creditors. At this point, he moved his wife and family—now four children, to the St. Louis headquarters, where the schools were better. In 1889, debt again overwhelmed the company and Fordyce was appointed receiver a second time. He stayed on as president as well until his resignation in 1899. Despite the financial failure of the line, "it built more mileage than any of its predecessors or followers, [and] it instituted cheap transportation in the Southwest."[8]

During his tenure at the Cotton Belt, Fordyce ran into an old acquaintance down on his luck and drew upon his legendary people skills to prevent a holdup. During an inspection tour of the railroad, Fordyce had his directors' meeting interrupted by a gang of train robbers. Faced with a masked man brandishing a pistol in his face, Fordyce recognized the man's voice as belonging to Shang Doland, a former employee whom he had assisted with a pardon from the penitentiary. Fordyce said, "Shang, aren't you ashamed of yourself to come over on the Cotton Belt and try to rob a road as poor as this one? Don't you know that no one with any money ever rides on the Cotton Belt? Why don't you go over and hold up the Iron Mountain [Railroad]?"[9] Doland apologized and called off the attack. A few nights later, he did hold up the Iron Mountain.

While he was building his businesses, Fordyce had a parallel career in politics although he never held office. Active in the Democratic Party, he was "a frequent counselor to every president of the United States from Abraham Lincoln down to Woodrow Wilson."[10]

According to a speech he made in 1897, he believed his legacy lay in the facts that "railways have abolished distance" and "concentrated capital has removed much of the drudgery of life."[11] In addition, the city of St. Louis owes him gratitude for the St. Louis Public Library. Fordyce was instrumental in raising money for the purchase price of the site as well as donating the $250,000 that was a condition of his longtime business associate Andrew Carnegie for his gift of $1 million for the library.[12]

1. Obituary, *St. Louis Globe-Democrat*, August 4, 1919.

2. Samuel Fordyce, *The Autobiography of Samuel Wesley Fordyce, Captain, First Ohio Calvary Army of the Cumberland, Railroad Builder Southwestern United States* (Bethesda, MD: Fordyce family, 1992), v.

3. Ibid., 79.

4. Ibid., 78.

5. Ibid., 79.

6. Samuel Wesley Fordyce, "Address to the Southern Industrial Congress," Atlanta, 1911, Fordyce family papers.

7. Fordyce, *Autobiography*, 93.

8. Jacob E. Anderson, *80 Years of Transportation Progress: A History of the St. Louis Southwestern Railway* (Tyler, TX: Story-Wright, 1957), Michael Tiemann files, Bellefontaine Cemetery, 39.

9. Ibid., 41.

10. David Thomas, *Arkansas and Its People*, vol. 3 (New York: The American Historical Society, 1930), Manuel Garcia files, Bellefontaine

11. "Col. Sam. W. Fordyce's Address," *Pine Bluff Eagle*, September, 7, 1897.

12. Letter from Fred K. Crunden, Public Library, June 10, 1902, Fordyce family papers.

DAVID ROWLAND FRANCIS

1850–1927

GIFTED WITH SUPERIOR business acumen, insatiable drive, and a talent for remembering the name of everyone he ever met, David Rowland Francis was destined for public life. He dreamed big for his beloved city of St. Louis, and those dreams found their apotheosis in the World's Fair of 1904. Francis's life could be divided into two parts: In the first and major part, he was brilliant and transcendent with business success leading to political success; in the second, his pragmatic nature struggled in vain against the chimera that was Russian politics.

Francis was born into a hardscrabble life in Richmond, Kentucky. He came to St. Louis for college to live with a prosperous uncle, David Rowland. Although he had wanted to go to law school, college debts of $450 sent Francis to work as a mud clerk, checking inventory on the docks for his uncle's commission trading house in 1870. Within seven years, he had parlayed this lowly position into his own firm, D. R. Francis and Brother.

In 1876, he married Jane Perry, the beautiful and intelligent daughter of railroad magnate John D. Perry. She was remarkable for a woman of the time because she had studied architecture in Germany and France. She bore him six sons. Although she was not the extrovert David was, Jane served as an admirable hostess for his many political and civic ventures.

In 1884 at age thirty-three, Francis was elected president of the Merchants' Exchange, a prestigious and powerful position in St. Louis that became his entree into politics. The next year, he became the successful Democratic candidate for mayor almost as a fluke because the three other potential candidates were deadlocked. He ran the city like a business, reducing debt, paving streets, and purchasing a waterworks site. His effectiveness as mayor led to his nomination for governor. In a rough campaign, the opposition accused him of being a grain speculator, an unpopular business in a farm state.

Francis won and brought his keen business sense to state government in 1889. In Jefferson City, he cut spending and taxes and got the state legislature to instate a secret ballot that gave Missourians more confidence in the fairness of state elections. As governor, however, Francis's most lasting influence was on the University of Missouri. The legislature carried out his recommendations to restructure the governance of the university to the present system of nine bipartisan curators. He is credited with saving the school after the 1892 fire that burned it to the ground. As a result, the university's Francis Quadrangle bears his name.

Following his stint as governor, he returned to St. Louis, where he had his hand in many businesses as owner, director, vice president, or president, including the *St. Louis Republic*, Mississippi Valley Trust Company, and Merchants-Laclede Bank.[1] In 1893 during an economic depression, he founded the Hospital Saturday and Sunday Association to provide funds for hospitalization for the poor.

St. Louis most honors Francis for his next venture: president of the Louisiana Purchase Exposition—a post for which he accepted no pay. In 1898, he began his relentless promotion and enthusiastic management of the 1904 World's Fair. Francis and fellow St. Louis magnates contributed $10 million to the fair's coffers, while Congress levied another $5 million. From April 30 to December 1, 1904, St. Louis became the most popular city in the world as 20 million visited the 1,275-acre site on what is today Forest Park and Washington University. In addition to the great exposition halls and the entertainments of the Pike (the local name for the midway), the 1904 Olympics were held on what is today known as Francis Field and Francis Gymnasium at Washington University. The university named them for Francis because they were purchased with rent that the fair paid the university for the use of its new campus.

To date, it is the only World's Fair to turn a profit. After settling accounts, the Louisiana Purchase Exposition had made $850,000, which it spent on public works, including the construction of the Jefferson Memorial building for the Missouri Historical Society. The *Chicago Tribune* attributed the fair's success mainly to Francis.[2] The city honored him on closing day, which was called Francis Day.

In 1916, after a lifetime of marching from triumph to triumph, Francis accepted a post where the results of his endeavors were ambiguous at best. Because President Woodrow Wilson sought a trade treaty with Russia, and Francis's abilities as a businessman seemed particularly suited to the mission, Wilson appointed Francis ambassador to czarist Russia. Francis never could negotiate the treaty because of the vast country's political turmoil caused by defeats in battle in World War I and the extreme contrast between the poverty of the masses and the wealth of the aristocracy. Unaccustomed to the conventions of diplomacy, Francis was widely criticized, sometimes with good reason. After initial success with the new Provisional Government, Francis floundered diplomatically during the two revolutions of 1917 when he misread the political importance of the Bolsheviks. It was due to his good offices that the United States was the first country to recognize the Provisional Government led by Aleksandr Kerensky.[3] In November 1917, the Bolsheviks under Vladimir Lenin and

Leon Trotsky assumed power, and the reign of terror commenced. Francis loathed the revolutionaries and advised his government not to recognize their government and to do everything to support the ousted Provisional Government.

Francis left Russia in 1918 in ill health, from which he never recovered. He died nine years later in St. Louis surrounded by five of his six sons. The old Francis mansion at Maryland and Newstead was opened for his funeral service. Following the service, thirty-five automobiles drove to Bellefontaine Cemetery, where Francis was interred next to his wife beneath one of the most compelling monuments in the cemetery. Francis had commissioned sculptor George Julian Zolnay to make the monument for his wife although it bears Francis's name. A bronze cast of a shrouded woman with bowed head and clasped hands sits within a stone niche bearing a Celtic cross. She seems the personification of grief, inviting the visitor to sit on the benches beside her to share her emotion.

---

1. Harper Barnes, *Standing on a Volcano: The Life and Times of David Rowland Francis* (St. Louis: Missouri Historical Society, 2001), 94.
2. Ibid., 163.
3. Ibid., 232.

ETHAN ALLEN HITCHCOCK
1835–1909

AFTER A SUCCESSFUL career in business, Ethan Allen Hitchcock entered public life at the age of sixty-two. Successfully fighting to keep land in the public domain during his eight years in public office, Hitchcock proved himself a leader of the conservation movement.

Ethan Allen Hitchcock was born in 1835 in Mobile, Alabama. When his father—the grandson of Revolutionary War hero Ethan Allen—died in 1840, his mother moved the family to Nashville, Tennessee. After studying at a military academy in New Haven, Connecticut, Ethan followed his older brother Henry Hitchcock to St. Louis in 1855. Henry enjoyed a successful career in law in St. Louis and is considered the model for the hero of Winston Churchill's novel about the city during the Civil War, *The Crisis*.[1] Brothers Ethan and Henry married sisters Margaret and Mary Collier, respectively.

Ethan achieved leadership and made a fortune in varied business interests, both in St. Louis and in the Far East. In 1874, he became president of several companies: Vulcan Steel Works, Big Muddy Coal and Coke Company, Grand Tower and Carbondale Railroad Company, the Chicago and Texas Railroad Company, and Bell Telephone Company of Missouri. He founded Crystal Plate Glass Works, the first successful manufacturer of plate glass in America.[2] It later merged with a company in Pittsburgh to form the Pittsburgh Plate Glass Company:

Thanks to Hitchcock's glass business, he would surprise much of Missouri by being appointed secretary of the interior. He became acquainted with the future president, William McKinley, while advising him about the glass schedule for the tariff of 1890. McKinley, who would later invite Hitchcock to join his cabinet, admired Hitchcock's "clear-headed, business-like ways."[3] In 1896, shortly before McKinley's inauguration, a group of Missouri congressmen visited him in Ohio to request he name a Missourian to his cabinet. He replied, "How would Mr. Hitchcock do?"[4] The congressmen incorrectly assumed that he meant Henry. Before appointing him to his cabinet, McKinley sent Ethan Hitchcock to Russia as the first U.S. ambassador to that country.

Hitchcock approached his cabinet post as a way to clean up corruption. Hitchcock soon dismissed the commissioner of the General Land Office because he was "convinced that the government was being systematically robbed of valuable lands and other natural resources."[5] According to his grandson John R. Shepley, "In order to bring about the prosecution of those who were cheating the government and the Indians, Hitchcock had a group of agents organized to do this work, which later became the Federal Bureau of Investigation."[6] He proved himself a great friend to the Indians, considering it his duty to guard "the Indians from exploitation and injustice."[7] He was able to retain oil and gas lands as well as mineral rights for certain tribes. Under his aegis, the government undertook land reclamation. "Roosevelt and Hitchcock were in entire accord in the sweeping executive orders of 1906–1907 which enlarged the forest reserves and withdrew the mineral lands from exploitation."[8]

Exhausted by his battles against graft, Hitchcock retired from the cabinet in 1907. When he died two years later, his remains were brought back to Bellefontaine Cemetery. President William Taft, who sat in Roosevelt's cabinet alongside Hitchcock, wrote his widow, "Your husband's record for honesty and high sense of official duty were deeply impressed upon the country by his efficient conduct of the interior department and his dignified and able representation of his country abroad."[9]

---

1. "Henry Hitchcock," obituary, Manuel Garcia files, Bellefontaine Cemetery.
2. *American Biography*, 74.
3. Walter B. Stevens, *Centennial History of Missouri* (St. Louis: Clarke, 1921), 165.
4. Ibid.
5. *American Biography*.
6. John Rutledge Shepley, *Our Family* (Venice, FL: Sunshine, n.d.), 15.
7. Margaret Leech, *In the Days of McKinley* (New York: Harper & Brothers, 1959), 384.
8. *American Biography*, 75.
9. William Howard Taft quoted in Stevens, *The Fourth City*, 639.

STEPHEN WATTS KEARNY served his country as an army commander for thirty-six years, guarding its western frontier and adding almost one-third to its territory in the form of New Mexico and California. As a result, cities are named for him in New Jersey, Texas, Arizona, Wyoming, and Nebraska.[1] New Mexico honors him with a monument in the Plaza of Santa Fe.

Although history has largely forgotten Kearny, he was honored in his day. More than seven hundred soldiers marched in his funeral procession, which was over a mile long,[2] the largest and most impressive St. Louis had witnessed up to that time.[3] A full military band led the procession to John O'Fallon's Athlone Farm, where Kearny's body was laid to rest alongside William Clark's. In 1861, Kearny's remains were reinterred in Bellefontaine Cemetery beneath a marble obelisk bearing his name on its base.

Stephen Watts Kearny was the youngest of fifteen children born to Philip and Susanna Watts Kearny in Newark, New Jersey. At fourteen, he entered Columbia University, then known as King's College, where he studied math and the classics.[4] He left school at sixteen and joined the army in 1810. In the battle of Queenstown Heights during the War of 1812, he distinguished himself for bravery. Kearny was later captured by the British but was released soon afterward in an exchange of officers.

After the War of 1812 was over, Kearny served along America's frontier on expeditions up the Missouri and Yellowstone rivers until he settled for a time in St. Louis. There, in 1826, he marched his troops out of Fort Bellefontaine to found what would be Jefferson Barracks, supervising construction of many of the early buildings there. From 1842 to 1845, he commanded the Third Military Department protecting the Great Plains region, headquartered at Jefferson Barracks.

In 1833, Kearny was appointed lieutenant colonel of the newly orga-nized dragoons, becoming their colonel in 1836. This crack unit developed into the U.S. Cavalry, thus earning Kearny the nickname "Father of the U.S. Cavalry."[5] Kearny devised the dragoons' drills and wrote a manual on the subject. As a handsome bachelor and commander of Jefferson Bar-racks, Stephen Watts Kearny was a sought-after guest at all the festivities St. Louis's gay society offered: "When he entered the ballroom, all female hearts were aflutter."[6] At the home of William Clark, he met his future bride, Clark's stepdaughter Mary Radford, whom he married in 1830. According to her cousin William Kennerly, Mary "was a young and beau-tiful girl and a great belle, for it seems that all the young men of St. Louis who had entree to her parents' home were her suitors."[7] The Kearnys became a devoted couple, raising nine surviving children.[8] Though she eventually settled in St. Louis with her large brood, immediately after their marriage Mary followed Stephen to many of his posts, including Fort Leavenworth in Kansas. There "she did not lay eyes on another white woman for over two years."[9]

In 1846, Kearny was promoted to brigadier general and given com-mand of the Army of the West with orders to take military possession of New Mexico and California.[10] Kearny's primary objective was to secure the Santa Fe Trail, an important trade route between St. Louis and Mexico. Setting off with 1,800 troops from Fort Leavenworth, Kearny master-minded a difficult forced march of almost eight hundred miles, averaging twenty miles a day. The New Mexicans surrendered without firing a shot. He brought a legal system to the territory in the form of the Kearny Code, written by four lawyers including the young politician Frank Blair. After six weeks of military rule, Kearny considered New Mexico pacified and named a civil government with Charles Bent as governor and Blair as dis-trict attorney.

Fresh from his bloodless victory in New Mexico, Kearny set off with his First Dragoons to conquer California. On the trail, Kearny encountered Kit Carson, who gave him the mistaken information that the territory had already been conquered. Kearny therefore sent three of five companies back to spare them the desert trek. Persuading Carson to guide him and the remaining one hundred soldiers, Kearny led a march through the des-ert that took its toll on his men and their mounts. Along the way, they met cowboys who gave them the bad news that Californians had revolted against Admiral Robert Stockton and Lieutenant Colonel John Charles Frémont's hold on their land. In December 1846, Kearny met the enemy at San Pasqual, California. Although his troops were exhausted and his horses spent, Kearny attacked, perhaps thinking a bold move would take the day. Historians have attributed victory to both sides in the ensuing battle. Wounded himself, Kearny lost eighteen men, the Californians, almost as many. Within short order, the territory was subdued and American rule instituted.

The question as to who would govern the new U.S. territory of California proved the crisis of Kearny's career. Within one week, one of the Mexican commanders received letters from three different officers, each signed "Governor and Commander-in-Chief of California."[11] Frémont laid claim to the title as much as his superiors, Stockton and Kearny, did.

In January 1847, Stockton arbitrarily appointed Frémont governor,[12] even though Stockton served in the navy and Frémont in the army, where Kearny was his superior. "This [Stockton] did in the face of the orders from the President that Kearny produced directing him to assume that position."[13] Kearny was determined to carry out his orders yet possessed insufficient troops to enforce his mandate. Although Kearny claimed the title of military commander of the conquered territory, Frémont continued to disobey explicit orders to relinquish the governorship. Kearny's men were outraged. Some speculated that Kearny's relationship with Frémont's father-in-law, Thomas Hart Benton, stayed his hand. Finally, Kearny sent Colonel Richard B. Mason to assume command and took Frémont with him under arrest to Washington, D.C., where he had Frémont court-martialed for mutiny.

Kearny testified as the government's witness in the Frémont mutiny trial from November 1847 to January 1848. Thomas Hart Benton defended Frémont and, according to Kearny's biographer, put the general on trial.[14] Kearny was forced to defend his every action, without benefit of a defense attorney since he was not a defendant. Nevertheless, Frémont was convicted of mutiny and two other charges and expelled from the army. President James K. Polk pardoned Frémont for the charge of mutiny and ordered him reinstated in the service, but Frémont resigned. Frémont later ran unsuccessfully for president and served a controversial stint as a Civil War general. Why did this victory damage Kearny's reputation? While Frémont managed to present himself as a romantic underdog, wronged by the powers that be, Kearny, taciturn and stern by nature, came off as stiff and unyielding. Popular works, such as Irving Stone's fictional *Immortal Wife*, portray Kearny as a villain.[15] Six months later when Kearny was promoted to major general, Benton harangued his son-in-law's opponent for a full thirteen days in the Senate.

In May and June of 1848, Kearny served as civil governor first of Vera Cruz and later, for a short time, of Mexico City. Unfortunately, like so many of his men, in Vera Cruz the major general caught a tropical disease, possibly yellow fever. He returned home to St. Louis and his family, eventually moving in with his wife's former suitor, Meriwether Lewis Clark, at whose house he died in October 1848. Shortly before his death, he contacted Jessie Benton Frémont requesting an interview, which she denied. According to one of her biographers, she refused because "a little grave lay between them."[16] She had lost a child after the court-martial.[17] Even the *Dictionary of American Biography* attempts to interpret the emotions on both sides: "It may be that some regret for this action troubled his last hours, for on his deathbed, according to Mrs. Frémont, he sent a request for her to come to see him, which she resentfully denied."[18]

Stephen Watts Kearny built more frontier posts than any of his contemporaries,[19] while protecting his country's frontiers and adding vast amounts of valuable territory to the United States. Yet his heroic deeds largely go unsung.

---

1. Kearney City, Nebraska, misspells his name.
2. Scharf, *History of St. Louis,* 388.
3. Ibid., 387.
4. Dwight Clarke, *Stephen Watts Kearny: Soldier of the West* (Norman: University of Oklahoma, 1961), 8.
5. Phyllis Roberts, "Stephen Watts Kearny," *Buffalo Tales* 2, no. 1 (January 1979).
6. William C. Kennerly, *Persimmon Hill: A Narrative of St. Louis and the Far West* (Norman: University of Oklahoma, 1948), 107.
7. Ibid.
8. Hyde and Conard, *Encyclopedia of St. Louis,* 1157.
9. Clarke, *Soldier of the West,* 49.
10. Scharf, *History of St. Louis,* 387.
11. Andrew Rolle, *John Charles Frémont—Character as Destiny* (Norman: University of Oklahoma Press, 1999), 91.
12. John S. D. Eisenhower, *So Far from God: The U.S. War with Mexico, 1846–1848* (New York: Random House, 1989), 230.
13. Ibid.
14. Clarke, *Soldier of the West,* 352.
15. Ibid., 349.
16. Ibid., 383.
17. Ibid.
18. American Council of Learned Societies, *Dictionary of American Biography* (New York: Scribner's, 1959), 273–274.
19. Phyllis Roberts, "Stephen Watts Kearny."

MANUEL LISA
1772–1820

MANUEL LISA was the only prominent Spaniard in the fur trade. To flaunt his national identity, he read *Don Quixote* on trapping expeditions. He came up the Mississippi River from New Orleans to St. Louis as a young man of eighteen. Called the "Father of Navigation" on the Missouri, Lisa would use the city as a base for thirteen trips up that river, taking 26,000 miles of the roughest voyages. A great trader, he understood the subtle differences between Indian nations. As a result of this understanding, Lisa managed to keep the Indians allied with the Americans rather than the British during the War of 1812. Lisa was the first to hire white men to hunt furs as well as trade with the Indians. To establish bases for white trappers and to deal with the Indians, he founded three trading posts, unimaginatively named Fort Lisa, in Nebraska; Lisa's Fort, in North Dakota; and Fort Manuel, in South Dakota. In each place, he also introduced the Indians to farming.

Formerly a sea captain, he started out in St. Louis in the mercantile business and helped outfit the Lewis and Clark expedition. Hearing the tale of the Voyage of Discovery, he fixed upon the idea of enriching himself with the furs found along the Lewis and Clark route and became the first to follow the explorers up the Missouri. Lisa competed with the Chouteaus, the St. Louis French fur trading family and city's founders. Lisa teamed up with some of St. Louis's leading citizens to form various fur trading companies, always named the Missouri Fur Company. William Clark, Reuben Lewis (brother of Meriwether), Pierre Chouteau, and Auguste Pierre Chouteau Jr., among others, joined the 1809 partnership. In 1810, Lisa built a warehouse for the Missouri Fur Company on the riverfront, improving it in 1818. The Old Rock House, as the warehouse was known, stood until 1959, when it was dismantled to make way for the Jefferson National Expansion Memorial.[1]

A shrewd and ruthless businessman, Lisa was hated as much as he was admired. In his own defense, he wrote to his business partner, Territorial Governor William Clark: "I go a great distance while some are considering whether they will go today or tomorrow. I impose upon myself great privations. Ten months of the year I am buried in the depths of a forest at a great distance from my house."[2] In 1811, Manuel Lisa set a keelboat record, traveling eighteen miles a day upriver, a feat that has never been matched.

Only Clark earned as much respect from the Indians as Lisa. In Lisa's case, he gained their confidence because he understood and honored tribal ways, so much so that in 1814 he took an Omaha wife named Mitain, who was the daughter of the chief Big Elk, thus cementing his relationship with that tribe. At the time, he was married to Polly Chew in St. Louis. When she died in 1817, he remarried within the year to widow, Mary Hempstead Keeney, from one of St. Louis's most prominent families. Although Lisa was a Roman Catholic and she a Presbyterian, and he spoke mainly Spanish and she only English, the marriage was a great success. Lisa said he never really knew domestic happiness until he married her. Mary Hempstead Lisa understood her husband's philosophy about Indian relations and accompanied him on his final 1819 expedition, thus becoming the first white woman to travel up the Missouri River. When he brought his new bride to Fort Lisa, he sent word that his Indian wife must be kept away from that trading post. At the fort, Mary gamely ate a feast of dog meat, with paws lapping over the bowl's edge. Lisa had no children with Mary, but he had a son and a daughter with Mitain, Christopher and Rosalie. Cemetery superintendent Michael Tiemann said Mary Hempstead Lisa "did not know he had an Indian wife so she was startled, naturally. Yet, after they returned to St. Louis a year later, he died; and she then invited his Indian wife and their Indian children to come join her in St. Louis. They did, and the children were educated in the St. Louis schools."[3]

As a trader, river man, and student of Indian affairs, Manuel Lisa had no rival in his day. His enemies were as legion as his admirers. From the mansions of St. Louis society to the Indian council fire, Lisa lived a life full of double cross and diplomacy. According to cemetery gatekeeper Manuel Garcia, Lisa's rich and adventurous life inspired James Michener to use it as the basis for the character Pasquinel in his novel *Centennial*, which became a television miniseries.[4] As the first commercial voyageur up the Missouri, plying his keelboats to compete for beaver pelts, Lisa had the idea of building forts in the Rockies as bases for the mountain men and for the Indian trade. These would guide the operations of all subsequent trappers and traders and foster settlement in the West.

Lisa returned from his 1819 expedition with an unnamed illness and died two months later at the age of forty-seven at the Sulphur Springs spa. First buried in a Roman Catholic churchyard, his remains were later moved beneath a sandstone obelisk next to his wife Mary on the Hempstead family farm, a property that later became part of Bellefontaine Cemetery.

---

1. In 2007, the stones were numbered and reassembled at 1200 S. Seventh Street, south of the original location.
2. David Sievert Lavender, *Westward Vision* (Lincoln: University of Nebraska Press, 1985), 169.
3. Tiemann, *Oral History*, tape XII, 175.
4. Garcia, *Oral History*, tape XXXVI, 645.

EDWARD MALLINCKRODT SR.

1845–1928

EDWARD MALLINCKRODT JR.

1878–1967

THE SON OF GERMAN immigrants, Edward Mallinckrodt Sr. worked the family farm in north St. Louis as a teen but aspired to accomplish more. He established Mallinckrodt Chemical Works, the first company to manufacture fine chemicals west of the Mississippi. Barely surviving in its early years, the company grossed $9 million annually by the time Edward senior retired in 1928. At that point, his only son, Edward Mallinckrodt Jr., stepped up to company leadership, and under his tenure sales rose as high as $47 million a year. The company's efforts were crucial to the development of the atomic bombs dropped at Hiroshima and Nagasaki.

In 1834, when Edward Mallinckrodt's father, Emil Mallinckrodt, emigrated from his native Prussia, fleeing political unrest, he first settled on a farm west of St. Louis. He and his bride, Eleanore Luckie Mallinckrodt, bought a thirty-nine-acre farm just north of the city in 1840. Clearly a go-getter, he laid out the town of Bremen near his farm in 1844, becoming "one of the first real estate dealers who operated extensively in St. Louis property."[1] The next year, his son Edward senior was born.

Helping his father on the farm, Edward senior developed a passion about the application of chemistry to agriculture as well as a lifelong love for all things that grow. In later years, he wrote "almost as many letters about seeds and plants as those regarding business transactions."[2] While he became farm manager as a young teenager, he was not content merely to reap the rewards of his father's real estate successes. Edward senior's discovery of Justus von Liebig's treatises on agricultural chemistry awakened in him a great hunger for knowledge that could only be satisfied by returning to Germany to study, along with his younger brother Otto.

EDWARD MALLINCKRODT SR.

Edward and Otto returned to St. Louis in 1867 determined to put their new knowledge to practical effect. Along with older brother Gustav, they set up a chemical company on the family farm on Mallinckrodt Street, using $10,000 in capital that their father had borrowed. They called it G. Mallinckrodt and Company. The days shortly after the Civil War were a difficult time to start a business. The three brothers had only one assistant, so Edward stoked the boiler himself, and Gustav sometimes fell asleep over his accounts. Because they could afford no truck of their own, they borrowed one from a wholesale druggist to deliver their chemicals. After his brothers died six months apart in 1876 and 1877, Edward came into his own as a businessman, giving personal attention to every detail of the firm's operation. He committed himself so tirelessly to running the chemical company that he rarely stopped longer for lunch than to eat a sandwich at his desk. Even on his brief vacations, he gave dictation about company matters every day. In 1882, under Edward's direction, the firm incorporated and its name was simplified to Mallinckrodt Chemical Works. Drawing in part on its president's contacts in Germany, the company began manufacturing such new products as morphine, codeine, hydrogen peroxide, and tannic acid, and it developed barium sulfate for X-ray analysis. In 1889, Edward formed a separate company, the National Ammonia Company, which manufactured that product and sold it all over the world. As a result, the press dubbed him the "Ammonia King."

Edward senior built a mansion on Vandeventer Place and bought a summer home in New York's Adirondack Mountains. There he lived with his wife, Jennie Anderson Mallinckrodt. Though he was a reserved man, he and his wife entertained frequently. Edward senior's reticence and apparent aloofness came to the fore in his philanthropy. Seeking no recognition for his gifts, he shunned all publicity.[3] Yet he had an exceedingly generous nature, and the wealth resulting from his diligence enabled him to give it full play. He made his largest single gift of $500,000 to provide Harvard with a chemical laboratory.[4] Among his gifts to Washington University in St. Louis was the Mallinckrodt Radiological Institute. He also endowed a ward at St. Louis Children's Hospital in memory of his wife. Serving as director or officer of the boards of the university, St. Luke's Hospital, Missouri Botanical Garden, and the Saint Louis Art Museum, Edward senior was a benefactor of all these institutions as well.

When Edward Mallinckrodt Jr. succeeded his father as president and chairman of the board of his company, he brought a solid background in chemistry to the table as well as a keen business sense "that guided his company's expansion from a small chemical producer to a major producer of fine chemicals for industry and medicine."[5] His research in anesthesiology led to sixteen patents. By improving the quality and stability of ether, his studies "contributed substantially to safer surgical operations."[6] His work advancing anesthesiology was cited when he received the Midwest Award from the St. Louis chapter of the American Chemical Society. Under his guidance, the company also developed chemicals for use in X-ray analysis.

Edward junior's friend Dr. Arthur Holly Compton inspired him to accept an undertaking that many other companies had refused—the manufacture of pure uranium. On a handshake over lunch at the Noonday Club on April 17, 1942, Edward junior committed his company to a course that allowed the United States to win the race for the atom bomb and thus prevail in World War II. Compton, later chancellor of Washington University, headed a project at the University of Chicago that required enriched uranium to prove the existence of self-sustaining nuclear reactions and thus the creation of nuclear weapons.

Because Compton's experiment required forty tons of enriched uranium, the company had to find a way to produce the element in bulk. In April 1942, no more than one-half cup of uranium of this purity existed in the entire United States. Within three months, Mallinckrodt Chemical Works was manufacturing a ton a day—a feat Compton later called "a technological and industrial miracle."[7]

Because of the critical need for complete secrecy, employees were not informed about what they were so frantically seeking until August 7, 1945—the day after the bombing of Hiroshima. They were given the day off, for many of them only the second or third day off in years. Secretary of War Henry Stimson sent all three thousand Mallinckrodt employees involved in the uranium enrichment project a silver medal bearing an *A* and a certificate saying that they "had participated in work essential to the production of the atomic bomb."[8]

Unlocking the secrets of the universe also unleashed its demons. In later years, workers' health would suffer and high cancer rates among employees would be cause for alarm. A 1989 *Post-Dispatch* article reported that Mallinckrodt's nuclear research and manufacturing left 2.3 million cubic yards of contaminated material throughout the city, the north St. Louis area, and St. Charles. By 2003, the waste at the Mallinckrodt plant in Weldon Springs, Missouri, had been contained, but another 230,000 cubic yards of soil remained scattered around the city. The Army Corps of Engineers recommended shipping it to Utah or Idaho for disposal.[9]

While the nuclear waste his company created cannot be easily wiped away, Edward Mallinckrodt Jr. did more than his share to improve the world. Mallinckrodt senior thrust his son into philanthropy by assigning $2 million ($108 million in 2006 dollars) to "such benevolent, scientific, charitable, literary or educational"[10] institutions as Edward junior saw fit to benefit. In his own name, Edward junior gave additional funds to the Mallinckrodt Radiological Institute and endowed the departments of pediatrics and pharmacology at Washington University. He gave Washington University and Harvard many grants for research. In memory of their son Henry Elliot Mallinckrodt, who died in 1945, he and his wife gave both medical schools a chair of anesthesiology. Like his father, Edward junior wished his benevolences to be as anonymous as possible.

Edward junior's personal life, although blessed with accomplishment, was marred by great tragedy. He married the former Elizabeth Elliott and had three sons, all of whom died young. Henry died from heart disease. Edward Mallinckrodt III was killed piloting a plane that crashed into the Massachusetts Bay in 1932 while he was a freshman at Harvard. The only son to survive his parents, George Elliot Mallinckrodt, met an untimely death the year after his father died. Just as his older brother had done, the forty-eight-year-old crashed in a private plane he was piloting.

All three sons are buried together with their parents and grandparents in the mausoleum at Bellefontaine Cemetery designed for their family by Henry Bacon, architect of the Lincoln Memorial in Washington, D.C. Appropriate for a family of high aspirations, all forms on the remarkable tomb reach upward, from the torchères flanking the door to the acanthus topping the roof. Even the proportions of the neoclassical building give a soaring feeling, as the mausoleum appears much taller than it is wide.

Edward Mallinckrodt Sr. and Jr. created a great legacy in their chemical company. Believing that science could and should benefit humankind, they dedicated much of their profits to the welfare of humanity. The firm where they labored so tirelessly and with such excellent intentions was sold to Tyco Industries in 2000. Ironically, these two men were succeded at the helm by Dennis Kozlowski, who was convicted in 2005 of stealing $600 million from the company. Today, Covidein, the company formed in November 2007 out of the old Tyco International Healthcare Division, proudly advertises the honorable name of Mallinckrodt as a division that manufactures pharmaceuticals and imaging and respiratory products.

---

1. Hyde and Conard, *Encyclopedia of St. Louis*, 245.
2. "Mallinckrodt Chemical Company," Manuel Garcia files, Bellefontaine Cemetery, 239.
3. Ibid., 242.
4. *American Biography*.

5. Ibid.

6. Ibid.

7. Carolyn Bower, Louis J. Rose, and Theresa Tighe, "A Miracle with a Price," *St. Louis Post-Dispatch*, February 12, 1989, 1D.

8. Ibid., 10D.

9. Harry Levins, "The Nuclear Age," *St. Louis Post-Dispatch*, December 14, 2003, 20.

10. *American Biography.*

WILLIAM McCHESNEY MARTIN SR.

1874–1955

WILLIAM McCHESNEY MARTIN JR.

1906–1998

WITH A TERM THAT stretched nineteen years, William McChesney Martin Jr. served the longest of all the chairmen of the Federal Reserve System and is credited with being "the Father of the Modern Fed."[1] His father, William McChesney Martin Sr., preceded him at the Federal Reserve System as the first head of the central bank's St. Louis branch. As the founding chairman of the Federal Reserve Bank of St. Louis, William senior used monetary policy to rein in both boom and bust. Sometimes opposing the will of the presidents he served, William junior spent his life maintaining confidence in U.S. financial markets. If that meant restraining a burgeoning economy, William junior was willing to be the hard-nosed guy "taking away the punch bowl just as the party gets going."[2]

Father and son, dedicated public servants, rest together beneath simple stones in the family plot at Bellefontaine Cemetery. Perhaps their most enduring monument is the confidence with which the government and the public view the monetary policy of today's Fed. William junior is also honored by the William McChesney Martin, Jr., Federal Reserve Board Building in Washington, D.C. When he broke ground for the edifice with a silver shovel in April 1971, he became the first living public servant to have a federal government building named for him.[3]

William McChesney Martin Sr.'s life was steeped in public service and finance. Both to escape the legacy of his father's bankruptcy in Kentucky and to take advantage of St. Louis's booming economy, William senior moved to the city in 1895. He had just graduated from Virginia's Washington and Lee College, an institution infused with the ethos of public service. In St. Louis, William worked for a bank, where he wrote speeches for the bank president, who eventually encouraged the young man to speak out on his own. In 1911, William spoke out in support of a new idea, a national reserve association to strengthen the nation's banks. During the nineteenth century, the country fluctuated constantly between boom and panic, with recessions occurring more than half the time and taking down many small businessmen like his father. Because he was relatively young and untried at age forty, William surprised the St. Louis banking community when he became the St. Louis Fed's first chairman in 1914.

WILLIAM McCHESNEY MARTIN SR.

As revered as the Fed is today, it is hard to conceive of the opposition William senior faced at the time of the central bank's inception. He spent five years on the road convincing the cautious bankers of the Eighth Reserve District, the fourth-largest banking concentration in the country, to join. At the end of that time, William's persuasive powers had converted most of the largest banks into members of the Federal Reserve System.

After graduating from Yale in 1928, a year before the stock market crash, William junior took his uncle Albert N. Edwards's offer of a position with the brokerage firm he headed, A.G. Edwards. Starting out as a board boy in November 1928, he was promoted two months later to head the firm's research department. At the time, with the market increasing almost a third of its value every year for five years, speculation in stocks was rampant. While most reserve banks were allowing investors to borrow as much as 75 percent of the value of stocks, William senior inveighed against such excesses and only allowed the St. Louis branch to loan from 22 to 25 percent. St. Louis banks complained mightily until October 1929 when William senior's dour predictions came true and the wisdom of his cautionary measures became evident.

During the Depression, William junior learned hard lessons about the market, seeing firsthand the pain caused by severe financial loss. Some short-selling, price-manipulation schemes, for example, he considered "just a type of stealing."[4] In 1931, he moved to New York to represent A.G. Edwards on the floor of the New York Stock Exchange (NYSE) and decided to complete his education in finance at night by earning a doctorate at Columbia University, focusing his studies on the NYSE. In 1932, when he was only twenty-six and still a junior stockbroker, he started a serious economics journal, *Economic Forum*. The first issue featured renowned economist John Maynard Keynes's first article for a U.S. publication.

While William junior did extremely well trading in securities during this time, he also had a passion to do good.[5] Keen to reform what he saw as a corrupt system, he ran for the presidency of the New York Stock Exchange. Although only thirty-one years old, he succeeded as a result of a compromise between the old guard who could accept him as a plainspoken pragmatist and the reformers who trusted his commitment to reform. He spent the next three years of his life fighting against entrenched interests to restore the stock market's tarnished reputation. He stated, "The exchange is a national institution. It isn't a private club anymore."[6]

William junior's career as president of the NYSE was cut short by a draft notice ordering him to report for basic training in 1941. Unlike all of his contemporaries on Wall Street who maneuvered appointments out of harm's way, his personal convictions moved him to enter the army as a private.

Independence despite the risk to his personal reputation would mark his years at the Federal Reserve. In 1951, William junior came to the Fed chairmanship "as the younger and comparatively unknown candidate."[7] In his relationship with President Harry Truman, William set what would become the Fed's policy ever after—a role in maintaining the economy that was above politics. William's nonrenewable term on the Fed's Board of Governors expired in 1970, slightly more than a year into Nixon's term. As head of the Fed, William "presided over a golden era of strong growth, low unemployment, low inflation and grand gains in the standard of living."[8] The resulting economic well-being of ordinary Americans stemmed directly from policies William fought selflessly to implement. In William's mind, sound monetary policy created confidence in the nation. As he put it, "Good money is Coined Freedom."[9]

1. Robert P. Bremner, *Chairman of the Fed: William McChesney Martin Jr. and the Creation of the American Financial System* (New Haven, CT: Yale, 2004), 294.

2. "Federal Reserve Bank of St. Louis and Missouri Historical Society Unveil William McChesney Martin, Jr., Web Site," *Missouri Historical Society Magazine*, November–December 2007, 3.

3. Bremner, *Chairman of the Fed*, 291.

4. Ibid., 23.

5. Andrew Brimmer, "William McChesney Martin Jr.," *Proceedings of the American Philosophical Society* 144, no. 2 (June 2000): 232.

6. Harry Levins, "Great Fed Chairman Martin Dies at 91," *St. Louis Post-Dispatch,* July 29, 1998, C2.

7. Bremner, *Chairman of the Fed*, 81.

8. Levins, "Great Fed Chairman," C1.

9. Bremner, *Chairman of the Fed*, 229.

JAMES S. McDONNELL JR.

1899–1980

AS A PILOT, ENGINEER, and corporation leader, James S. McDonnell Jr. dedicated his life to humans' flight. His special genius lay not only in designing and building aircraft but also in motivating others to work almost as hard as he did. He was born in Denver to James S. McDonnell and Susan Belle Hunter McDonnell, who came from Arkansas. After moving around the United States working for other aircraft companies, he selected St. Louis as the place to build his own company—McDonnell Aircraft Corporation. This would become McDonnell Douglas Corporation in 1967, which merged with Boeing Company in 1997. He started out in offices at St. Louis's Lambert Airfield with fifteen employees. During World War II, the company grossed $60 million, and by 1964, at the quarter-century mark, the company's gross rose to almost $5 billion. The business that had been housed on one floor now sprawled over a 383-acre campus and was the state's biggest employer.

By the time McDonnell graduated from Princeton with honors in physics in 1921, he had already set his sights on a career in aeronautics. He next went to Massachusetts Institute of Technology, then the only school offering a master's degree in aeronautical engineering. The next year, with theoretical studies under his belt, he went to Brooks Field in San Antonio, Texas, to learn to fly with the army. Charles Lindbergh had graduated from the same program the year before. At Brooks Field, McDonnell flirted with death by volunteering to be one of the first six men ever to parachute from a plane.

After working for several other aircraft companies, he moved on to Baltimore and the Glenn L. Martin Company in 1933. He rose to be chief project engineer for land planes and married Mary Elizabeth Finney in 1934.

In 1939, he formed his third successful business, choosing to locate in St. Louis away from the eastern seaboard.[1] He started McDonnell Aircraft (MAC) with $30,000 of his own savings and $135,000 of invested capital, including $5,000 from Laurence Rockefeller, who invested based upon a half-hour interview with the great salesman.

During World War II, McDonnell Aircraft worked primarily on parts and subcontracts for other airplane manufacturers. Yet while subcontracting, the always-forward-looking "Mr. Mac" had been delving into the new jet propulsion engines. This led to the company's first significant contract with the navy. In 1943, MAC was asked to design the first jet fighter plane able to take off and land from aircraft carriers. The Phantom I jet fighter was completed in 1945, and the navy and air force awarded contracts for two more planes that would become the Banshee and the Goblin. Later fighters would be named the Voodoo and the Demon, reflecting McDonnell's interest in the supernatural. When the Phantom II was completed in 1958, this high-performance, adaptable plane contracted by the navy was also commissioned by the Marine Corps and the U.S. Air Force, making it the first to be used by all three. According to his nephew Sanford McDonnell, "With U.S. Government approval, it was also sold to the air forces of 11 other nations. By the time production ended in 1979—more than 20 years after the first flight—over 5,000 F-4 Phantoms had been produced. I think it fair to say it is the best-known jet fighter in the world."[2]

Tragedy struck on the tenth anniversary of the founding of McDonnell Aircraft when Mary Elizabeth McDonnell died of cancer, leaving the widower with two young sons, James S. McDonnell III and John Finney McDonnell. Seven years later, McDonnell married Priscilla Brush Forney.

Perhaps the McDonnell Aircraft Company's most celebrated undertaking was Project Mercury. Via television, everyone in the United States watched the MAC-designed capsules that initiated manned space flight. After this success, MAC was awarded contracts for Project Gemini, manufacturing a series of two-man space capsules. Mercury and Gemini laid the groundwork for Project Apollo, which landed men on the moon in 1969.

In the early 1960s, Mr. Mac made an offer to buy Douglas Aircraft Company. He was interested in diversifying into passenger planes since military contracts could be fickle. Donald W. Douglas refused the offer until the budget-busting success of the DC-9. Because Douglas's salespeople had priced the plane too cheaply, a huge rush of orders proved devastating financially. The company's bankers said Douglas needed more capital to survive; a merger was the answer. On April 27, 1967, the two companies consummated the deal, with Mr. Mac in the chairman's seat—and that seat was in St. Louis.

In 1972, Sanford McDonnell took over as CEO, but Mr. Mac stayed on as chairman of McDonnell Douglas. As his company prospered, Mr. Mac gave his time and money with increasing generosity to St. Louis institutions. As early as 1959, McDonnell received the St. Louis award for public service. At the ceremony, when he was handed a certificate and a check for $1,000, he reciprocated by giving Mayor Raymond Tucker a check for $20,000 to purchase the equipment for the McDonnell Planetarium in Forest Park. He had previously put up $200,000 for the building. At Washington University in St. Louis, he served as chairman of the board and gave the medical school a $4.7 million gift of a new building, completed in 1969.

James S. McDonnell Jr. was a man with the vision, talent, and leadership ability to change the world. He dreamed of making a career of flight at a time when planes were considered "flivvers"—insubstantial, cheap, whimsical contraptions. He lived to build planes that took men around the world and spaceships that aimed for the stars.

---

1. James J. Horgan, *City of Flight: The History of Aviation in St. Louis* (St. Louis: Patrice Press, 1984), 341–342.
2. Sanford N. McDonnell, *This Is Old Mac Calling All the Team* (St. Louis: Author, 1999), 7.

JOHN BERRY MEACHUM
1789–1854

BORN INTO SLAVERY, John Berry Meachum purchased his own freedom, as well as that of his wife, his parents, and twenty other men and
women of his race. He succeeded in three careers: businessman, preacher,
and educator. He was much more than a minister to his congregation.
Meachum believed in working within the laws of the time, though after
his death, his wife was arrested for participating in the Underground Railroad that helped slaves escape to freedom.

John Berry Meachum was born in Virginia, on May 3, 1789. He
learned the trades of carpenter and cooper (barrel maker) and was thus
able to save money to buy his freedom. His father, Thomas, a Baptist
minister, and his mother, Patsy, were taken by slave owner Paul Meachum
to Kentucky. There, John was able to buy his parents' freedom as well.
In Kentucky, he married a slave named Myra. When her master took her
to the Missouri Territory, John followed with the intention of setting her
free.

Meachum arrived in St. Louis in 1815 with $3 in his pocket. By
1835, his talent, industry, and thrift had made him a wealthy man. Contemporary accounts list him as owning two brick houses in St. Louis and a
farm in Illinois. He worked as a carpenter and a cooper, and he built and
owned two steamboats. One was a "temperance boat," equipped with a
library warning of the evils of liquor. He used his wealth to purchase other
slaves, whom he taught a trade to enable them to support themselves and
to buy their freedom from him.

Already a prominent member of the black community of St. Louis,
Meachum's star ascended even farther when it came in conjunction with
a white Baptist minister, John Mason Peck, who arrived in St. Louis in
1818. The Baptist Missionary Convention that had met in Philadelphia

in 1817 sent Peck as a missionary to the West. In St. Louis, he met with Territorial Governor William Clark. Peck started a Baptist church with a congregation of about one hundred, with blacks and whites worshipping together.

In 1822, the black congregation separated from the white to worship under the leadership of Meachum, still a layman, under the supervision of Peck. Three years later, Peck ordained Meachum as a Baptist minister. In this same year, Meachum founded the First Baptist Church, the first church established in St. Louis for African Americans. An 1825 diary account tells of Meachum baptizing hundreds of people in Chouteau's Pond. In 1827, the church was able to erect its first building at Third and Almond. At this time, the congregation numbered 220, with 200 of those being slaves worshipping with the permission of their masters.

Soon after the church was built, Meachum and Peck began teaching black children reading, writing, and arithmetic in the basement. They charged tuition of $1 a month but turned no one away for lack of funds. One of Meachum's students was James Milton Turner, founder of Lincoln University in Jefferson City. Turner became the first black ambassador of the United States when President Ulysses S. Grant appointed him ambassador to Liberia.

In 1847, the Missouri legislature passed a law making it a crime to instruct "negroes or mulattoes in reading or writing in this STATE."[1] In response to this edict, Meachum took a brave and clever step. According to James Neal Primm in *Lion of the Valley*, "Meachum had then opened his 'Freedom School' on a steamboat anchored in the middle of the Mississippi. During the late 1840s and 1850s, dozens of black pupils rafted back and forth daily to these water-borne classes taught by teachers imported from the East."[2] As there are no contemporary accounts of the Freedom School, this wonderful story may be apocryphal.

On February 19, 1854, John Berry Meachum dropped dead in his pulpit, preaching on a Sunday morning. He died as he lived, serving the spiritual, educational, and vocational needs of the African American population of St. Louis.

While the only monument to Meachum is his marble tombstone in Bellefontaine Cemetery, his memory is celebrated annually with a parade to the cemetery. According to cemetery gatekeeper Manuel Garcia, the First Baptist Church honors its founder's accomplishments by riding to his grave in a fire truck.

---

1. N. Webster Moore, "John Berry Meachum (1789–1854)," *Missouri Historical Society Bulletin,* January 1973, 101.
2. Primm, *Lion of the Valley,* 317.

VIRGINIA MINOR
1824–1894

BEAUTIFUL, INTELLIGENT, and charming, Virginia Louisa Minor assumed leadership, along with such feminists as Susan B. Anthony and Elizabeth Cady Stanton, in the struggle for women to obtain the vote. So strong was her conviction that she and her husband took her case to the U.S. Supreme Court.

One of seven children born to Warner and Maria Minor in Goochland County, Virginia, she was educated at home except for a short stint at an academy for young ladies in Charlottesville where the family had moved when her father was appointed hotel keeper to the University of Virginia. There she met and married, in 1843, an attorney who was a distant cousin, Francis Minor, a nominal coincidence that allowed her to keep her maiden name, much like twentieth-century feminists. In 1845, Virginia and Francis followed other family members to St. Louis, where they bought a farm. Their son, Francis Gilmer Minor, was born in 1852.

Virginia Minor took up political activism during the Civil War. Despite their southern background, both Minors supported the Union cause wholeheartedly. Virginia became one of the first members of the St. Louis Union Aid Society, a women's group organized in 1861 to help wounded soldiers and their families obtain food and supplies. News that Union soldiers suffered from scurvy inspired Minor to comb the countryside seeking fruit to alleviate their condition. She personally made preserves for the soldiers from a wagonload of cherries.

Public service did not stop after the war for many patriotic women, Minor among them. They turned their attention to the vote, believing that both women and blacks should be enfranchised. On October 3, 1866, Virginia Minor's life was irreversibly changed when her only child, fourteen-year-old Francis, was accidentally shot and killed. According to cemetery gatekeeper Manuel Garcia, "The transformation from a wife and bereaved mother to a dedicated activist occurred the following year."[1]

In 1867, Minor obtained 355 signatures on a petition seeking that the proposed amendment to the U.S. Constitution giving blacks the vote be extended to women. The Missouri legislature dealt the measure a resounding defeat, 89–5. On May 8 of that same year, she assumed the presidency of the first organization in the world dedicated solely to the political enfranchisement of women. The Woman Suffrage Association of Missouri was founded by Minor along with several other women; sympathetic men such as William Greenleaf Eliot and James Yeatman eventually joined as well. The first meetings were held in the Mercantile Library, but membership grew to the point where rooms were rented in the Pickwick Theater. Despite the fact that women did not gain the vote until 1919, the Woman Suffrage Association made great progress in Missouri.

Two and a half years later, the third annual national convention of woman suffragists met in St. Louis. The convention adopted Francis Minor's three resolutions that the rights of citizenship are national, the Constitution does not give electors the right to deprive any citizen the right to vote, and laws that exclude women from the right to vote are unconstitutional because women are citizens.[2] Thus, Francis believed a special amendment allowing female suffrage was unnecessary because the newly passed Fourteenth Amendment to the Constitution had already given them the vote. One of the Reconstruction Amendments, the Fourteenth intended to extend the full rights of citizenship to former slaves: "All persons born or naturalized in the United States and subject to the jurisdiction thereof, are citizens of the United States and of the State wherein they reside."

Virginia Minor put her beliefs to the test on October 15, 1872, when she attempted to register to vote for the presidential election of Ulysses S. Grant versus Horace Greeley. Reese Happersett, the election district registrar, refused to allow her to register, citing the Missouri Constitution's limiting of the vote to males. In December, Francis Minor filed suit for $10,000 in damages in the St. Louis County Circuit Court as coplaintiff with his wife because at that time married women had no right to sue in their own names. The Minors contended that Happersett was depriving her of a privilege of U.S. citizenship to which she was entitled as a native-born, tax-paying, property-owning citizen and thus he was condemning

Virginia Minor to "a position of involuntary servitude."[3] Happersett claimed he had simply enacted the provision of the Missouri Constitution, which stated, "Every male citizen . . . of the United States shall be entitled to vote." After losing in the circuit court, the Minors took their suit to the Missouri Supreme Court in March 1873, where they also lost.

The Minors next took their case to the Supreme Court of the United States, again arguing that the Fourteenth Amendment granted women the vote. On March 29, 1875, the Supreme Court issued a unanimous decision in the case of *Minor v. Happersett*. Chief Justice Morrison R. Waite wrote the opinion that "if the law is wrong, it ought to be changed, but the power is not with us. . . . The Constitution of the United States does not confer the right of suffrage upon anyone," nor did it prevent states from giving "that important trust to men alone."[4]

Undaunted, Virginia Minor continued her campaign. She testified repeatedly before the legislature. In 1876, she petitioned the St. Louis City government that women be exempted from paying property taxes as long as they could not vote; her request was denied. In 1879, she refused to pay her own taxes, writing the St. Louis Board of Assessors, "The principle upon which this government rests is representation before taxation. My property is denied representation and therefore cannot be taxable."[5] Every session of the Missouri legislature was presented a petition for woman suffrage. Most legislators did not even entertain debate. On July 4, 1876, the one hundredth anniversary of the Declaration of Independence, Minor joined Susan B. Anthony, Lucretia Mott, Elizabeth Cady Stanton, and twenty-four others in signing the Declaration of Rights for Women.[6] That same year, she organized and led a second woman suffrage group affiliated with the national Woman Suffrage Association. In 1892, just two years before she died, she took her last post as honorary vice president of the Inter-State Woman Suffrage Convention in Kansas City.

Even in death, Virginia Minor proclaimed her principles: She left $1,000 to Susan B. Anthony and $500 each to two nieces, provided they not marry. Her funeral took place at her house, without religious services, because she felt the clergy had not supported the cause of woman suffrage. According to a newspaper account of the time, "Mrs. Minor was one of the most noted advocates of female suffrage in the country," and "the cortege was a large one,"[7] following the hearse to Bellefontaine Cemetery where she was laid to rest on Memory Hill alongside her husband and son. (Ironically, Reese Happersett is buried in an unmarked grave across the street.)

Virginia Minor spent her life trying to win the vote for women. Her failures eventually led to success, for they shed light on the struggle and made the public aware of the issues at stake. In 1919, all that she had worked so hard to achieve finally came to fruition in the Nineteenth Amendment to the Constitution, granting women the right to vote.

---

1. Manuel Garcia, unpublished biography, Bellefontaine Cemetery
2. Laura Staley, "Suffrage Movement in St. Louis during the 1870s," *Gateway Heritage*, Spring 1983, 38.
3. Katherine Corbett, *In Her Place: A Guide to St. Louis Women's History* (St. Louis: Missouri Historical Society, 1999), 133.
4. Leslie Friedman Goldstein, *The Constitutional Rights of Women: Cases in Law and Social Change* (Madison: University of Wisconsin, 1988), 82.
5. Corbett, *In Her Place*, 134.
6. Ibid.
7. Virginia Minor obituary, March 1, 1894, Missouri Historical Society Vertical Files.

JOHN O'FALLON
1791–1865

THE SON OF a penniless and disgraced Irish gentleman-speculator and William Clark's sister, John O'Fallon aspired to wealth and respectability. O'Fallon had an aching need to prove himself worthy of his mother's distinguished family and to restore the name his father had tarnished by double-dealing land speculation.

Though John O'Fallon barely knew him, his father played a critical role in shaping his character. Dr. James O'Fallon was born in Ireland and came to America in 1774, serving as a surgeon in George Washington's army during the American Revolution. After the war, Dr. O'Fallon became involved in land speculation in what is now Mississippi. He soon embroiled himself in double-dealing by playing the Spanish governor of New Orleans against President Washington and was able to draw William Clark's brother George into his schemes. O'Fallon cemented their business relationship with his 1791 marriage to Clark's youngest sister, Fanny. Their son John was born that same year, and Benjamin followed in 1793. By that time, Fanny had suffered a nervous breakdown and had left her husband to return to the Clark homestead. After George learned that the doctor had physically abused his sister, he broke a cane over O'Fallon's head, calling him "a Rogue, Rascal and Villain."[1] Dr. O'Fallon died soon afterward in 1794, leaving William Clark to become the guardian of his twenty-one-year-old sister's infant sons. Clark kept the unruly Benjamin home with him but sent the more scholarly John off to an academy in Kentucky.

Steered by his uncle into a career in law, O'Fallon abruptly broke off this path to enter the army after reading law for a year with Robert Todd, father of Mary Todd Lincoln. O'Fallon joined in 1811 as a private and eventually rose to captain. (In later life, he was known as Colonel

O'Fallon, but he seems to have promoted himself.[2]) Serving under General (later president) William Henry Harrison in his Indian campaign, O'Fallon was severely wounded at the battle of Tippecanoe. Harrison had such a high opinion of the rising star that he said, "Whenever O'Fallon is on duty I can sleep sound and secure."[3] Despite his successes, army life did not suit O'Fallon. His true aptitude was revealed in the shrewd (and perhaps envious) eye for business he cast on the quartermaster's department. Although

he believed he would not advance in the army, he feared to leave it because his poverty would hold him back in life. Nevertheless, after resigning in 1818, O'Fallon headed for St. Louis "with the ambition, which he frankly avowed, of making a fortune in business."[4] He decided St. Louis was the spot to pursue a career as a merchant because "more goods are sold in St. Louis than in any other part of the United States of equal population."[5] Through his army contacts, O'Fallon soon secured the post of sutler[6] to a military expedition up the Missouri. Within the year, his incredible business ability came to the fore. He bragged to his mother that he was making money "at the rate of $1000 a month,"[7] a fortune at the time. It is improbable that O'Fallon could turn such a huge profit by selling trinkets to the officers' wives.[8] Although Congress had decreed it illegal to sell whiskey to the Indians, he likely engaged in this lucrative trade.

Returning to St. Louis, the shrewd businessman built a fortune as a merchant, then reinvested his profits in real estate, banking, and railroads, among many other diverse interests. Always one to ferret out opportunity, O'Fallon helped his uncle William Clark execute his responsibilities as Indian agent. When President Andrew Jackson signed the Indian Removal Bill into law in 1830, Clark oversaw moving all Indians east of the Mississippi to land he supervised in the West. O'Fallon made another fortune supplying the equipment, food, and clothing that the government purchased for the tribes. Because of his good reputation, he was appointed president of the St. Louis Bank of the United States in 1828. According to St. Louis historian James Neal Primm, "By 1831, the branch's discounts (loans—represented by notes in circulation) exceeded $400,000, and by late 1832 they reached $883,000. This increase in its money supply was a boon to the city as well as its merchants."[9] When the bank closed in 1835, under O'Fallon's excellent management, his branch had lost only $125, while other branches had lost tens of thousands of dollars[10] during an era of unregulated banking in which failure was a regular occurrence. As a result, economist J. Ray Cable said, "John O'Fallon deserves to be remembered as perhaps Missouri's first teacher of sound banking principles."[11]

A progressive capitalist, O'Fallon was among the first to seek railroads for Missouri in 1835, a time when only a few hundred miles of track existed in the entire United States. As a result of his considerable investments in the lines, he eventually became president of two, the Ohio and Mississippi along with the North Missouri, as well as a director of the Missouri Pacific.

O'Fallon's commercial instinct always prevailed, even in affairs of the heart.[12] His first wife, Harriet Stokes, was the wealthy sister of Englishman William Stokes, who had settled in the city in 1819 or 1820.[13] O'Fallon married again three months after Harriet's death. Caroline Sheets O'Fallon had her own fortune as the daughter of a Baltimore merchant.

Together they built a mansion on a six-hundred-acre park, named Athlone after James O'Fallon's Irish birthplace.

As a philanthropist and business advocate, O'Fallon became one of the city fathers who set the tone for the "future great city."[14] John O'Fallon's philanthropy reflected his station in life. He gave his city Fairgrounds Park and the site for the city waterworks, and he endowed Washington University in St. Louis, Saint Louis University, and the O'Fallon Polytechnic College. Proud of his son-in-law Charles Pope, who became president of the American Medical Association in 1854, O'Fallon built a medical school for him called St. Louis Medical College, which would later became the medical school of Washington University. Biographer Mary Ellen Rowe was skeptical of his motives: "Although a human being lived inside the calculating businessman, even at his most human, O'Fallon's life centered around the quest for status."[15] Still O'Fallon gave openhandedly in private. In 1830, he covered a $12,000 note his uncle William Clark had borrowed[16] and made arrangements four years later to sell 919 acres of his uncle's land to help Clark get out of debt.[17] As banker and merchant, he staked many others to success.

By the time O'Fallon died in 1865, the son of the "reckless, debt-ridden adventurer"[18] had accumulated an estate of $8 million (as much as $1 billion in 2007 dollars), and the City of St. Louis suspended all business on the day of his burial.[19] Pallbearers included such St. Louis luminaries as Henry Shaw, Robert Campbell, and General William Harney. O'Fallon is buried in the largest lot in Bellefontaine Cemetery—almost an acre, with room for six hundred graves, according to cemetery superintendent Michael Tiemann.[20] Much of Bellefontaine was originally part of the O'Fallon estate. The lot is circular and divided into quadrants, one for each of his four children, Caroline (Pope), John, James, and Benjamin O'Fallon. The most noted architect of the day, George Ingham Barnett, designed the fifty-foot-tall granite monument with its crowning, thirteen-foot female figure holding an anchor, the symbol of hope,[21] which weighs eighty tons and cost $20,000. O'Fallon and his second wife are laid to rest in an underground burial chamber beneath the figure of hope. A good seventy of their descendants join them in the lot and the mausoleum.

John O'Fallon was blessed with exceptional business acumen that propelled his rise from gentile poverty to great wealth and high social position. Thanks to his philanthropy and private generosity to friends and business associates, he died respected and beloved, the first citizen of St. Louis. The region honors his name in many ways: O'Fallon, Missouri; O'Fallon, Illinois; O'Fallon Park; and O'Fallon Street.

---

1. Jones, *Shaping of the West*, 87.

2. Mary Ellen Rowe, "A Respectable Independence: The Early Career of John O'Fallon," *Missouri Historical Review*, July 1996, 407.

3. Hyde and Conard, *Encyclopedia of St. Louis*, 1664.

4. *Dictionary of American Biography* (New York: Scribner's, 1936), 633.

5. Rowe, "A Respectable Independence," 400.

6. A sutler is a camp follower who sells minor provisions to the troops.

7. *American Biography*, 633.

8. Mari Sandoz, *Love Song to the Plains* (Lincoln: University of Nebraska, 1966), 61–62.

9. Primm, *Lion of the Valley*, 136.

10. Hyde and Conard, *Encyclopedia of St. Louis*, 1663.

11. Floyd C. Shoemaker, *Missouri, Day by Day* (Columbia: State Historical Society of Missouri, 1942), 361.

12. Rowe, "A Respectable Independence," 405. At an 1822 Fourth of July celebration when others waxed enthusiastic for flag and homeland, O'Fallon gave a speech titled "The Lead Mines of the Upper Mississippi—Among the greatest resources of the Western Country; a wise policy demands their immediate development."

13. John F. Darby, *Personal Recollections* (St. Louis: G. I. Jones, 1880), 82.

14. Logan Reavis in *Seeking St. Louis*, ed. Lee Ann Sandweiss (St. Louis: Missouri Historical Society Press, 2000), 297.

15. Rowe, "A Respectable Independence," 407.

16. Foley, *Wilderness Journey*, 252.

17. Jones, *Shaping of the West*, 324.

18. Rowe, "A Respectable Independence," 395.

19. Landmarks Association, *Tombstone Talks*, 14.

20. Tiemann, *Oral History*, tape XII, 198.

21. George Ferguson, *Signs and Symbols in Christian Art* (London: Oxford, 1971), 169.

JOHN QUEENY

1859–1933

EDGAR MONSANTO QUEENY

1897–1968

TWO GIANTS TOOK the fate of chemical company Monsanto into their hands. First came the hard-driving father, John Francis Queeny. He had the courage to commit his entire life savings to found the chemical works while still working a day job. He named the company after his beloved wife, Olga Monsanto Queeny. When he developed cancer, he passed the reins of leadership to his suave and sophisticated son, Edgar Monsanto Queeny, who proved an intuitive and charismatic leader. By the time he retired in 1962, Edgar had transformed a good company with 1,000 employees and sales of $5.5 million into a great company with 45,000 employees and sales of over $1 billion. His life was so closely intertwined with Monsanto's fate that on the day he retired, he cried.[1] This shocked employees, who called him "Old Stone Face" behind his back.

The early life of John Francis Queeny is a tale of struggle and persistence in the face of adversity. He was born in 1859 in Chicago, the son of prosperous Irish immigrants. The Great Chicago Fire in 1871, however, wiped out his father's income from rental property. As a result, John, the eldest of five, had to drop out of school at age twelve to help support his family. He had completed just six years of formal education. Never feeling sorry for himself, John persisted in looking for a job until six months later he found one for $2.50 a week as an office boy for a drug company. He rose through the company ranks by a combination of determination and hard work, moving to New York in 1894 as sales manager for the Merck drug company. There, in 1896, he married Olga Monsanto. She was the daughter of a Spanish aristocrat and had been raised on the family's sugar plantation on St. Thomas, one of the Virgin Islands. Her effect on her ambitious husband helped build the company that bears her name.

St. Louis–based Meyer Brothers Drug Company, one of the country's largest wholesale drug houses, hired John, bringing him to the city in 1897. After the Queenys moved, John started his first moonlighting venture, which would lead to his founding Monsanto. Two years later, he was sufficiently established to take his life savings of $6,000 and invest it in a sulfur refinery. The factory burned down on its first day of operations. Because it was not insured, he lost everything. Not wishing to upset Olga, who was giving a party the night of the fire, he did not tell her about the tragedy until the next day.

Although he had twice seen his family fortunes go up in smoke, John was undaunted. In two years, he saved another $1,500 and was able to borrow enough to come up with the $5,000 needed to found the Monsanto Chemical Works. He saw an opportunity to manufacture the artificial sweetener saccharine in this country to sell to Meyer Brothers, which had bought a lot of the sweetener from a German concern, the only worldwide producer. John, a Swiss chemist, and one helper formed the entire workforce, and John came in after working from seven to three o'clock at Meyer Brothers. He would not commit himself to Monsanto full-time until 1906.[2] While sales grew steadily, the fledgling company ran into powerful opposition from the German manufacturers, who tried to wipe him out by cutting prices below the cost of what it cost to make the product. By 1904, Monsanto had lost $2,000, so John sold his horse and buggy and borrowed on his life insurance. The next year, his resolve paid off: Monsanto turned its first profit. By 1970, Monsanto had grown from its initial product—saccharine—to over five hundred products manufactured in plants around the world.

World War I brought Monsanto prosperity, but its aftermath almost drove the company out of business. During the conflict, Monsanto developed new technology to manufacture such crucial products as antiseptic and aspirin,[3] formerly imported from Germany. Although John was no chemist, he was prescient enough to hire three Swiss chemists who were able to come up with the necessary formulas. Unfortunately, after the war, Monsanto was hit by a quadruple whammy of debt, excess inventory, price wars, and depression. Wartime growth had been fueled by significant debt that had to be repaid. At the armistice, Monsanto was left with stockpiles of wartime materials unnecessary to a peacetime economy. Because German chemical manufacturers were soon back in business and cutting prices, Monsanto's sales fell. When the postwar depression hit in 1921, the company's sales fell to a third of their wartime highs. The 1,100-man workforce had to be cut to 25 people. By 1926, however, the economy stabilized, sales rose, and Monsanto survived.

EDGAR QUEENY

But John Queeny would not. When he came down with incurable throat cancer in 1928, he handed over company leadership to his son Edgar. Edgar started out at the company after serving as a lieutenant in the navy after World War I. The man who would turn out to be a brilliant leader of industry had not had a brilliant academic career. Because he had not succeeded academically at prep school in Pawling, New York, he was sent to a special tutoring institute, Sturgis School Preparatory Department. When the United States entered World War I, he had matriculated only through his sophomore year at Cornell University, but he was given a special wartime degree after he dropped out to serve in the armed forces. While stationed at a naval base in California, he met his future wife, Ethel Schneider, whom he married in 1921.

John did not give his son credit, saying, "Edgar wants to change everything; he's going to ruin Monsanto."[4] Yet, according to John Ingham in the *Biographical Dictionary of American Business Leaders*, "it was Edgar Queeny who was primarily responsible for building Monsanto into a major industrial power."[5]

When Edgar joined the company, he became its first advertising manager, a position where he could use his creative talents. "In this position he inaugurated an extensive advertising and promotional program that helped spur Monsanto's expansion during the 1920s."[6] In response to the antibusiness ethic of the New Deal, Edgar published *The Spirit of Enterprise* in 1934.

While the country writhed in the throes of the Depression, Edgar courageously expanded and diversified his product lines, taking risks that would lead to Monsanto's playing a critical role in the World War II effort. He acquired new companies around the world and paid for extensive research, making decisions based on his intuitive grasp of the economy rather than tedious calculations. When war came and the Japanese cut off rubber imports from the Pacific, the company manufactured a synthetic replacement for rubber that would continue to put tires on aircrafts and cars. The company had three other factories dedicated to the war effort: two for chemical warfare and one for the army's ordinance department. In 1943 and 1944, Monsanto scientist Dr. Charles Allen Thomas, who would later serve as the company's president, led the group of scientists who refined plutonium, the element necessary for the atomic bomb.

The postwar period inspired even greater growth, with Monsanto producing hundreds of chemicals necessary for the economic boom. In the 1970s, Monsanto chemists developed Roundup herbicide, which became the star of the lineup. A 1985 acquisition of G.D. Searle and Company brought Monsanto full circle with a significant new artificial sweetener, NutraSweet: "a replacement for saccharin, the first product Monsanto ever produced."[6]

When Edgar Queeny stepped down as chairman of the board in 1960, he devoted himself full-time to philanthropic and civic work. In 1961, he took over as chairman of the board at Barnes Hospital and focused his attention on expanding and improving the medical center. He and his wife donated $4 million to a seventeen-story ambulatory care center that would be named Queeny Tower. The bulk of both of their estates also went to Barnes Hospital. Before her death, Ethel Queeny donated $1 million to the county park named Edgar M. Queeny Park. The 570-acre site was formerly the Queenys' country estate.

At the time of Edgar Queeny's death in 1968, Monsanto was the fifth-largest chemical company in the world,[7] with assets of almost $2 billion.[8] The president of the company at the time, Charles H. Sommer, issued a statement calling Edgar the "symbol of Monsanto." When Ethel died in 1975, she joined Edgar and their son, who had died in infancy, in the family plot at Bellefontaine Cemetery.

1. Dan J. Forrestal, *Faith, Hope, and $5,000* (New York: Simon and Schuster, 1977), 47.

2. John N. Ingham, *Biographical Dictionary of American Business Leaders* (Westport, CT: Greenwood Press, 1983), 1132.

3. Ibid.

4. Forrestal, *Faith, Hope, and $5,000*, 48.

5. Ibid.

6. *Monsanto*, Manuel Garcia files, Bellefontaine Cemetery.

7. Ingham, *American Business Leaders*, 1133.

8. "Edgar Queeny Dies, Community Leader," *St. Louis Post-Dispatch*, July 8, 1968.

IRMA STARKLOFF ROMBAUER
1877–1962

WHEN IRMA STARKLOFF Rombauer's husband died, leaving her in financial straits, she decided to write a cookbook to earn some money. Behind her back, her friends scoffed; she wasn't much of a cook. Irma had left most of the household cuisine to her hired help. In fact, her daughter wrote to a friend, "Mother's hobby is beginning to embarrass me, she carries it to such lengths."[1] But Irma had such confidence in herself that she spent half of her inheritance to have her cookbook printed. She was a born saleswoman, and the edition of three thousand sold out quickly, inspiring her to seek a publisher. She met the editor of Bobbs-Merrill at a bridge party at her Indianapolis cousin's home. After initially rejecting it, he decided to publish it in 1936, suggesting a title change, but she held firm to *The Joy of Cooking*.

With more than 15 million copies in print, *The Joy of Cooking* is considered the best-selling trade cookbook ever. It was the only cookbook chosen as one of the 150 most-influential books of the twentieth century by the New York Public Library.[2] In 1997, *New York Times* food writer Molly O'Neill called *The Joy of Cooking* "an icon."[3] Moreover, it has continued in the family; Irma's daughter, Marion Rombauer Becker, first worked with her and then carried on alone. Marion's son, Ethan Becker, next picked up the pot and pen.

The unlikely author was born in St. Louis to Dr. Hugo Maximilian von Starkloff and Emma Kuhlmann von Starkloff. Dr. von Starkloff, a surgeon who had served in the Union army, was born and educated in Germany as was his wife, who came to this country to work with Susan Blow in setting up the nation's first public school kindergartens. Irma's half-brother, Dr. Max Starkloff (the second generation dropped the "von"),

126 • IRMA STARKLOFF ROMBAUER

served as the health commissioner of St. Louis, keeping the death rate in St. Louis far lower than in any other major city during the 1918 outbreak of the Spanish flu by maintaining strict quarantines.

Irma attended art school at Washington University in St. Louis. Diminutive, attractive, and clever, Irma had many boyfriends, among them an unemployed author named Booth Tarkington to whom she was introduced by her Indianapolis cousins. Although Irma and Tarkington were at first serious about each other, her family considered an aspiring author an inappropriate suitor and discouraged the affair. The handsome Edgar Rombauer finally won her hand in 1899. He was the son of Roderick Rombauer, a judge and Hungarian immigrant, and Augusta Koerner Rombauer, daughter of Gustave Koerner, lieutenant governor of Illinois and an intimate of Abraham Lincoln.

When Irma married her "impecunious, young lawyer," she was, in her own words, "ignorant, helpless and awkward"[4] around the kitchen. She taught herself to cook and to direct the cook, though she "placed many a burnt offering upon the altar of matrimony."[5] The Rombauers had two children, Marion and Edgar Jr. While her husband was not as successful as the ambitious Irma might have liked, she was "always the life of the party,"[6] said *Post-Dispatch* society columnist Marguerite Martyn in 1936. Her charities were not all fun and games: With suffragist Edna Fischel Gellhorn, she instituted a clinic to test prostitutes for venereal disease.[7]

Life changed for Irma on February 3, 1930. Edgar had suffered bouts of what he called "nervous breakdowns"[8] throughout his life. Deep in the throes of depression, he put a Purdy double-barreled shotgun in his mouth and pulled the trigger with a string attached to his toe while Irma was out shopping. Even though Edgar had been relatively successful as a lawyer, he left only a modest estate of $6,000 and stock worth less every day during the Depression. Irma began casting about for something to do: write a cookbook.

Once Bobbs-Merrill decided to publish *The Joy of Cooking* in 1936, it marketed the book with extreme skill, leading in part to its success. Yet the relationship between publisher and author was not a triumph in any sense of the word. When Irma signed her contract with editor Laurence Chambers, she thought she was meeting with a gentleman and took neither lawyer nor agent to protect her interests. She signed a contract assigning copyright of both the 1936 and the 1931 edition that she had self-published to Bobbs-Merrill. It "cost Irma Rombauer and her heirs hundreds of thousands (perhaps millions) of dollars."[9]

The Joy of Cooking was so successful in large part because of the wit and charm of Irma Rombauer. For example, in the first chapter of the 1936 edition she wrote: "The chief virtue of cocktails is their informal quality. They loosen tongues and unbutton the reserves of the socially diffident. Serve them by all means, preferably in the living room and the sooner the better."[10] Marion's revisions starting in 1953 turned *Joy* into the teaching manual that it has become.

Irma spent the last eight years of her life debilitated by strokes. Nevertheless, she made her opinions known in the ongoing revision of her book. She died October 14, 1962, on the sixty-third anniversary of her marriage to Edgar. She was cremated, and her remains were buried in Bellefontaine Cemetery. On October 17, at a reception following a memorial service held at the First Unitarian Church, Marion was greeted not only by mourners but also by the news that their longtime nemesis, Bobbs-Merrill, had put out a rush copy of her latest revision full of unacceptable mistakes.

More a hostess than a cook, Irma Rombauer felt that conversation should take precedence over cuisine at a party. She captivated generations of women by not talking down to them and by deeming the culinary arts the means to an end, rather than an end in itself. Indomitable, charming, Irma Rombauer made her book a success by putting her personality on every page.

---

1. Marion Rombauer Becker quoted in Anne Mendelson, *Stand Facing the Stove* (New York: Henry Holt, 1996), 88.

2. "Joy of Cooking 75th Birthday," http://recommendedreading.suite101.com/article.cfm/joy_of_cooking_75th_birthday.

3. Molly O'Neill, "There's a New 'Joy' in Cookbook Land, But Will It Inspire the Same Kind of Love?," *St. Louis Post-Dispatch*, November 10, 1997.

4. Irma Rombauer, *Joy of Cooking* (Indianapolis: Bobbs-Merrill, 1936), preface, quoted in Marion Rombauer Becker, "Irma Rombauer: The Joy of Cooking, 1877–1962," *Notable American Unitarians*, http://www.harvardsquarelibrary.org/unitarians/rombauer.htmail.

5. Allen Johnson, *Dictionary of American Biography* (New York: American Council of Learned Societies, 1946), 656.

6. Marguerite Martyn, *St. Louis Post-Dispatch*, March 25, 1936.

7. Lorin Cuoco and William H. Gass, eds., *Literary St. Louis* (St. Louis: Missouri Historical Society Press, 2000), 112.

8. Mendelson, *Stand Facing the Stove*, 38.

9. Ibid., 151.

10. Ibid., 237.

HENRY SHREVE

1785–1851

WHILE ROBERT FULTON is widely known as the "Father of the Steamboat" for his 1803 invention, most would only recall the name of Henry Shreve as part of the name of Shreveport, Louisiana. Yet if any one man could be honored for making the Mississippi River teem with trade, surely he would be Henry Shreve. Fulton's invention was not really suited for the Mighty Mississippi, where it would only run downstream swiftly. A brilliant river man, Shreve designed one steamboat that could travel both up and down the Mississippi in record time and another that cleared the river of fallen trees. A patriot, he ran the British blockade to bring munitions to the Battle of New Orleans in the War of 1812. A shrewd and principled businessman, he won a long lawsuit to end a monopoly's control of the waterways. Shreve's influence was so pervasive that the name he gave the passenger cabins on his first great "floating palace" has been applied ever since. He named each cabin after a different state of the Union, hence the term "stateroom."[1]

Henry Shreve virtually grew up on the river. He was born in New Jersey, but his family moved as pioneers to the "western wilderness" of Pennsylvania when he was two years old. Israel Shreve, his Quaker father who had fought in the American Revolution, bought land from his commander, George Washington, in 1787. The property was located on the frontier of civilization between two rivers that joined to feed into the Ohio River at Pittsburgh fifty miles south. Three years after his father died, at the age of seventeen, Shreve first took to the river on a flatboat. By the time he was twenty-one, he was the captain of his own keelboat.

Shreve's trading skills brought him wealth and knowledge of the waterways. His career on the river took him from Pittsburgh to St. Louis to Louisville to New Orleans and back to St. Louis. With his keelboat laden with supplies, he made his first trip as captain of his own ship in 1806 to the outpost of St. Louis. He traded these supplies for furs on which he turned a tidy profit. Later, he went farther up the river to Galena, Illinois, where he traded with the Indians for lead, earning $11,000, an exorbitant sum in 1810.

Shreve paid keen attention when Fulton's *New Orleans* made it down the Mississippi in a little over four weeks in 1811. Though the hue and cry was "Old Mississippi has met her master,"[2] the river showed its dominance when Fulton's deep-hulled ship could go upriver no farther than Natchez, Mississippi. Better understanding the ways of the river, Shreve was able to correct the deficiencies of Fulton's boat with a design that became the prototype for all riverboats to follow. Shreve's steamboat had a flat bottom like a keelboat so it could float on shallow rivers rather than attempt to plow through the water as Fulton's boat did. The Mississippi is such a fickle stream that sandbars can rise up overnight, and a few inches of a boat's hull can mean the difference between getting stuck or not. Shreve gave his engine more steam pressure and thus more power than Fulton's and put it up on deck, making it easier to stoke with wood and leaving the hold free for cargo. In 1817, in his steamboat the *Washington*, Shreve shortened the downriver trip to sixteen days from the six weeks it took with a keelboat and made it upriver to Louisville in twenty-four days, a vast improvement over the four months a keelboat took to travel the same route. A contemporary account said, "This was the trip . . . which convinced the despairing public that steamboat navigation would succeed on the western waters."[3]

Shreve was honored for his accomplishments throughout the Mississippi Valley. Immediately after the *Washington* reached Louisville, the citizens gave a public dinner for him. At this banquet, he predicted that the twenty-four-day journey would soon be cut to ten days. "Although this may have been regarded as a boastful declaration at that time, the prediction has been more than fulfilled; for in 1853, the trip was made in four days and nine hours,"[4] said Captain Emerson Gould in his nineteenth-century *History of River Navigation*. In 1806, a mere six keelboats and two barges plied the Ohio. By 1819, the number of ships on the river had increased to twenty-five—all steamboats, and an additional twenty-six were in the process of being built.[5] In 1842, nearly two thousand steamboats stopped at the port of St. Louis, and the steamboat tonnage on the Mississippi equaled that of the British empire.[6] Throughout the Mississippi Valley, Shreve was recognized as the father of this growing fleet. With the advance of steam power, trade on the river grew at a furious pace; Shreve prospered accordingly. He was owner or part owner of the first sixty steamboats running on the Ohio-Mississippi waterway.[7]

In 1817, Shreve was arrested and his boat seized upon docking at New Orleans. Robert Fulton and his financial backer Robert Livingston had been granted exclusive rights to all steamboat trade in the Louisiana Territory. "The prospect of becoming entangled in expensive litigation . . . held back steamboat navigation for years. But the Fulton forces received a rude awakening . . . for they had reckoned without Captain Henry Shreve."[8] During the war, New Orleans had been under martial law, enabling Shreve to ply the river with impunity, but once hostilities ceased, the monopoly was back in effect. The Fulton group pressed charges. As a matter of principle, Shreve refused to post bail. The sheriff offered to pay the bond himself rather than take the hero to prison in front of a crowd demonstrating on his behalf. Thus began a protracted legal battle between Shreve and the Fulton-Livingston interests. During the course of this dispute, the monopoly's representatives offered Shreve's lawyer a payoff of $3,000 and Shreve himself half of the profits of the monopoly if they would drop their suit. Neither, however, succumbed to the temptation.

Shreve did more than unseal the Mississippi legally; he also unclogged it physically from the snags and sawyers, old trees and tree trunks that could smash a steamboat's hull. Between 1822 and 1827, snagged boats and cargoes resulted in a loss of $1,362,500 ($30,747,101 in 2007 dollars).[9] That final year, the War Department named Shreve superintendent of western river improvement. He immediately started pulling sawyers out of the river with his steamboats. Two years later, he finished building the snag boat he had designed and patented. Popularly known as "Uncle Sam's tooth-puller,"[10] it had twin hulls with an iron jaw in between for ramming snags. After winches pulled the trunks out of the water, a sawmill on board ground them up. Within five years, the Mississippi was so clear that not a single steamboat was lost to snags in the year 1832. By 1834, boats could run at night through channels that had once been dangerous by daylight.[11]

In 1833, Shreve was ordered to clear the Red River, and as a result, the town of Shreveport on its banks was named in his honor. This important potential waterway to the West had become so clogged with snags that driftwood was jammed into a "raft," a solid mass where trees even grew. Except for summers off when the river ran too shallow, Shreve and his crew of 160 worked five years to clear the Red River. The project cost $300,000 ($6,896,075 in 2007 dollars) and cleared some of the country's richest corn and cotton land previously subject to flooding. Shreve "estimated that the opening of the river added fifteen million dollars to the worth of the public domain"[12] because he had opened the only quick route to Texas and reclaimed vast areas of rich land.

St. Louis City hired Shreve for his final project on the Mississippi in 1837. Changing currents were moving the channel to the Illinois side, away from St. Louis, and threatening to leave the city landlocked. Shreve turned the work over to the War Department engineer Robert E. Lee (later the Confederacy's commanding general), who largely followed Shreve's plan to build dikes that diverted the current back to the city's waterfront.

In his later years, Shreve even became an advocate of the railroad because he believed it would bring more of the country in touch with the Mississippi. Along with friends such as Pierre Chouteau Jr. and John O'Fallon, he organized the Pacific Railroad Company.[13]

Shreve spent his final years overlooking the Mississippi on a farm named Gallatin Place.[14] Because his innovations had made the "Father of Waters" flush with commerce and St. Louis's fortunes shine, the city considered Shreve its leading citizen. The city honored him in its naming of Shreve Avenue in north St. Louis and by selecting Shreve to send the first cable to the president in Washington, D.C., when telegraph service was established in St. Louis in 1848. Tragically, the cholera epidemic of 1849 claimed three of his grandchildren as well as his own infant daughter, and it broke his spirit. He died in 1851 and was buried in Bellefontaine Cemetery on a bluff overlooking the Mississippi River.

Although steamboats no longer travel the Mississippi except as historical novelties, Henry Shreve's ships improved life for the entire population of the Mississippi Valley and contributed to the growth and prosperity of the city of St. Louis. While there are many reasons for the exponential growth in population of the city of St. Louis from 10,000 in 1820 (three years after the first voyage of Shreve's innovative riverboat) to 105,000 in 1850[15] (the year before he died), the significance of the steamboat to the city's economy was certainly a driving factor. Shreve's clever engineering applications made the river grow prosperous with trade, and settlement flourished along its banks.

---

1. *Engine on a Raft*, Manuel Garcia files, Bellefontaine Cemetery, 57. The officers' cabins on the third deck are known as the texas because these staterooms were added later to steamboats just as the state of Texas joined the Union in 1845.

2. Edith McCall, "The Man Who Tamed the Mississippi," *The American Legion Magazine*, March 1978, 30.

3. "Political Portraits with Pen and Pencil: Henry Miller Shreve," *The United States Magazine and Democratic Review* XXII (January 1848), 168.

4. Emerson Gould, *Fifty Years on the Mississippi; Or, Gould's History of River Navigation* (St. Louis: Nixon-Jones, 1899), 166.

5. Ibid., 169.

6. Florence L. Dorsey, *Henry Shreve and the Conquest of the Mississippi* (New York: Houghton, 1941), 208.

7. Harry Sinclair Drago, *Steamboaters: From the Early Sidewheelers to the Big Packets* (New York: Dodd, 1967), 16.

8. Ibid., 8.

9. Walter Havighurst, *Voices on the River: The Story of the Mississippi Waterways* (New York: MacMillan, 1964), 71.

10. *American Biography*.

11. Havighurst, *Voices on the River*, 72.

12. Ibid., 75.

13. Dorsey, *Henry Shreve*, 242.

14. Shreve's farm was named after Albert Gallatin, the U.S. secretary of the treasury who lived on a neighboring farm to the Shreve family during Henry Shreve's childhood.

15. "Genealogy Articles, Tips, and Research Guides," www.genealogybranches.com, 2003–2008.

LUTHER ELY SMITH
1873–1951

WHILE HE IS JUSTLY honored for securing the Jefferson National Expansion Memorial and the Arch for St. Louis, Luther Ely Smith devoted his life not only to the creation of a more beautiful city but also to the creation of a more just society. As an attorney, he worked hard to sweep out corruption in city government. To clean up St. Louis's blighted downtown, in 1933 he came up with the idea of a riverfront memorial to westward expansion. He spent the remaining years of his life fighting against all odds to realize his vision. Sadly, Smith died in 1951, fourteen years before the Arch was completed. St. Louis remembers his name with a small park between the Old Courthouse and the Arch grounds.

Born in 1873 in Downers Grove, Illinois, outside of Chicago, Smith settled in St. Louis after earning his law degree from Washington University in 1897. He married SaLees Kennard in 1909, and together they had three children. Always public spirited, he joined the U.S. Army as an artillery captain in World War I.

At the turn of the century, he served on a commission that brought the city its first playgrounds. In 1914, along with three other civic leaders, he was a chief instigator of the Pageant-Masque, which would develop in 1919 into the Muny, Forest Park's open-air theater that continues to this day. In 1916, as chairman of the City Plan Commission, he brought architect Harlan Bartholomew to St. Louis to work on an urban plan.

When he returned from the war, Smith, in addition to his successful law practice, devoted his considerable energies to a vision of civic progress. To this end, he served on commissions to take the appointment of appellate judges out of the hands of political bosses and combated the political spoils system. A lifelong Republican, he was also a director of the St. Louis Committee of the American Civil Liberties Union. At that time,

St. Louis was a big, dirty city, so he set out to improve downtown through slum clearance and smoke abatement.

But Smith wanted more for St. Louis. Looking at St. Louis's decaying warehouses along the river, he came up with the idea of beautifying the riverfront with a monument that recognized the historic significance of the city. Here was the place where all settlers of the western United States started out, and to Smith, the riverfront was "historically sacred ground."[1] While he felt the monument should honor Thomas Jefferson and the Louisiana Purchase, he wanted "a memorial not to any one man, but to the men who made it possible."[2]

Today, St. Louis is unimaginable without the riverfront park and its soaring monument, but in 1934 Smith fought an uphill battle to establish it, not only nationally but locally as well. He immediately enlisted the support of Mayor Bernard Dickmann and other civic leaders to join the new Jefferson National Monument Expansion Association. Smith served as its president from 1934 to 1949 and as chairman until 1950. Others fought hard against condemning the ninety acres of riverfront property: Smith won thirty-nine lawsuits that attempted to block the project. Although the project died many deaths before and after President Franklin Roosevelt signed the executive order permitting its development on December 21, 1935, Smith never gave up.

The city voters approved a $7.5 million bond issue to provide one-quarter of the costs, with the federal government furnishing the rest of the funds.[3] Creating much-needed jobs for unskilled laborers, the $9 million demolition of the riverfront property began in 1939 and was completed in 1942. However, the cleared land existed only as a parking lot until 1961 when work on the monument began.

In 1946, Smith's committee held a design competition for the monument. When fund-raising fell $40,000 short of the $225,000 needed for the competition, Smith wrote a check to make up the difference.[4] He sought a monument of "transcending spiritual and aesthetic values."[5] In February 1948, the winner was chosen: Eero Saarinen's Arch, a bold symbol of St. Louis as the Gateway to the West. Just before the dedication of the Arch in 1966, President Lyndon Johnson said that St. Louis "faced a hard choice and . . . made it. The people of Saint Louis chose progress—not decay. A new spirit of Saint Louis was born. And today you look forward to the future with pride and confidence."[6]

Smith died of a heart attack while walking to work on April 2, 1951. His legacy soars 630 feet above the St. Louis riverfront, drawing 3 million people a year[7] and giving the city a proud focus.

---

1. "The St. Louis Scene," *Gateway Heritage*, Fall 1998, 24.

2. Ibid., 23.

3. Harry Levins, "Arch of Triumph," *St. Louis Post-Dispatch Magazine*, October 28, 1990, 8.

4. National Park Service, U.S. Department of the Interior, "Jefferson National Expansion Memorial," http//www.nps.gov/jeff/historyculture/upload/luther_ely_smith.pdf.

5. Ibid.

6. Lyndon Johnson quoted in Elinor Martineau Coyle, *Saint Louis: Portrait of a River City* (St. Louis: Folkestone, 1966), 175.

7. Mary Delach Leonard, "Arch reflections: The next ten years," *St. Louis Post-Dispatch*, October 23, 2005, EV5.

SIR PETER SMITHERS
1913–2006

CONSIDERED THE MODEL for the character James Bond in Ian Fleming's 007 novels, Sir Peter Smithers was a true Renaissance man. He served England and Europe as spy, legislator, diplomat, and executive, in addition to achieving renown as a historian, photographer, and master gardener.

After he died on a June day in his garden outside Lugano, Switzerland, his ashes were brought to Bellefontaine Cemetery. They lie alongside those of his wife, Dojean Sayman Smithers, and her parents, Thomas and Luella Sayman of the Sayman Products Company. They all rest inside the columbarium of the Sayman monument, which is shaped like a fainting bench. Cemetery superintendent Michael Tiemann explained, "Back in the 1870s to 1880s, women wore tight corsets, . . . so tight that they would take their breath away. Most of the large homes had a bench that the ladies could recline on to catch their breath. . . . It's the only fainting bench in the cemetery."[1]

During World War II, Sir Peter Smithers served under Ian Fleming in MI6, the British equivalent of the CIA. It led to his being considered the inspiration for the elegant spy James Bond. Although seven other colleagues have also been proposed as Bond types, the Fleming-Smithers connections are significant. "When the *Daily Express* asked the novelist to advise one of its cartoonists on Commander Bond's appearance for a new comic strip, the face that emerged resembled the younger Smithers."[2] Smithers became a spy in spite of himself. He volunteered for the Royal Navy, but a severe case of measles took him off ship and relegated him to shore duty. Both he and Fleming were assigned to Paris, narrowly escaping to Bordeaux before the Nazi invasion. There, Smithers and Fleming commandeered seven merchant ships and used them for the escape of British refugees. Upon return to London, both worked in naval intelligence. "Fleming was taught how to kill a man in combat by biting him on the back of the neck. . . . Smithers was taught how to pick locks."[3] They collaborated in designing a dagger, and Fleming gave Smithers a gun shaped like a pen.

Smithers was posted to Mexico City to spy on German U-boat refueling stations because U-boats and mines had sunk 397 Allied boats in the Caribbean in 1942.[4] He met and, after a whirlwind, three-week courtship, married Dojean Sayman, an heiress who at the time owned a solid gold typewriter. Fleming borrowed the idea of a gold typewriter and used it as a detail in his novel *Goldfinger*. In the same 1959 novel, the villain Colonel Smithers serves the evil Goldfinger as his undercover agent at the Bank of England. A character named Smithers also appears as assistant to Q, Bond's quartermaster, in Fleming's *For Your Eyes Only* and *Octopussy*.

Dojean was accustomed to colorful eccentrics. Her father, Thomas "Doc" Sayman, had started a multimillion-dollar firm as a traveling medicine man selling soaps and salves from a horse-drawn wagon. Novelist Williams S. Burroughs II, who grew up near the Sayman mansion, said, "[Sayman] was a famous old character who used to bring people in off the street and challenge them to butt heads. He had a horse stuffed in the front hall. When he started selling his soap, he had a cart, and this was the horse that pulled the cart."[5] He also carried a pistol that he called "Ol' Becky Trueheart," which he brandished more often than he should have. Despite his aggressive instincts, he was a great public benefactor. Sayman donated Roaring River State Park to Missouri and supported many St. Louis charities.

Following the war, the much-decorated spy returned to Oxford, England, to earn his doctorate in history, and he was eventually elected to Parliament. From 1960 to 1962, he served as the British delegate to the United Nations, and in 1964 he was elected secretary general of the Council of Europe in Strasbourg, France.

In 1970, Smithers and his wife accepted the invitation of the Swiss government to become citizens. An original thinker, his advice continued to be sought by prime ministers, in particular by Margaret Thatcher. The Smithers bought a one-acre former vineyard on the shores of Lake Lugano, where he spent the rest of his life hybridizing plants and developing his garden. He designed it as an ecosystem that would grow increasingly self-sustaining as he grew older. By the time of his death at ninety-two, it contained more than ten thousand plants that he photographed using one of the first digital cameras.

Sir Peter Smithers brings notoriety to Bellefontaine Cemetery as an alter ego to the glamorous agent 007. Through the years, he and his wife, Dojean, visited her parents' final resting place and chose to join them inside the Sayman "fainting bench" when their time came.

---

1. Michael Tiemann, *Oral History*, tape II, 9.

2. "RIP Agent 007s unlikely alter ego—Sir Peter Smithers," *MI6 News*, http://www.mi6.co.uk/news/index,php?itemid=3882&catid+4.

3. Ibid.

4. *MI6 News*; in *A World at Arms: A Global History of World War II* (Cambridge, England: Cambridge University Press, 1994), 379, Gerhard Weinberg puts the figure at 485 ships sunk between January and August 1942.

5. Harper Barnes, "William Burroughs Comes Home," *St. Louis Post-Dispatch*, n.d.

JAMES YEATMAN
1818–1901

COMING TO ST. LOUIS at the age of twenty-four, James Erwin Yeatman established himself in business and then spent the rest of his life passing on his own good fortune to the poor, the sick, the wounded, the orphaned, and all who hungered for knowledge. His influence on St. Louis continues to this day in institutions such as Bellefontaine Cemetery and the Mercantile Library that he established and led. His name lives on in the Yeatman-Liddell Junior High School, a descendant of the former Yeatman High School that was named after him and dedicated in 1903 after his death. Though he had built up great wealth in banking, business, and railroads, his considerable generosity left him with little except for an extensive library when he died.

Dying of natural causes at age eighty-three, he had outlived two wives and three of his five children. "His city mourned him as its first citizen," claims *The Dictionary of American Biography*.[1] His *New York Times* obituary reads: "Probably no person in St. Louis was more widely known and generally loved than Mr. Yeatman, whose life was coincident with the life of St. Louis."[2] Consistent with the humility with which he lived his life, he was buried in Bellefontaine Cemetery beneath a simple stone that bears only his name and dates. According to cemetery gatekeeper Manuel Garcia, "Flowers are still placed on his tombstone throughout the year."[3] Nearby, a monument to his first wife is one of the sculptural highlights of the cemetery. While the marble is badly worn, the sculpture by Robert von der Launitz has an elegant silhouette of Angelica Charlotte Thompson Yeatman on one side and on the other an image of angels ascending to heaven, bearing babies in their arms.

James Yeatman was born at an estate called Beechwood near Wartrace, Tennessee, the son of Thomas and Jane Erwin Yeatman. His mother's second husband was John Bell, who ran for president against Abraham Lincoln in 1860. James was educated by tutors and at the New Haven Commercial School. He came to St. Louis from Nashville as a representative of his father's iron business in 1842 and immediately founded a commission business of his own. Making a name for himself with his honesty, keen business sense, and courtly manners, within five years he became a real estate developer with Yeatman's Row, an elegant housing project. Within eight years, he became a proponent of the railroad, petitioning Congress for a right of way through the state for the Missouri Pacific Railroad, of which he was an incorporator, and securing a $500,000 subscription from the city of St. Louis for the Ohio and Mississippi Railroad. In 1849, he, along with several other prominent St. Louisans, founded the Merchants' Bank. Ten years later, he put aside all of his other business to become president of this bank when it was reorganized as Merchants' National Bank. He headed it for thirty-five years, taking it to a position of leadership in the region.

But it was in philanthropy that Yeatman made his lasting mark upon the city. He approached charity with as much vision, organization, and discipline as he did business. For example, he was a leader in establishing the Provident Association to aid the "deserving" poor. The story goes that he was called to his door on a bad night by a woman seeking alms, saying she had a child who might not live until the next day, for whom she had no money. He gave her the money for food or medicine, but, still troubled by her tale of woe, he contacted a doctor to help the sick child. When they arrived at her home, Yeatman found her serving a party with beer bought with his charity. The next day, he gathered a group of businessmen to set up an agency to determine need and distribute only food, clothing, and shelter, not money, to the deserving poor. Its effectiveness was such that Archbishop Farley of New York commented, "In St. Louis, the workingman and poorer classes are much better taken care of in their homes than similar classes in New York."[4] In addition to the other institutions he founded and served, he incorporated a hospital for the insane and was the first head of the trustees of the asylum for the blind as well as first president of the soldiers orphans' home, secretary of the St. Louis medical college, and president of the eye and ear infirmary.[5]

Despite the fact that Yeatman had lived in St. Louis only seven years, he was one of the first people William McPherson and John F. Darby asked in 1849 to join the movement for establishing a rural cemetery. He became the first president of the Bellefontaine Cemetery Association and in this capacity traveled to the East Coast in search of a landscape architect. The cemetery is fortunate that he found Almerin Hotchkiss at Brooklyn's Green-Wood Cemetery. The gentle hills of Bellefontaine were laid out by Hotchkiss, who served as its superintendent for the next fifty-three years.

Unfortunately, Yeatman was among the first to use the cemetery when Angelica, his wife of eleven years, died during the cholera epidemic of 1849. Two years later, he married Cynthia Ann Pope, daughter of Nathaniel Pope and sister of General John Pope. Three years afterward, she also died. Yeatman's personal life was marred by these tragedies; nevertheless, he lived with great style and entertained many friends in his mansion that he named Belmont. The American writer Winston Churchill changed that name to Bellgarde when he depicted it in his best-selling novel *The Crisis*, a tale of St. Louis during the Civil War. Churchill modeled his character Mr. Brinsmade on Yeatman.

The hour when Yeatman's fine and patriotic character cast its brightest light was during the darkest days of the Republic. While the army had its surgical corps to minister to wounded soldiers at the battlefront, no organized system transported the wounded to hospitals; no Red Cross tended to the needs of the sick and battle scarred or to the civilian refugees; and no government agency tended to the sanitary needs of the soldier—good food, sanitary supplies, and drainage ditches for waste. In response, the government created the U.S. Sanitary Commission, but its reach did not extend beyond the eastern seaboard. In the summer of 1861, General John C. Frémont, commander of the Western Department headquartered in St. Louis, established the Western Sanitary Commission (WSC) and appointed Yeatman its president. Yeatman took no pay and worked until after midnight, night after night, often sleeping on a bed in his office. Supported almost entirely by donation, the Western Sanitary Commission provided $4,270,998 in supplies and services ($58 million in 2007 dollars) and did so with the utmost efficiency.

The WSC set up fifteen military hospitals in and around St. Louis and five floating hospitals on steamships. The St. Louis medical centers alone treated 61,477 soldiers, with a 10 percent mortality rate. Yeatman personally visited the battlefields and inspected the distribution of supplies. The soldiers fondly called him "Old Sanitary."

Moreover, following Yeatman's directives, the Western Sanitary Commission ministered to Confederate as well as Union victims. While the WSC distributed more than 1 million articles of aid to soldiers who wore both blue and gray, it gave some five thousand articles to refugees and more than eighty thousand to freedmen. Yeatman's group established an orphanage for white children and another for blacks that exists to this day as the Annie Malone Children's Home. During one of his tours of the battlefields, Yeatman began investigating the situation of the freedmen in the Mississippi Valley. He questioned thousands, finding, "They all testify that if they were only paid their little wages as they earned, they could stand it, but to work and get poorly paid, poorly fed, and not doctored when sick is more than they can endure."[6] Yeatman recommended that abandoned plantations be leased to blacks. The commission sent doctors, nurses, and teachers, as well as medicine, food, and clothing, to their aid. In St. Louis, the WSC granted the Ladies' Freedmen's Relief Association $1,000 a month to set up nine schools. Yeatman recommended the creation of a Freedmen's Bureau to minister to their special difficulties. He already had the president's ear as he served on a commission to report to Lincoln about the situation in St. Louis.[7] Heeding his recommendation, Lincoln asked him to lead the new bureau, but he declined.

Yeatman saw his success in business as an opportunity to become a benefactor for the common good. He is truly a father of today's St. Louis. Many of the city's finest institutions, Washington University, the Missouri Botanical Garden, Bellefontaine Cemetery, the Mercantile Library, and the Annie Malone Children's Home, to name but a few, were founded upon the bedrock of his generosity and leadership. During the Civil War, his patriotism inspired him to work tirelessly for the sick and the wounded, and afterward to tend to the needs of the returning soldier and the newly freed slaves.

---

1. *American Biography*, vol. 20, 60.
2. Obituary, *New York Times*, July 8, 1901.
3. Manuel Garcia, *Oral History*, tape LXVII, 985.
4. Yeatman file, Manuel Garcia files, Bellefontaine Cemetery.
5. Shoemaker, *Missouri Day by Day*, 133.
6. Allan Nevins, *The War for the Union*, vol. 3 (New York: Scribner's, 1971), 438.
7. Obituary, *New York Times*.

PART TWO

SCALAWAGS
AND
NOTORIOUS
WOMEN

Scalawags and notorious women interred in Bellefontaine Cemetery represent the flip side of St. Louis's movers and shakers. Ironically, some of the city's leading citizens were also scalawags. In a city founded for the purpose of trade, money motivated surprisingly few of the cemetery's bad boys. Robber baron Henry Clay Pierce built a great fortune but watched it dwindle away. Ellis Wainwright, now renowned for the architectural masterpieces he commissioned, spent ten years on the lam. He was caught paying a bribe to a city official.

Lust motivated many of Bellefontaine's rakes and roués. Infidelity ranks high. Benjamin de Bonneville (see Part 4) and Herman Luyties (see Part 13) were guilty of this sin. Arthur Duestrow's infidelity led to murder.

Duestrow is not the only murderer interred in Bellefontaine. John Cockerill, Joseph Pulitzer's prize editor, may have gotten away with murder (see Part 7). William S. Burroughs II, author of *Naked Lunch*, accidentally shot and killed his wife while drunkenly demonstrating a William Tell stunt, a martini glass instead of an apple on her head (see Part 9).

In some cases, eccentricity verged on insanity. Alfred Plant's family had him committed to St. Vincent's Insane Asylum after he married a prostitute. The Lemp brewing dynasty boasted "Lavender Lady" Lillian Lemp. Perhaps because three of the four family suicides occurred there, ghosts supposedly still haunt the family mansion.

Among Bellefontaine's notorious women are a madam, a belle, and a lady who died for her vanity. If the cemetery's stones could talk, they would tell tales of murder and infidelity, vanity, and greed.

KATE BREWINGTON BENNETT
1818–1855

ATOP A HILL OVERLOOKING the Mississippi River stands one of Bellefontaine Cemetery's most beautiful and romantic monuments. An elegant arched canopy with spiked Gothic details protects a recumbent figure guarded by an angel. The marble figure, whose features have worn away, represents the beautiful Kate Brewington Bennett. Her husband, William Bennett, one of the cemetery's founders, erected this tribute to their love when she was tragically poisoned at the age of thirty-seven.

Bennett was "regarded as the most beautiful woman in St. Louis."[1] Commitment to her own good looks brought about her early demise. During the mid-nineteenth century, a pallid complexion was considered the height of loveliness. To whiten the complexion, some women took drafts of arsenic. While not fatal in small dosages, the poison has a cumulative effect. The arsenic built up in her system until it killed her.

Esley Hamilton, preservation historian for the St. Louis County Department of Parks and Recreation, doubts the story's validity. "This story may be true, but no contemporary source for it has been found. The notice in the newspaper says only that she died after a short illness."[2] Whether true or not, the fable of the beautiful Bennett's fatal pursuit of vanity seems appropriate to this monument to lost love.

---

1. John A. Bryan, *Touring Bellefontaine Cemetery* (St. Louis: Bellefontaine Cemetery Association, 2005), 13.
2. Esley Hamilton, "Winfield Scott Hancock's St. Louis Connections," *The Jefferson Barracks Gazette* 7, no. 1 (January–March 1999), 6.

ARTHUR DUESTROW
1868–1897

ON THE AFTERNOON of Valentine's Day 1894, twenty-five-year-old Dr. Arthur Duestrow came home in his sleigh from a three-day spree with a woman of the night. Taking out his revolver, this scion of a wealthy family murdered his wife and baby son, Louis, in the upstairs hall of their mansion and promptly turned himself in to the police. According to the *St. Louis Chronicle*, the act was premeditated because he had told his mistress, Clara, just beforehand that "there would soon be a change in his condition."[1]

Three years and two days later, he was executed by hanging outside the jail in Union, Missouri, before a crowd of five hundred people. Just before he stepped off the platform into eternity, he declared that he "was dying for another man."[2] In a final interview granted moments before to Miss Ada Patterson of the *St. Louis Republic* (the first female reporter to cover a state execution), Duestrow maintained that he was actually Count Van Brandenburg, one of several identities, including that of a Roman Catholic cardinal, that he had assumed since the murder.[3] Earlier that morning in his prison cell, he had broken down and cried, admitting, "I did wrong. I killed my wife and child, but it was not my fault. It was something within me that made me do it. I was not myself."[4]

His defense attorney, Charles P. Johnson, a former lieutenant governor of Missouri and defender of Jesse James's brother Frank, pled that Duestrow was innocent due to insanity. However, "the St. Louis newspapers, apparently a great majority of their readers, and most importantly, the last of three juries to hear the murder case, believed that Arthur Duestrow was merely feigning madness."[5]

In a bizarre attempt to vindicate his client, Johnson insisted upon a postmortem investigation of Duestrow's brain to prove the convicted murderer was indeed non compos mentis. Finding "milky spots"[6] in his brain, the doctors, with one exception, concluded that Duestrow's brain was abnormal. Others argued that his brain might not have been so diseased three years previously when the murders took place. One of the medical examiners kept the skull as a trophy and used it to hold his pens and pencils.[7]

The public reveled in the lurid details of the heinous crime. People were fascinated by the failings of the "$20,000-a-year"[8] heir of Louis Duestrow, director of one of St. Louis's most important insurance companies and a primary stockholder in a lucrative mine. The *Post-Dispatch* pointed out that Louis Duestrow "sent Arthur to a medical college, hoping that he would become a doctor. The boy was dissipated and stupid, and old Duestrow realized that unless he tied up the money so that Arthur could not get at the principal he would make ducks and drakes of his fortune."[9] People even sang a popular ditty with the lyrics "Cigarettes drove Duestrow crazy—killed his wife and little baby."[10] When Johnson gave an extemporaneous eulogy at Duestrow's graveside, the local papers and two contemporary books carried the entire text.[11] However, only Johnson, Duestrow's doctors, and an attorney representing his sister, Hulda Duestrow, attended the burial. No tombstone marks his grave.

---

1. *St. Louis Chronicle*, September 17, 1894, 1.

2. "Milky Spots on His Brain," *St. Louis Post-Dispatch* 48, no. 192, 1897.

3. Marshall D. Hier, "Arthur Duestrow's Brain: An 1897 Autopsy," *St. Louis Bar Journal* (Fall 2005): 38.

4. "Duestrow Sheds Tears," *St. Louis Post-Dispatch*, February 16, 1897, 1.

5. Hier, "Duestrow's Brain," 38.

6. "Milky Spots."

7. Manuel Garcia, *Oral History*, tape III, 43.

8. Hyde and Conard, *Encyclopedia of St. Louis*, 526.

9. "Duestrow's Awful Crime," *St. Louis Post-Dispatch*, February 16, 1897, 3.

10. William J. Kuehling, letter to the editor, October 27, 2005, *St. Louis Bar Journal* (Winter 2006): 3.

11. Hier, "Duestrow's Brain," 39.

ELIZA HAYCRAFT

1820–1871

ELIZA HAYCRAFT was a "soiled dove." In 1840, she came to St. Louis from Callaway County, Missouri. Over the next thirty-one years, she used her considerable charms to make a living, first as a courtesan, then as a madam. Despite the fact that she was illiterate, she had a keen business sense and attained great wealth. Her funeral procession to Bellefontaine Cemetery was attended by a crowd of thousands,[1] black as well as white, many of them recipients of her charity. The *Daily Democrat* declared that the newspaper seldom gave space to a "social outcast" like Haycraft,[2] but her generosity and kindness as well as her great wealth, not to mention the way she earned it, made her one of the town's most notorious citizens.

Her last will proved her a feminist. She left a fortune of a quarter of a million dollars (as much as $28 million in 2006 dollars[3]), largely composed of real estate. She had six sisters, two of whom she gave $100 apiece. Among the remaining four, Haycraft divided the bulk of her estate, stipulating that her bequest be "free from any interference" from their husbands. Bellefontaine Cemetery superintendent Michael Tiemann believes "this is the most important part . . . because females had no way of earning a living in those days."[4]

Eliza Haycraft came to St. Louis alone and penniless, with no means of supporting herself except by selling herself as a courtesan.[5] According to the *Daily Democrat*, "Possessed of unusual personal attractions and a warm and confiding nature, she fell prey to the arts of the seducer and became an outcast from home and society."[6] She was cast out of her home at the age of twenty by her "humble and honest parents."[7] The beauty and charm that caused her downfall as a young woman would later prove her means of support. Haycraft rode a canoe down the Missouri River to St. Louis[8] seeking employment in the big city. In the nineteenth century, the only respectable jobs for a young woman were servant, seamstress, and teacher. Uneducated, Haycraft could not teach, and the other jobs could not provide a comfortable livelihood. Therefore, when it came to the choice between prostitution and starvation, Haycraft chose to pursue "a life of degradation."[9]

Haycraft proved a success in her chosen field. She rose from courtesan to madam, proprietor of several brothels. Bellefontaine Cemetery gatekeeper Manuel Garcia traced her progress through St. Louis real estate directories: "After the Civil War she owned five."[10] The year before she died, Haycraft sold her business and moved to a private residence. She had risen so high that she was able to buy the house where she died from the Chouteau family,[11] descendants of the founders of St. Louis and one of the wealthiest and most prominent families in town. Having diversified her business interests, she was able to bequeath nineteen pieces of choice city real estate, both commercial and residential properties, to her sisters. Yet canny as she was, Haycraft signed every deed with an X.

Her generosity as well as her wealth inspired the respect of her contemporaries. During the nineteenth century, without pensions or social security to provide a safety net, widows and orphans were often left destitute. When the poor begged at her door, Haycraft turned no one away. As early as 1859, a local newspaper recounts her donating $125 for the poor (as much as $21,000 in 2006 dollars).[12]

Eliza Haycraft was in the right place at the right time. The phenomenal growth of St. Louis contributed to her success as much as her business acumen did. Between the years of 1840 and 1870, when Haycraft was plying her trade, the population of St. Louis increased almost tenfold from 36,000 to 350,000.[13] Moreover, this population was disproportionately made up of young men, attracted to the city to make their fortune. By 1865, when the city's population had swollen to 300,000, "by police estimate," the city's population of prostitutes had grown to 2,500.[14]

Haycraft took advantage of this business boom. One author found that St. Louis police seldom bothered houses of ill repute for "they recognized that brothels provided a valuable service in a large city."[15] In addition, city officials had long taken a laissez-faire attitude toward the sex trades. Madams were thus able to offer their employees "protection from the police, regular wages, and the ability to work under the shroud mandated by municipal officials."[16] Indeed, starting in 1870, St. Louis made prostitution legal under the terms of the Social Evil Ordinance, which licensed bawdy houses and regulated the health of prostitutes. A campaign by clergymen and respectable citizens, led by William Greenleaf Eliot, brought an end to this social experiment four years later.

Although her profession placed her outside of the boundaries of polite society, Haycraft earned a certain amount of respect within the community because she used her wealth to help the poor and afflicted. When death approached, Haycraft wanted to be buried in Bellefontaine Cemetery, the place where her most important clients rested eternally. According to cemetery legend, the trustees at first resisted selling her a lot but finally yielded to pressure from her personal representative as long as no headstone designated her grave.[17] She rests in an unmarked grave beneath a sweet gum tree, alone and in peace in a lot large enough for twenty-one people.

1. "Funeral of Eliza Haycraft, Remarkable Career of a Remarkable Woman," *St. Louis Daily Democrat*, December 8, 1871.

2. Ibid.

3. "How Much Is That?," *Economic History Services*, http://eh.net.

4. Michael Tiemann, *Oral History*, tape V, 91.

5. "Funeral of Eliza Haycraft."

6. Ibid.

7. Ibid.

8. Ibid.

9. Ibid.

10. Manuel Garcia, *Oral History*, tape LXVII, 984–985.

11. Manuel Garcia, *Oral History*, tape LVIV, 934.

12. "City Council, Remembering the Poor," *Daily Missouri Republican*, December 1, 1858.

13. "Population of St. Louis and Missouri, 1820–2000," www.genealogybranches.com/stlouispopulation.

14. Lawrence Meier Friedman, *Crime and Punishment in American History* (New York: Basic Books, 1993), 224.

15. Jeffrey S. Adler, "Streetwalkers, Degraded Outcasts, and the Good-for-Nothing Huzzies: Women and the Dangerous Class in Ante-Bellum St. Louis," *Journal of Social History* (Summer 1992): 741.

16. Ibid., 747.

17. Michael Tiemann, *Oral History*, tape VIII, 135; Manuel Garcia, *Oral History*, tape LV, 898.

ADAM LEMP

1798–1862

WILLIAM J. LEMP SR.

1836–1904

WILLIAM J. LEMP JR.

1867–1922

LILLIAN HANDLAN LEMP

1877–1960

THE NAME "LEMP" conjures up vivid images: opulence and decay, success and suicide, mansions, caves, ghosts, and beer. Four members of this tortured family committed suicide, all using pistols, three under the same roof. Except for Adam, who rests beneath his own headstone in a separate part of the cemetery, and Charles, whose ashes were buried in an unknown location, they all lie together in Bellefontaine's Lemp Mausoleum, even the divorced Lillian and Billy, on either side of their son William.

Adam Lemp came to St. Louis in 1838 and established a small grocery store, distilling vinegar and brewing beer for his customers. His beer became so popular that he soon discontinued all of his other businesses. There were several reasons for its popularity. One was the city's growing German population with a thirst for beer. In 1842, Lemp was among the first in the country, which was flowing with English ales and porters, to produce German lager. St. Louis's south side is riddled with caves, a necessity for the lager process in the days before factory refrigeration. He called his business, which sat on the site of what is today the Gateway Arch, the Western Brewery. By the time he died in 1862, it had made him a wealthy man: In the census of 1860, his estate was valued at $20,000, quite a bit of money at the time.

ADAM LEMP

In the second generation, William J. Lemp Sr. was to take the business to the heights of prosperity and the family to the depths of despair. He was born in Germany in 1836. Twelve years later, his father brought him to St. Louis, and he took full control of the business upon his father's death. The small brewery no longer fit his plans. Rather than continue to transport the beer from the plant to the caves for fermentation, William moved the brewery to the caves. A brewery of three stories above ground sat atop three more stories below of cellars and caves. Renamed Lemp, the new brewery was built of the handsomest architecture and would eventually fill five blocks and contain the newest equipment, making it "one of the largest and most modern in the world."[1] William senior built his mansion a block north of his kingdom and connected it by tunnel to the caves.

While Adam was deemed a success by turning out 26,000 barrels of beer a year in 1862, by 1886 the Lemp Brewery turned out 300,000 barrels annually with sales of over $3 million. By 1895, the brewery employed seven hundred people and was the eighth largest in the country, with Lemp's Falstaff outselling Anheuser-Busch's Budweiser in St. Louis. Not only was Lemp beer sold across the nation, but it could be bought in Calcutta, the West Indies, London, Paris, and Berlin.[2]

Deciding to go into partial retirement and travel the world with Julia, his wife and the mother of his nine devoted children, William turned over power to his sons, naming William junior, vice president; Louis, superintendent; Charles, treasurer; and Frederick, assistant superintendent. But it was Fred who was "widely known to have been William's favorite"[3] and his father's choice to be his successor as leader of the firm. A dedicated worker, twenty-eight-year-old Fred took time off to go to California for his health. His parents thought him recovering nicely on an early December visit only to learn that he had died of heart failure on December 12, 1901. According to the Lemp company secretary, Henry Vahlkamp, "suddenly the grief of the father was most pathetic. He broke down utterly and cried like a child. It was the first death in the family. He took it so seriously that we feared it would completely shatter his health and looked for the worst to happen."[4] William senior had the Lemp Mausoleum built for his heir apparent in 1902 on Prospect Avenue, the street where the captains of industry built their monuments in Bellefontaine Cemetery. Designed by Frank Henry Kronauge, it is the largest mausoleum in the cemetery and cost $60,000, an amount estimated to be worth $1.6 million in 2005. Like the Lemp company logo, it has the strength and simplicity of modern design, a surprising attribute in an era of artistic excess.

William senior was struck another crushing blow on January 1, 1904, when Milwaukee brewer Frederick Pabst, his best friend and the father-in-law of his daughter Hilda, died. Despondent, on February 13, 1904, William took his revolver and shot himself in the head in the bedroom of his home. His estate, valued at $10 million, would pass in equal shares to his children upon the death of his wife, Julia, in 1906.

The oldest son of the third generation, William J. Lemp Jr., or "Billy," succeeded his father as president of the brewery, turning the family mansion where his father had shot himself into the company's offices. He came up with the name Falstaff for the company's most popular beer, naming it after the rakish friend of Shakespeare's Prince Hal.

In 1899, Billy married Lillian Handlan at her family home, under two interlocking hearts of white roses with "Lemp" spelled out in purple violets. He had captured the belle of St. Louis society, daughter of a wealthy manufacturer of railroad supplies. She became known as the "Lavender Lady," for she not only wore this color exclusively, employing a staff of full-time seamstresses, but even kept seven carriages, one for each day of the week, all leather-upholstered in her signature color. She created a sensation wherever she went.

LILLIAN HANDLAN LEMP

It was this sensation, her husband told the court, that caused him to want a divorce in 1909. According to Walker, Billy charged his wife with "the excessive wearing of the color lavender to attract public attention."[5] In addition, he claimed she used profane language and was unfaithful to him. She charged that he brought women to her apartments and had beaten her up and threatened her with a revolver. Needless to say, the courtroom was a circus, and the newspapers delighted in salacious stories of millionaires at war. The presiding judge awarded the Lavender Lady a divorce with sole custody of their son and alimony of $6,000 a year. Billy was awarded weekly visitation, in effect tying Lillian to him. She sued for a retrial within weeks and took her suit to the Missouri Supreme Court, which awarded her a lump sum alimony of $100,000—"the largest such sum ever awarded in Missouri"[6] up to that point.

Six years later, Billy married a widow, Ellie Limberg, daughter of Caspar Koehler, president of the Columbia Brewing Company. Lillian never remarried and lived to the age of eighty-three. St. Louis author Elizabeth Benoist said, "The Lavender Lady was pitiful after that [divorce]. She still wore lavender, but she never got over the divorce."[7] Benoist also said, "She was right pretty, but crazy as a coot."[8]

Billy was not the only Lemp to be divorced. His youngest sister, Elsa, had married Thomas Wright, president of the More-Jones Brass and Metal Company, in 1910. In 1919, Elsa filed for divorce and her petition was granted on the same day. Though it stated that "her husband had destroyed her peace and happiness,"[9] she did not parade the ugly details of the dissolution before the public. The two reconciled and remarried March 8, 1920. Elsa, who suffered from bouts of depression, had a bad night on March 19 and told her husband she wanted to stay in bed the next morning. Her husband described a quiet morning, taking a bath when he heard a "sharp sound."[10] Thinking his wife was trying to attract his attention, he investigated only to find that she had killed herself with a shot in the heart. Her brothers rushed to the scene, where Billy commented, "That's the Lemp family for you."[11]

But the Lemp family had more trouble ahead. In 1919, the Eighteenth Amendment to the Constitution was ratified, outlawing the manufacture, sale, and transportation of intoxicating liquors. The Lemp Brewery tried to keep operating with a nonalcoholic beer called Cerva but found it wasn't profitable enough to sustain its huge brewery. The plant closed abruptly in June 1919. Billy simply gave up. All of the owners of the plant were family members who did not always see eye to eye, and they were all independently wealthy. None of them had the mettle to make it through Prohibition. Moreover, Billy had never modernized operations; he clung to traditional methods. On June 28, 1922, the buildings were sold at auction, mostly to International Shoe Company. Three years before, they had been estimated to be worth $7 million, but they sold for $585,000.

Despondent over having to dismantle his family's business, Billy grew increasingly depressed. On December 29, 1922, putting a revolver to his chest, he shot himself through the heart in his office in the mansion where his father had committed suicide. Like his father and sister, he left no suicide note. Within minutes, his son, William J. Lemp III, was kneeling over his body, crying, "I was afraid this was coming."[12] Two days later, the funeral was held in the company offices where William senior's services had taken place eighteen years earlier.

William III attempted unsuccessfully to revive Lemp beer after the repeal of Prohibition in 1933, even though Falstaff and the Lemp shield had been sold to Joe Griesedieck, who was making a go of it. In 1939, William entered into an agreement with Central Breweries of East St. Louis, Illinois, which changed its name to William J. Lemp Brewing Company. While initial sales figures looked good, a year and a half later the company went bankrupt. William III dropped dead of a heart attack at age forty-three in 1943.

Charles Lemp, Billy's brother, was the fourth family suicide. While he had been treasurer and later vice president of the brewery, he withdrew from the family business and went into banking. In 1911, he moved out of the family mansion and into the Racquet Club. In 1929, still unmarried, he moved back into the Lemp mansion. He became increasingly reclusive, arthritic, and ill. At age seventy-seven, he, too, took his life. On May 10, 1949, he lay down in bed and put a bullet through his head. He was the only Lemp to leave a suicide note, which read: "In case I am found dead, blame it on no one but me."[13] He had prepaid for his funeral and requested that his ashes be buried at his farm.

The fortunes of the Lemp mansion have ebbed and flowed similarly to those of the family. The year after Charles died, the once elegant mansion was turned into a boardinghouse. In 1975, Richard D. Pointer and family bought the boardinghouse and renovated it to become a restaurant. In 1980, *Life* magazine included the Lemp mansion in an article on America's nine most haunted houses.[14] Almost everyone involved with the house has had an encounter with a ghost, all of them friendly. Elizabeth Benoist imagines "it must be the Lavender Lady and Charlie that haunt it.

They were both so unhappy, maybe they're still down there, looking for the happiness they never found while they were alive."[15]

---

1. Stephen P. Walker, *Lemp: The Haunting History* (St. Louis: Lemp Preservation Society, 1988), 16.

2. Don Crinklaw, "The Lemps of St. Louis," *Post-Dispatch Pictures*, December 2, 1973, 18.

3. Walker, *Haunting History*, 35.

4. Ibid.

5. Ibid., 45.

6. Ibid., 68.

7. Elizabeth Benoist quoted in Adrian Cornell, "The Lurid Legacy of the Lemps," *St. Louis Post-Dispatch Sunday Magazine*, October 30, 1994, 13.

8. Ibid.

9. Walker, *Haunting History*, 76.

10. Ibid., 77.

11. Ibid.

12. Crinklaw, "The Lemps of St. Louis," 25.

13. Walker, *Haunting History*, 90.

14. Troy Taylor, "Haunted Places of St. Louis," http://www.prairieghosts.com/lemp.html.

15. Elizabeth Benoist quoted in "The Lurid Legacy of the Lemps," 13.

NELLIE HAZELTINE PARAMORE
1856–1884

THE BELLE OF ST. LOUIS, Nellie Hazeltine entertained ninety-nine unsuccessful suitors, including a candidate for president of the United States and a second-class tenor, until she settled on Frederick Paramore, the son of cotton and railroad magnate Colonel James Paramore. Tragically, she and her infant son died shortly after childbirth when she was but twenty-seven years old.

Nellie was beautiful, wealthy, and intelligent, and she was an accomplished pianist. Newspapers covered her every indiscretion the way today's grocery-store tabloids fabricate stories about movie stars. According to a biography of Joseph Pulitzer, "When Nellie settled down by marrying Frederick Paramore . . . it was a loss to journalism."[1]

Nellie Hazeltine first titillated readers of St. Louis newspapers during the Democratic Convention held in St. Louis in June of 1876. The party's unsuccessful nominee for president, Samuel Tilden, had his name linked to hers. Two years later, papers around the country carried tales of their engagement. Her obituary in the *Missouri Republican* related:

> The joke proved a world-wide advertisement. . . . She was besieged by an army of interviewers wherever she went. Her denials of the foolish report were unheeded. Her protests against the painful notoriety were mocked. . . . Finally Mr. Tilden issued a card denying the truth of the rumor. Then many of the newspapers declared that she herself had started the story . . . and for many months she was shamefully and inexcusably decried.[2]

Clearly, the life of a belle was not easy.

Nellie received even worse treatment when she became involved in what the *Post-Dispatch* termed a "social scandal." When she had a fling with John Anweg, a tenor who sang at the popular St. Louis watering hole known as Uhrig's Garden, "this piece received greater prominence [for that day] than a story concerning President Garfield lying mortally wounded from an assassin's bullet."[3] A study of the *Post-Dispatch* found that the paper played the two stories appropriately as far as reader interest: "A boost of several hundred copies accompanied the Haseltine [*sic*] sensation."[4] The paper splashed out sensationalistic headlines to tell the tale that "Nellie's Papa Pays $1,000 and Costs for His Daughter's Flirtation."[5] Moreover, the *Post-Dispatch* concocted a tale of perennial bachelor Tilden rushing to comfort Nellie with dowry in hand.

When Nellie died shortly after giving birth on Valentine's Day, the *Post-Dispatch, Globe-Democrat,* and *Missouri Republican* relayed to their readers every detail from the wedding dress she wore as her shroud to the elaborate floral display. Her infant son died a few days later. Today, Nellie rests in the Paramore Mausoleum with her son, her husband, and his second wife, no longer hounded by the sensationalistic press.

1. J. A. Swanberg, *Pulitzer* (New York: Scribner's, 1967), 60.

2. P. Donan, "Nellie Hazeltine," *Missouri Republican*, March 22, 1884.

3. Julian S. Rammelkamp, *Pulitzer's Post-Dispatch, 1878–1883* (Princeton, NJ: Princeton University, 1967), 169.

4. Ibid.

5. Ibid., 170.

HENRY CLAY PIERCE lived large in the Gay Nineties. His Vandeventer Place mansion stood out for its gaudiness on the city's most fashionable street, where extravagance reigned. He entertained regally in a ballroom large enough to hold one hundred people, with an elevator that carried up iced champagne from the hotel-sized kitchen. To build his manse, he spent $500,000 (some even say $800,000), a sum almost inconceivable at the time (more than $10 million in 2006 dollars). It boasted nothing as common as wallpaper: Only silk tapestries and wood paneling covered its walls. His life practically defines the term "robber baron."

The story went that he rode into town in 1864 at age fifteen to work in a cracker factory and by the time he left for New York in 1910, he was the second-wealthiest man in St. Louis, one of the richest in the country. In reality, Pierce was the well-educated son of a doctor from Upstate New York whose uncle, J. O. Pierce, owned a cracker factory. When J. O. went into banking, his nephew followed as a clerk.

In 1869, Henry Clay Pierce advanced his career in the time-honored fashion of marrying the boss's daughter. Minnie Finlay Pierce was the daughter of John R. Finlay, who owned an oil company that refined petroleum for lamps. Finlay soon took his capable son-in-law into partnership. While Finlay managed the manufacturing, Pierce put his ambition to the task of bringing the local company into the national market.

Upon the death of his father-in-law in 1877, Pierce entered into a partnership with William H. Waters, who had directed the bank where Pierce clerked. Pierce became president of the Waters-Pierce Oil Company and soon drove it to national prominence, expanding its Missouri refinery to one of the largest in the nation and eventually owning pipelines and storage tanks all over the Midwest as well as refineries and railroads in

Mexico. The company sprawled over several acres near Union Station. Business boomed with earnings increasing 600–700 percent each year of the 1880s,[1] according to the *St. Louis Business Journal*.

In 1878, John D. Rockefeller's Standard Oil Company bought 40 percent of the Waters-Pierce stock. In 1903, Henry Ford made automobiles financially accessible to middle-class Americans and lit the petroleum industry on fire—a conflagration that would bring Pierce both great fortune and great shame.

The Sherman Antitrust Act brought down Pierce like a bolt of lightning. In 1896, Texas was one of four states trying to bust the Pierce trust (now known as Pierce Oil). After four years of litigation costing $1 million, Texas won. Pierce Oil was allowed to continue in business in that state upon the sworn oath of its founder that the company was not part of a trust. The arrogant Pierce had lied; Standard Oil owned a majority of the firm at that time.

In the course of Missouri's antitrust case against him, Pierce testified that Standard Oil owned a majority of his company and was the only source of its petroleum. When the state of Texas got wind of his testimony, the ax dropped. To keep the company operating in that state, Pierce Oil paid a fine of $1.7 million. Texas then went after Pierce personally for lying under oath, but he got off on a technicality. Pierce was forced to sell the company at a price of $1.5 million, $200,000 less than the fine. Standard Oil forced him out, and the company's worth dwindled.

Despite a life of excess, scandal, and financial upheaval, Henry Clay Pierce died peacefully, surrounded by family. Yet he died without a will, causing his heirs to squabble for a decade. His second wife sued her own grandchild and stepchildren for a $300,000 trust promised at her wedding that had never been set up. In 1938, eleven years after his death, with his mansions sold for a fraction of their value and his stocks rendered worthless by the crash, his estate was declared bankrupt.

This scalawag rests eternally surrounded as he was in life by great opulence.

The Eames and Young–designed mausoleum is embellished with a bronze, lion-headed door knocker and such rich neoclassical details as lion-legged, big-breasted, winged harpies as well as five windows designed for the tomb by the great Louis Comfort Tiffany himself. Exquisite in detail, they depict a female figure picking flowers beside a river and four angels representing truth, salvation, peace, and understanding—virtues to which Pierce hardly seemed to aspire. According to Bellefontaine Cemetery superintendent Michael Tiemann, it had been built for $60,000 in 1902,[2] a time when a laborer earned $148 a year. That same year, Pierce added an entrance passage 40 feet wide by 114 feet long to his family plot. It gives the mausoleum an importance unprecedented in the cemetery.

Despite the impressiveness of this mausoleum, Pierce was initially laid to rest in Woodlawn Cemetery in New York in 1927. He did not come to his opulent Bellefontaine digs until 1934 when the family reinterred him in the mausoleum he had built nearly twenty-five years before his death. The surviving heirs placed his first wife, who had been buried on the lot earlier, beside him in a double sarcophagus.

---

1. "Henry Clay Pierce," *St. Louis Business Journal*, February 1995, Missouri Historical Society Vertical Files.
2. Michael Tiemann, conversation with the author, August 26, 2008.

ALFRED H. PLANT

1851–1923

ALFRED H. PLANT scandalized his family on December 20, 1889, when he married Mollie Murphy, a local prostitute. The next day, his relatives had him committed to St. Vincent's Insane Asylum, where he lived until his death at seventy-two. He is buried in the family plot at Bellefontaine, and his bride rests eternally a short distance away.

A newspaper account of June 6, 1890, related: "The sequel to a sensational marriage in which figured a well-known and prominent citizen of St. Louis occurred in Judge Fisher's court yesterday . . . annulment of the marriage on the grounds that one of the parties was non compos mentis when it took place."[1] It described Mollie Murphy as "an inmate of Mme. Burke's house of ill-fame."[2] Alfred was identified as "the brother to the well-known mill owner of that name."[3] The town of Alton, Illinois, was named after his grandfather Colonel Alton Easton because of his efforts in settling the area.

---

1. Newspaper article dated June 6, 1890, Manuel Garcia files, Bellefontaine Cemetery.
2. Ibid.
3. Ibid.

ELLIS WAINWRIGHT
1850–1924

WHEN ELLIS WAINWRIGHT died in 1924, he was finally laid to rest beside his bride in the monument built to her beauty thirty-two years earlier. He had gone from the heights to the depths of society. Because of his shady dealings, his name appears in *The Shame of the Cities*, the 1904 muckraking exposé by Lincoln Steffens. But his name truly survives on two buildings that have gone down in architectural history: the Wainwright Building and the Wainwright Tomb.

When Wainwright inherited the family business, Wainwright Brewery, from his father, Samuel, an English immigrant, he doubled its profits. Later he joined forces with an English syndicate that bought out small breweries in St. Louis, becoming president of the resulting St. Louis Brewing Association. His mother, Catherine Dorothy Wainwright, bought several lots at Seventh and Chestnut in the city of St. Louis to build an office building. At first skeptical, Wainwright became a partner in the enterprise. In 1890, he hired the renowned Chicago architect Louis Sullivan to design the Wainwright Building, considered the first true skyscraper. An art collector and socialite, Wainwright probably met Sullivan on one of the architect's trips to St. Louis. Sadly, Wainwright's beautiful wife, Charlotte, died suddenly of peritonitis at thirty-four before the building was even completed. To honor his bride, Wainwright commissioned the monument that art historian Hugh Morrison says "is unmatched in quality by any other known tomb."[1] He is not alone in his assessment, for it earned a place on the National Register of Landmarks. Completed in 1892, it fits easily amid the Greek and Egyptian mausoleums on Prospect Avenue. Yet its simplicity sets it apart. Cemetery superintendent Michael Tiemann explained, "Frank Lloyd Wright was on the staff at Louis Sullivan's firm at the time the tomb was built, and Frank Lloyd Wright takes as much credit for the tomb as Louis Sullivan."[2] The geometric masses of the exterior reflect the style of Wright, but the interior is pure Sullivan.

The Wainwright Tomb derives its beauty from geometry: A half sphere rests upon a cube. On the exterior, ornament is restrained to simple bands with stylized plant forms, with each side of the building depicting a different flower. Compared to the severity of the exterior, the interior is a lavish riot of color and design, though it was meant for family eyes only. Writhing, stylized floral designs interlace the two simple graves set in the floor. Above them rises the inside of the dome, where delicate, Raphaelesque angels float in a field of maize topped with a stylized sun. Gold tiles fleck the interior dome and appear and disappear like twinkling stars as the viewer walks around and gazes at the dome from different points of view. This apotheosis of the arts includes literature. Ellis's grave bears lines from Alfred, Lord Tennyson: "But O for the touch of a vanished hand / And the sound of a voice that is still." Charlotte's bears lines from a minor English poet of the nineteenth century, Anna Laetitia Barbauld: "Say not Good-night, but in some brighter clime / Bid me Good-morning."

Wainwright's own star sputtered soon afterward. When his signature turned up on a $135,000 note intended to be used as a bribe for municipal officials, he was indicted along with several cronies. He heard about his indictment in the Suburban Railway scandal while traveling in Egypt. He found it convenient to live for a decade in a magnificent Parisian residence, where he lived the high life with $4 million in the bank and an income of $60,000 a year from the Wainwright Building. Maintaining ties with St. Louis, he remained on the boards of the public library and the art museum.

Meanwhile, journalist William Marion Reedy persisted in a campaign in his influential periodical *The Mirror* to exonerate Wainwright. Friends claimed Wainwright did not know what he was signing when he affixed his signature to the bribery bond. In 1911, he returned to St. Louis after the principle witness for the prosecution had died. All charges were dropped. Proclaiming, "My God, I am glad to be back in the best town in the world,"[3] he soon took off for New York, where he bought a place on Park Avenue.

On a trip to Florida, he met a lovely divorcée, Rosalind Velva Kendall, whom he adopted when he was seventy-two and she was twenty-two.

Although she called herself Miss Wainwright and they maintained separate residences, they spent most of their time together until he wrote his will six months after the adoption. Disinheriting Rosalind, he left bequests to Children's Hospital and to Bellefontaine Cemetery for the maintenance of his wife's monument, with the bulk of the estate going to Washington University in St. Louis. Soon after the will was written, Marion Early, the attorney for the university, took up residence at Wainwright's Park Avenue suite and banished Rosalind from the premises. In 1924, suffering from a stroke and hardening of the arteries, Wainwright returned to St. Louis to live as a recluse in the Buckingham Hotel. When the maids came to clean, he moved ahead of them from room to room so he could not be seen. Shortly after he passed away, Rosalind successfully contested the will and was awarded an inheritance of $215,000.

With the indignities of his declining years now mostly forgotten, Ellis Wainwright is remembered for the splendor of his commissions: the mausoleum and the Wainwright Building, two of the nineteenth century's great works of architecture. Cemetery gatekeeper Manuel Garcia said, "Someone always puts flowers on the tomb at Christmas time"[4]—a tribute to the two lovers Charlotte and Ellis.

---

1. Hugh Morrison, *Louis Sullivan: Prophet of Modern Architecture* (New York: W. W. Norton, 1935).
2. Michael Tiemann, *Oral History*, tape I, 7.
3. William Woo, "Story Behind the Wainwright Building," *St. Louis Post-Dispatch*, January 23, 1966.
4. Manuel Garcia, *Oral History*, tape III, 58.

PART THREE

SUFFRAGETTES

 Women of Missouri fought hard for the vote. Without that right, they were not even second-class citizens, according to the inspiring Edna Fischel Gellhorn.[1] St. Louis bred many leaders of the national suffrage movement, such as Virginia Minor, who sued for the right to vote (see Part 1); attorney Phoebe Couzins, who barnstormed the country advocating the enfranchisement of women; and Rebecca Naylor Hazard, who served as president of the American Woman Suffrage Association in 1878.

While the first recorded event of the suffrage movement in the state took place in 1854 with a visiting lecturer,[2] the Civil War provided the impetus for many women to reconsider their place in society. With their husbands at war, many women ran businesses or farms. Moreover, future leaders of the suffrage movement gained leadership experience working for the major relief organization located in St. Louis, the Western Sanitary Commission.

Although today we consider it self-evident that women deserve the vote, there was initially great resistance to the idea. In the nineteenth century, women's suffrage "seemed revolutionary, sinful, and destined to ruin the home, church, and state."[3] Many of the early suffragists were well-educated, upper-class women who believed the vote would improve the lot of humankind. (Although commonly known as "suffragettes," the women of the St. Louis movement did not like this diminutive. They preferred the more assertive term "suffragists.") They were willing to face public scorn at a time "when most people considered it a crime to believe in women's rights and those brave women who did were hooted and jeered at in the streets."[4] Even as late as 1914, "the word 'suffragette' was not even whispered in polite society . . . and it was like throwing a bomb in conservative St. Louis to repeat the new slogan 'Votes for Women.'"[5]

In 1867, Hazard, Lucretia Allen Hall, Penelope Pope Allen, and Anna Clapp held a meeting at the Mercantile Library to organize the Woman Suffrage Association of Missouri, and they elected Virginia Minor president. In a history of the movement published posthumously in 1920, Allen's granddaughter Christine Orrick Fordyce wrote that it was "the first organization in the world having for its sole object the political enfranchisement of women,"[6] because other suffrage organizations took on additional agendas. It would be fifty-two years before their goal would be achieved. With St. Louis a hotbed of suffragist activity, the American Woman Suffrage Association held its convention there in 1869 and the National Woman Suffrage Association did the same in 1879, electing Minor president.

In 1867, Missouri suffragists first petitioned the state legislature for the vote. That same year, U.S. senator B. Gratz Brown advocated at a national level the franchise for women as well as blacks. Resigning weeks later due to illness, Brown did nothing to make his words become reality. Dedicated Missouri women continued to petition the state legislature at every session without success until 1919. Up until that time, not only did women not have the vote, they also had "no property or parental rights, and almost no economic freedom, since professions, trades, and most businesses were closed to them."[7] Yet their efforts did result in liberal state laws for women.[8] Happily, according to Fordyce, "their many visits to the State Legislature of Missouri resulted in so many good laws for the protection of women that . . . one man was led to say that the women of Missouri were better protected than the men."[9]

In 1916, St. Louis suffragists succeeded in convincing the Democratic Party to put a plank for women's suffrage in their platform. Edna Gellhorn, Florence Wyman Richardson, Luella Sayman, Bertha Rombauer, Christine Fordyce, Marie Garesche, and Mrs. Ernest Stix dreamed up the "Golden Lane." While they hoped for 3,500 women to turn up, the organizers were pleased to find 7,000 women with yellow sashes and parasols lining the street leading from the delegates' hotel to the convention hall. Proud and silent, they inspired the delegates to understand their message as conventioneers walked this gauntlet daily. Afterward, the "golden" sashes and parasols the St. Louis suffragists sported became a symbol of the movement nationally.[10]

The suffragists' efforts came to fruition at last in 1919. In April, Missouri governor Frederick Dozier Gardner persuaded the legislature to grant presidential suffrage, making Missouri the eleventh state to allow women to vote in presidential elections. Three months later, with lawmakers dismissed for the summer, Gardner called a special session of the legislature in order to ratify the Nineteenth Amendment to the Constitution, making it illegal to deny anyone the right to vote on the basis of gender.

But the struggle did not end with the vote.

In March 1919, before the Missouri legislature had even granted presidential suffrage, the national convention of the Equal Suffrage League held its golden jubilee in St. Louis, and the five hundred delegates called for an organization to educate the anticipated new voters in their rights as citizens. Thus was born the League of Women Voters. Their mission, according to Edna Fischel Gellhorn, was for women "not merely to vote but to vote for something."[11]

1. Olivia Skinner, "Edna Gellhorn: Long-Time Civic Worker," *St. Louis Post-Dispatch*, December 18, 1967.

2. Corbett, *In Her Place*, 130.

3. Ibid., 222.

4. Christine Orrick Fordyce, "History of Woman Suffrage in Missouri," *Missouri Historical Review* 14 (1920): 288.

5. Florence Atkinson, "History of Woman Suffrage in Missouri," *Missouri Historical Review* 14 (1920): 300.

6. Stevens, *Centennial History*, 509.

7. Cheri Thompson in *Show Me Missouri Women*, ed. Mary K. Dains (Kirksville, MO: Thomas Jefferson University Press, 1989), 223.

8. Hyde and Conard, *Encyclopedia of St. Louis*, 2530.

9. Fordyce, "History of Woman Suffrage," 289.

10. Thompson, 223.

11, Edna Gellhorn, "History of Woman Suffrage in Missouri," *Missouri Historical Review* 14 (1920): 357.

LUCY VIRGINIA SEMPLE AMES was a woman ahead of her time. Known as the "Queen of St. Louis society,"[1] she was also a businesswoman, a suffragette, an advocate for women's education, and a feminist. She was fortunate to be the daughter of James Semple, a senator from Illinois and founder of the town of Elsah, Illinois, and the wife of pork-packer millionaire Edgar Ames. As a pioneering businesswoman, it is not surprising that she also used her wealth to back her belief that females deserved the same education as men and a place in the voting booth beside them.

When Edgar died in 1867 at the age of forty-three, he left his thirty-year-old widow with four young children and a fortune invested in several businesses. In 1841, he and his brother had followed their father, Nathan Ames, to St. Louis when he moved his pork-packing business from Cincinnati. The War Department made them a primary supplier to the troops during the Civil War. In addition, the brothers held interests in the Lindell Hotel, a sugar refinery, a grain elevator, steamship lines, and insurance and banking concerns.

Lucy Ames not only took over management of these extensive business interests but also added a real estate development company to them. The Ames Realty Company, with Lucy as president and her son Henry Semple Ames as secretary, developed the Ames Place residential district in University City, Missouri. Lucy's daughter Ada also married a realtor, Henry Turner, grandson of philanthropist Ann Lucas Hunt, who was head of Turner Realty Company. According to St. Louis County preservation historian Esley Hamilton, "An indication of Mrs. Ames's business acumen is that she is said to have required a prenuptial agreement to protect the half-million dollars her daughter [Mary Ames Cushman] brought to [her] marriage."[2]

Lucy Ames placed a high value on education and the rights of women. She became a member of the Equal Suffrage Society in 1869[3] and had her own children educated in Germany and France. In addition to her mansion on Lucas Place, the most prestigious address of her time, she maintained an estate known as Notch Cliff on the hills overlooking Elsah, Illinois.

Lucy Ames lies alongside her father, husband, and four children at Bellefontaine Cemetery in a lot distinguished by a fifteen-foot-tall late Gothic monument that resembles a cathedral spire. William Rumbold, the architect of the dome of St. Louis's Old Courthouse, designed the stone that was notched and cut until it looked like lace. Perhaps Edgar commissioned the handsome monument for his older brother, Henry Ames, who had predeceased him by sixteen months. Edgar was known as a patron of art and literature; perhaps Henry also had a penchant for art because between his tomb and that of his wife, Jenny Marmaduke Ames, kneels an angel with long, graceful limbs and a wistful expression.

1. Patricia Rice, "Glory Days: Exhibit Looks Back to Long-Lost Lucas Place," *St. Louis Post-Dispatch*, July 15, 1990, 4C.

2. Esley Hamilton, *Ames Place: A Brief History of Its Planning and Development* (University City, MO: Historical Society of University City, 1991), 3.

3. Rice, "Glory Days," 11C.

PHOEBE COUZINS
1842–1913

A COMPLEX AND DIFFICULT woman, Phoebe Couzins lived a life of triumph and tragedy. She blazed trails for women as the third female law school graduate in the United States, the first female U.S. marshal, the first female to address a presidential nominating convention, and the first woman to pass the bar in Utah, Arkansas, the Dakota territories, and the federal courts. Her mission was the enfranchisement of women, and she was so highly regarded among the nation's suffragettes that her picture graced the inside cover of an important tome on the movement.[1]

In 1842, Couzins was born in St. Louis to parents John E. D. and Adeline Couzins, who were not wealthy but were prominent civic activists. Her parents' public service inspired Phoebe's commitment to social and political causes. Her father served the city as the pro-Union chief of police during the Civil War and later as U.S. marshal. Her mother was wounded in the leg while nursing soldiers for the Western Sanitary Commission. Mother and daughter proudly joined the Ladies' Union Aid Society.

Following the war, Phoebe Couzins gained admittance to the Washington University School of Law in 1869. Washington University was among the very first law schools in the nation to admit women. Even though she graduated twelfth in a class of twelve, in her 1871 graduation address she said that she pursued her studies in order "to open new paths for women."[2]

She practiced law little, if at all, but dedicated most of her life to the lecture circuit, advocating the vote for women as well as equal rights and responsibilities. She joined Susan B. Anthony and Elizabeth Cady Stanton in the first rank of women's rights advocates. Large crowds attended lectures given by Couzins and Anthony, who traveled together across the country. The *Missouri Republican* praised her speaking style, which "appealed to the heart" because she spoke "with a deep, rich voice" in a "calm, dignified manner."[3] She testified at least three times before the House Judiciary Committee.

The decade of the 1890s saw her shooting star plummet to earth. When two woman suffrage associations joined, Couzins resigned, along with Minor. Couzins "had so antagonized the more conservative . . . association that she wielded little power in the combined group. Her hostility to the wealthy, socially prominent [members] swelling the combined group's ranks also helped ensure the demise of her power."[4] After she was fired from her post as secretary of the Board of Lady Managers for the World's Fair Columbian Exposition in Chicago, Couzins's ire deepened at the movement that had left her behind. From this point forward, she became a bitter critic of the suffragists. Author Karen Morello says: "Once the most powerful speaker in a room, [Couzins] began to snipe from the back of lecture halls, bringing up previous slights and generally refusing to cooperate with the new order."[5] In 1897, she hit the lecture circuit, denouncing the enfranchisement of women. The newspapers loved it, but her friends were dismayed. The press paid scant heed when she had a change of heart in 1902, telling a Kansas City audience, "I have been guilty of speaking in slurring disrespectful language of all those noble women."[6] Formerly a temperance advocate, which went hand in glove with the women's rights movement, she renounced this movement as well. Desperate for money, she took a stipend from the United Brewers Association to lecture nationally against the prohibition of alcohol.

In 1895, Couzins's life took another strange turn, and the newspapers made sport of it. She claimed, after he died, that aging millionaire and former U.S. senator James G. Fair had promised to marry her. *The Mirror* doubted it and went on to doubt Couzins's sanity: "What's the matter with Phoebe Couzins? Is she all right? I'm very much afraid not. . . . The last time I saw her, . . . she appeared to me to be a bit queer."[7]

Confined to a wheelchair by rheumatism, she lost her position with the brewer's association and returned destitute to St. Louis in 1908. Overcome by bitterness, in 1911 she sadly wrote to family friend William Bixby asking for financial aid and closed her letter with, "If you care to see me, I shall be glad to explain further, but I hate to ask busy men to stop and hear this tale of misfortune."[8] Couzins died impoverished and alone, seemingly without resources.

The headline of her obituary read: "First Woman Lawyer in United States Succumbs in Poverty."[9] A childhood friend paid for her burial on the family plot at Bellefontaine Cemetery, and only six mourners attended the ceremony. Her grave remained unmarked until 1950, when a headstone was erected by the Women Lawyers of Missouri. In recent years, academics have studied her life, and Washington University in St. Louis honors her name with a professorship in its law school.[10]

What may have been Couzins's proudest moment was her interim appointment after her father's death to fill his term as U.S. marshal, making her the first woman to hold this position. Though she served a scant two months, she wore the marshal's badge until she died and requested that it be buried with her. The U.S. Marshals Service, the oldest law enforcement agency in the United States, enforces the federal courts. Perhaps in her mind her appointment symbolized a breakthrough for women within the legal system. At the same time, as she opened new doors for women, she closed them for herself.

---

1. This publication was the third volume of *History of Woman Suffrage, 1876–1885*, written by women's rights leader Elizabeth Cady Stanton.
2. Matthew J. Sanders, "An Introduction to Phoebe Couzins," 2000, unpublished thesis available at womenslegalhistory.stanford.edu/profiles/CouzinsPhoebe.html, 7.
3. *Missouri Republican*, October 26, 1873.
4. Sandra Davidson Scott in *Show Me Missouri Women*, 174.
5. Karen Morello, *The Invisible Bar: The Woman Lawyer in America, 1638 to the Present* (New York: Random House, 1986), 49.
6. Patricia Rice, "Golden-Tongued Champion of Equal Rights," *St. Louis Post-Dispatch*, n.d., Manuel Garcia files, Bellefontaine Cemetery.
7. *The Mirror 5*, no. 6 (March 28, 1895): 4.
8. Sanders, "An Introduction," 35.
9. Ibid., 36.
10. The official title of the professorship is Lemma Barkeloo and Phoebe Couzins Professor of Law, honoring the first two female students at the university's School of Law.

EDNA FISCHEL GELLHORN
1878–1970

IN THE INTEREST OF bettering humankind, Edna Fischel Gellhorn became a powerful force for reform in St. Louis and in the nation, espousing causes from clean water to woman suffrage, from safe milk to the United Nations, from slum clearance to Civil Rights. She said, "I was inspired by the message that women had something to contribute."[1] She served as regional director of Herbert Hoover's food program during World War I and of the food-rationing program during World War II and was Eleanor Roosevelt's right-hand woman in St. Louis. While she never worked for pay outside her home, she started many other women in their careers, recommending them for jobs.

Edna Gellhorn showed promise as a leader early on, and she had social welfare bred in the bone. She served as president of both her Mary Institute and Bryn Mawr College classes. Ahead of their time, her parents urged their one daughter to excel as much as they urged her three brothers. Although Edna's father's family was Jewish and Edna's mother's Christian, both parents became atheists and were among the founders of the Ethical Society. Her father, Dr. Washington Fischel, was a professor of medicine at Washington University in St. Louis and the founder and first president of the Barnard Skin and Cancer Hospital. As one newspaper reported, her mother, Martha Ellis Fischel, became "one of the first [women] of social standing to earn her own living."[2] Before she married, Martha Fischel trained disadvantaged young women in homemaking skills.

Edna was blessed with a happy marriage and four successful children, three of whom were listed in *Who's Who in America*. After she died, among her papers was found a letter asking her to be the first president of the League of Women Voters. She turned this position down, instead serving as vice president and later president of the St. Louis and Missouri chapters of the league because the national position would have taken her away from her young family. Edna Gellhorn dedicated herself to the struggle for woman suffrage. When the Democratic National Convention was held in St. Louis in 1916, she determined to get the party to put a plank in their platform to secure the vote for women. Along with other redoubtable suffragists, she dreamed up the walkless, talkless parade. More than seven thousand women, including her eight-year-old daughter, wearing yellow sashes and carrying yellow parasols to form the "Golden Lane," lined the path to the convention center to impress the delegates with the strength of their cause. They succeeded in their mission. With women's suffrage a part of the Democratic platform, in just three more years the Nineteenth Amendment was ratified and women were finally allowed to enjoy the full benefits of citizenship.

Gellhorn committed herself to the cause of educating all citizens through the League of Women Voters with the same zeal as she had to the suffrage movement. She rode the milk train throughout Missouri, bringing her message to women throughout the state. The league pushed for such worthy causes as advances in child welfare, joint guardianship of children, and a new state constitution.

Moreover, the St. Louis league, with Gellhorn's help, led the nation in its acceptance of minorities. Beatrice Grady served as the first black officer in 1919 thanks to a tie-breaking vote cast by Gellhorn. During the 1920s, league organizational meetings of black women were held in the Gellhorn home, "an occurrence unheard of at the time."[3]

Edna Gellhorn loved St. Louis and did everything she could to make it the best city possible. In her own humble yet principled manner, she replied, when asked at a meeting to identify herself and her affiliation, "Edna Gellhorn—citizen."[4]

---

1. Corbett, *In Her Place*, 235.
2. Carl Rollyson, *Beautiful Exile: The Life of Martha Gellhorn* (London: Aurum, 2001), 1
3. Corbett, *In Her Place*, 234.
4. Mrs. Aaron Fischer, Mrs. George Gellhorn Commemorative Meeting, St. Louis, October 11, 1970.

PART FOUR

FUR TRADERS

 The quest for beaver pelts inspired it all. From the early nineteenth to the mid-twentieth century, St. Louis was the world's center of the fur trade. Every respectable European gentleman wore a good beaver-felt hat, so the lowly beast generated money, power, treaties with the Native Americans, and exploration of the West. Because the fashion of felt hats started in the 1400s, by the nineteenth century, beavers were hunted almost to extinction on the European continent. The felt hat inspired more exploration of North America than the quest for gold.

"It is not an easy thing, at this period in American history, to appreciate how great a place in the affairs of former times the fur trade occupied,"[1] said Hiram Martin Chittenden in 1903. Trappers opened the West because they braved the wilderness to find trails, discover landmarks, and make the maps to lead the way for settlers. They lived among the Indians and adapted some of their ways. Trading with Indians led not only to skirmishes but to treaties and alliances as well. In Oregon, American fur traders kept the Northwest Territory from going to the British. Following the imperative of the fur trade, Americans came to believe that it was their country's Manifest Destiny to expand to the Pacific. All nineteenth-century fur trade emanated from St. Louis. Every expedition began there with provisions and maps and ended there when the furs were brought back to the exchange on the riverfront. The city's dominance in the trade extended into the twentieth century. Thus, many of the great names of the trade have come to lie eternally among the hills of Bellefontaine Cemetery. When William Clark (see Part 1) and Meriwether Lewis returned from the Voyage of Discovery with stories of streams teeming with beavers, inspired trappers took to the wilderness. Bellefontaine Cemetery gatekeeper Manuel Garcia proudly pointed out the important trading posts on the map of the West because so many of them are named after Bellefontaine's people. Fort Lisa in North Dakota and Fort Manuel in South Dakota were founded by Manuel Lisa, while Fort William in North Dakota was founded by William Sublette, Fort McKenzie in Montana by Kenneth McKenzie, and Fort Bonneville in Wyoming by Benjamin de Bonneville. Fort Clark in North Dakota and Fort Benton in Montana were named for William Clark and Missouri's first great senator, Thomas Hart Benton, respectively.

Beaver pelts created great wealth not only for the fur traders but also for St. Louis merchants and bankers. Hunters obtained supplies at the emporiums of Sublette and Robert Campbell. They had to stop to get a license to trade at the office of Joshua Pilcher, U.S. superintendent of Indian affairs, who gained his experience with the Indians in the field, hunting. Both Campbell and Pilcher also engaged in banking, funding the fur trade among many other ventures. Every mountain man stopped at the gun shop of Samuel Hawken, whose rifles were considered sine qua non. If they were lucky, they might get to see the magnificent paintings of Carl Wimar, who accompanied traders so he could document the ways of the Indians (see Part 9).

It was a brave new world beyond Missouri. These men were ready to make their fortunes there. They relished the adventure.

---

1. Hiram Martin Chittenden, *The American Fur Trade of the Far West* (New York: The Press of the Pioneers, 1933), 3.

BENJAMIN LOUIS EULALIE de Bonneville's life stretched from the American and French revolutions to the Civil War and beyond. Thanks to his exploration of the West, his name lives today. He grew up the son of a French revolutionary, living in a household with Thomas Paine, author of *Common Sense*, a pamphlet that inspired American patriots. Thanks to his discoveries while engaged in fur trading, Oregon's Bonneville Dam and Utah's Bonneville Salt Flats and Bonneville Lake, as well as the Pontiac Bonneville automobile, all bear his name.

Bonneville was born outside Paris during the Reign of Terror to Nicholas, a radical journalist, and Margaret, his beautiful and well-educated wife. His father eventually offended Napoléon with his outspoken ways, but he befriended the Marquis de Lafayette and Paine. In 1797, when the American philosopher-revolutionary was visiting France and down on his luck, Nicholas offered him lodging. A few days turned into five years. Benjamin grew up above his father's printing press along with his two brothers, his parents, and Paine. Historians speculate whether Paine might be the natural father of Benjamin and his brothers. Margaret followed Paine to New York in 1803 while her husband remained in France. Called by some his housekeeper, she lived with Paine on and off until his death in 1809.

Possibly due to his connection to Paine, Benjamin secured an appointment to West Point when he was seventeen and embarked upon a military career. He graduated after two years in 1815. In 1825, he served as aide to his father's friend the Marquis de Lafayette during his visit to this country. At his next post at Fort Smith, Arkansas, he heard tales of the fortunes to be made in the West and determined to take advantage of the situation. In New York, he secured the financial backing of Alfred Seton, an associate of John Jacob Astor, to go into the fur trading business. In 1831, Bonneville received a two-year leave of absence from the army. Even so, Major General Alexander Macombe of the War Department wrote Captain Bonneville charging him with collecting "any information which may be useful to the Government" while exploring the territories "between our frontier and the Pacific."[1]

The instructions were problematic because Great Britain and Mexico owned the territory between what had been the Louisiana Purchase and the Pacific. Thus, asked to seek information about a foreign country under the guise of fur trading, Bonneville was in effect charged with being a spy. Although any documents pertaining to espionage have been lost, other details back up this interpretation of his journeys. Fort Bonneville, built in Wyoming on this expedition, was located at such an impractical spot for fur trading that the mountain men called it "Bonneville's Folly"; it did, however, stand at a strategic location for military defense. When cemetery gatekeeper Manuel Garcia told a Bonneville descendant who visited the cemetery, "I read several things that said he was the only fur trader who failed to make money," the relative replied, "That's not true. He wasn't a fur trader. He was working for the government; he was a spy."[2]

Bonneville's reputation rests on the accomplishments of his wanderings from 1832 to 1835. Among these are the first map of the Great Basin of the Great Salt Lake, the pathfinding expedition from the Great Salt Lake to California,[3] and the first wagon train through the South Pass on what would become the Oregon Trail. The War Department rewarded Bonneville's services by making him the first American military commander on the Columbia River in 1852.

After Bonneville returned from the West in 1835, he met the author Washington Irving while visiting Astor's Hellgate estate. Although known for fiction such as *The Legend of Sleepy Hollow*, Irving was writing a history of Astor's fur trading empire, to be titled *Astoria*. Three or four months later, he visited Captain Bonneville in Washington, D.C., where the explorer was attempting to write a book based upon his journals. Irving bought the journals from Bonneville for $1,000 and used them as the basis for his book, published in 1843. Washington Irving made Bonneville's reputation with *The Adventures of Captain Bonneville*, in which Irving portrays Bonneville as an intrepid and daring explorer.

At the outset of the Civil War, Bonneville appealed to General Ulysses S. Grant to serve in the Union army. In 1861, he was reinstated to take charge of the Benton Barracks in St. Louis as a recruitment and mustering officer. In 1865, he was given the rank of brevet brigadier general in recognition of "his long and faithful service."[4] The next year, he retired for good.

At the time of his death at age eighty-two, Bonneville was the oldest retired officer in the U.S. Army. He was, therefore, accorded full military honors at his burial in Bellefontaine Cemetery. Bonneville takes his eternal rest beneath a worn marble monument upon which can barely be read: "Here lies a noble man whose noble deeds have not escaped the page of fame. The generations yet unborn shall know the record of his name." He joined his first wife, mother, daughter, and son in the family plot. His daughter, Mary, died at age eighteen in 1862. His wife, Ann, died eleven days later, some said of grief. Her tombstone reads: "My husband, I follow our precious daughter, yet a little while you also will be among us. Oh, where is our little angel boy?" That boy, their son, Nicholas, died one month after birth, and his remains were moved to Bellefontaine the year after Ann and Mary died.

---

1. *Exploration and Empire*, Manuel Garcia files, Bellefontaine Cemetery, 149.
2. Manuel Garcia, *Oral History*, tape XX, 298.
3. According to an account written by Washington Irving, Bonneville sent out a party of 40 of his 110 men under the leadership of Joe Walker to make a circuit of the Great Salt Lake and ended up in California. While other traders had gone overland to California, the Walker party discovered the central route along the Humboldt River.
4. *American Biography.*

ROBERT CAMPBELL
1804–1879

ROBERT CAMPBELL immigrated to St. Louis from Ireland to build great wealth in the fur trade of the far West. He was neither as bold nor as ambitious as his partner and friend William Sublette. Yet, according to scholar Harvey L. Carter, his steadiness and integrity were such that at one time "anywhere on the frontier, among Indians or whites, his credit was considerably better than that of the government of the United States."[1]

Robert Campbell was born in 1804, a Protestant of Scottish descent in North Ireland. When he and his brother, Hugh Campbell, emigrated, they landed in Virginia in 1822. Robert left two years later for St. Louis, where he had heard great fortunes were to be made; Hugh settled in Philadelphia where he operated a dry goods business that would later supply Robert's Indian trade. Robert Campbell suffered from consumption and was prescribed a trip to the mountains for relief. In 1825, Campbell joined one of General William Ashley's fur trading expeditions led by Jedediah Smith, who would establish a partnership the next year with Sublette and David Jackson.

When the Smith, Jackson, and Sublette partnership split up in 1832, Campbell had proven so capable that Sublette selected him as his next partner. Their friendship was cemented that year during a battle at Pierre's Hole with the Blackfeet Indians in which Campbell dragged the wounded Sublette to safety. In 1833, Campbell built a trading post in Wyoming named Fort William, after his partner. In 1835, he and Sublette decided to retire to St. Louis so that they could enjoy life with the fortunes they had built. They remained in partnership as bankers and suppliers to the fur trade. They further grew their wealth because St. Louis was the point of departure and return for most expeditions to the far West.

Campbell invested the wealth he had earned from the fur trade in city real estate, and its value increased greatly as St. Louis grew and prospered. His skill as banker to the fur trade led to a position as president of the Bank of the State of Missouri and the Merchant's National Bank. He also owned the Southern Hotel. The government would draw upon his good reputation with the Indians: In 1851 and again in 1870, he helped negotiate treaties with the Plains Indians at Fort Laramie (previously known as Fort William). In another act of public service, he raised, equipped, and drilled four Missouri regiments that served in the Mexican War under General Stephen Watts Kearny (see Part 1). Although his own regiment did not see active duty, he was known as colonel for the rest of his life. He and his brother Hugh sent so much food, clothing, and money to their native land during the Irish potato famine that they were honored with triumphal arches and a cannon salute during an 1851 visit there.

For all Campbell's adventures in the West and success in business, finance, and philanthropy, his name endures because of his family life. In 1836, returning from the Rockies, he went to recover his health at his brother's home in Philadelphia. There he met Virginia Kyle, the fourteen-year-old cousin of Hugh's wife. He was captivated, but her mother felt he was too old for her daughter. At the same time, Hugh believed "that [Robert] mistook this familiarity on the part of Virga, for love."[2] Five years later, they married when she was nineteen and he was thirty-seven. Hugh wrote to Sublette that Virginia had already been "four times courted and twice engaged."[3] Both brother and partner opposed the marriage because they thought she was too young and "fond of admiration."[4] Yet the marriage was a long and happy one despite the great sorrow of burying ten of their thirteen children. Throughout their lives, they wrote letters to each other that were tender and affectionate.

In 1854, the Campbells used their great wealth to buy a mansion on Lucas Place, where the city's most prominent citizens resided. Two years later, they bought the lot next door to use for a garden and carriage house. (The address is now Locust Avenue at Fifteenth Street.) They sumptuously entertained such friends as General William Tecumseh Sherman, Henry Shaw, Henry Taylor Blow, and James Buchanan Eads at an oak dining table that seated thirty-six. Mrs. Campbell's handwritten recipes have been preserved, and they reflect her elegance and style. The apogee of her career as a hostess occurred in 1872 when President Ulysses S. Grant dined with them. He and his wife had come to town to ride a train across the newly opened Eads Bridge.

Robert Campbell's death occurred in 1879, followed by his wife's in 1882. They were buried in Bellefontaine, together with the children who had preceded them, beneath a marble obelisk erected in 1855 that would be replaced by a granite copy in 1926. Their vast estate was left to their three surviving sons.

Robert Campbell lived a life of great contrasts, from the wild adventures of the mountain man to the staid respectability of the St. Louis burgher. He was at one point considered the city's wealthiest man.

---

1. Harvey L. Carter, "Robert Campbell," in *Mountain Men and Fur Traders of the Far West*, ed. LeRoy Hafen (Glendale, CA: Arthur Clarke, 1965), 60.
2. "Campbell House," *McCall's,* July 1957, Manuel Garcia files, Bellefontaine Cemetery.
3. Carter, "Campbell," 58.
4. Ibid.

PHILIP FOUKE
1872–1951

LIKE CITY FOUNDERS Pierre Laclede and Auguste Chouteau, Philip Bond Fouke III came up the Mississippi River from New Orleans to St. Louis to trade furs. Unlike the French fathers of the city, Fouke did not ride in open boats or kill animals for their pelts. His efforts took place on the auction block, at his desk, and in government negotiations. As a result, he made St. Louis "the largest primary fur market in the country"[1] and the capital of the United States sealskin industry.

Born in New Orleans in 1872, Fouke started his career in St. Louis at age fourteen in 1885, earning $5 a week as an office boy for a fur company, rising to president in 1907. In 1921, he founded the firm that bore his name.[2] Understanding St. Louis's potential as a fur market, Fouke began a successful effort to bring northern furs to the city, with trappers and dealers eventually sending their furs directly there rather than to London.

In 1913, Fouke himself served as auctioneer for the country's first fur auction. Successfully lobbying the U.S. government to eliminate the London middle market, his firm obtained the government contract as "exclusive agent in taking, processing, and selling Alaskan sealskins"[3] that same year. From the end of World War II until the 1950s, St. Louis fur auctions brought in $4 million annually[4] with "the Fouke Fur Company [claiming] credit for having made sealskin one of the outstanding fashion furs of the country."[5] The company closed its doors in 1988 after animal protectionists stirred up public opinion against killing baby seals.[6]

Fouke's efforts at capturing the Alaskan fur trade for St. Louis were so successful that the *Globe-Democrat* proclaimed itself "the newspaper of the 49th state"[7] on its masthead from 1920 until 1959. With St. Louis founded and built by the fur trade, it is fitting that the city remained a great center for the trade well into the twentieth century thanks to the efforts of Philip Fouke.

1. McCune Gill, "Philip Bond Fouke III," *The St. Louis Story* (St. Louis: Historical Record Association, 1952), 1122.
2. "Philip B. Fouke, Fur Dealer, Dies," *St. Louis Globe-Democrat*, March 25, 1951.
3. Ibid.
4. Ibid.
5. Gill, "Philip Bond Fouke," 1122.
6. "John T. Fouke, 81; Was Executive Here," *St. Louis Post-Dispatch*, December 7, 1992.
7. Primm, *Lion of the Valley*, 437.

SAMUEL HAWKEN
1792–1884

A DESCENDANT of Swiss gun makers, Samuel Hawken set up shop in St. Louis to manufacture the Hawken Rocky Mountain Rifle. The preferred weapon of such legendary characters as Kit Carson, Jim Bridger, General William Ashley, "Buffalo Bill" Cody, Davy Crockett, and John C. Frémont, the Hawken guns "were made to kill at 200 yards,"[1] noted Hawken.

The mountain men were free white trappers who lived like Indians. They hunted beavers in the spring and fall and sold the pelts at the trading companies' summer rendezvous. They wore buckskins and carried few possessions except for a bullet pouch, powder horn, skinning knife, and rifle. In the eyes of a mountain man, his rifle was equivalent to his survival and his livelihood.

Samuel Hawken came to St. Louis from Hagerstown, Maryland, in 1822, a veteran of the War of 1812. He followed his brother Jacob, also a gun maker, who had arrived in St. Louis four years earlier; they became partners. When his brother died in 1849 during the cholera epidemic, Sam carried on alone in the shop on Washington Avenue near what would become the entrance to the Eads Bridge. Production never exceeded 120 rifles a year, and the price, $20–$40, was considered quite expensive. Today, the 2,500 existing Hawkens each sell for around $40,000, and good imitations cost $2,000. A small crew made the rifles by hand. The Hawken brothers were so particular about quality that they refused Sam Colt in 1847 when he asked them to be the St. Louis distributor for his guns.

Sam Hawken was known not only for firearms but for fire prevention as well. In a town built of wood, fires could wipe out many city blocks, as they did during the Great Fire of 1849. Each of the city wards recruited volunteer fire companies made up of leading businessmen. Chided by

Gil Chouteau that there was no uptown fire company, Hawken—fondly known to the crew as 'Uncle Sammy"—founded the second fire brigade in St. Louis, Union Company Number 2, and served proudly for thirty-three years. On a night in the winter of 1841–1842, when the temperature was 12 degrees below zero, the water froze in the hose until Uncle Sammy primed the pumps with whiskey. In his honor, the company's next fire engine was dubbed the Sam Hawken.

Always the adventurer, Hawken made a brief foray even farther west than St. Louis. In 1859, he joined an expedition to Pikes Peak to seek gold. It was unsuccessful. He proved himself a writer when St. Louis's *Weekly Missouri Democrat* published his account of the trip. He set up a gun shop in Denver for two years but returned to St. Louis to retire to his farm west of the city. There he died in 1884 at the age of ninety-two.

Hawken's grandsons erected a granite monument above his grave in Bellefontaine Cemetery as a tribute to him and his brother Jacob. Beneath the image of a rifle, it says they are

> makers of the famous "Hawken Rocky Mountain and Plains Rifle" which for nearly half a century preceding the Civil War was the outstanding choice of the old Mountain Men, trappers and fur traders. General William Ashley, the famous scout Kit Carson and Buffalo Bill Cody were among the many of these men who would have no other make if it was possible to get a "Hawken."

---

1. "Kit gave me an order for a rifle," from unknown book, Manuel Garcia files, Bellefontaine Cemetery.

WILLIAM SUBLETTE
1799–1845

WILLIAM SUBLETTE, known to the Indians as "Cut Face," was the oldest of five brothers, all involved in the fur trade that inspired so much of St. Louis's early prosperity and opened the West for eventual settlement. Many landmarks would bear his name, such as the Sublette Cutoff on the Oregon Trail, Sublette Lake, now known as Lake Yellowstone, and Fort William, which became Fort Laramie, all in Wyoming. Although the mountains were considered impassable to Conestoga wagons at the time, he led the first wagon train over the Oregon Trail, opening the trail for 250,000 settlers. St. Louis's Sublette Street and Sublette Park also honor his name, not because he first discovered them but because they ran through the vast estate he bought with the fortune he accumulated from trading fur.

Born in Kentucky in 1799, William Sublette moved in 1817 with his family to St. Charles, Missouri, where his father kept a tavern and he became constable. He sought adventure and fortune with General William Ashley, who advertised in the *Missouri Republican* for one hundred "enterprising young men"[1] in 1822. Ashley and his partner Andrew Henry had a new idea: Instead of depending solely upon trade with the Indians, they would provision trappers, send them into the mountains, and pay them per skin. To answer Ashley's call, citizens of St. Charles fitted out Sublette with a rifle and buckskin suit, his sole possessions. On the Ashley expedition, the young Sublette, along with such greats as Jedediah Smith and Tom "Broken Hand" Fitzpatrick, learned the ways of the mountain. In 1826, when Ashley was ready to retire from the fray to the role of bankrolling other traders, he sold the company to his best subalterns, Sublette, Smith, and David Jackson.

For four years, Smith, Jackson, and Sublette trapped and traded for pelts. In 1830, Sublette led one last expedition of the threesome into the mountains, this time using wagons to haul goods in and furs out. He got as far as the Wind River Mountains, within fifty miles of trails following rivers that flowed into the Pacific, a feat previously considered impossible. The news that wagons could penetrate the Rockies was heralded in papers from St. Louis east, inspiring many brave souls to undertake the passage to the Pacific.

The wagon train and the party that accompanied it stretched out nearly a mile when it returned to St. Louis to much fanfare. The furs from this trip yielded $84,000 ($2 million in 2007 dollars), making the partners so wealthy that they considered it time to sell out. Moreover, there were fundamental problems with their most important product—problems that also behooved them to cease trapping. Not only was the beaver overhunted and thus verging on extinction, but silk was becoming more fashionable than beaver for hats in the capitals of Europe and America.

The partnership sold out to Sublette's brother Milton and four partners who formed the Rocky Mountain Fur Company. Shrewd and bold, Sublette, along with a new partner, Robert Campbell, would serve as banker and purveyor to the company that succeeded his. When Sublette went into partnership with Campbell in 1832, they had so much capital that they presented themselves as serious rivals to John Jacob Astor's American Fur Company. In 1834, the astute Sublette effected an agreement with Astor that divided the territory, with Sublette and Campbell trading in the Rocky Mountains and the American Fur Company working the land south and west of the mountains.

In 1835, Sublette retired from the field to lead a civilized life in St Louis. He and Campbell maintained a store with a wigwam in the back where Sublette supported a family of Indians. He bought an estate of 779 acres from the heirs of merchant Charles Gratiot. There he built a great stone house that commanded a hill above the Des Peres River. On his domain, which is bounded roughly by today's Kingshighway, Manchester, Tamm, and Southwest avenues, he kept a zoo of wild animals and surrounded himself with Indian retainers. He built cabins where as many as sixty boarders could indulge themselves in the sulfur springs on his property. The St. Louis Jockey Club, which he had helped organize, also held races there. He then entered public life. In 1841, he was appointed colonel on the staff of the Missouri governor. Three years later, he served as a presidential elector and ran unsuccessfully for Congress.

At age forty-five, he married Frances Hereford of Alabama. He died the next year in Pittsburgh on a trip east. Historians dispute whether he was traveling to Cape May, New Jersey, to take the sea air for his health, or heading to Washington, D.C., to petition Senator Thomas Hart Benton for the position of superintendent of Indian affairs. He was buried on the grounds of his estate. Sublette willed his fortune to his wife providing that she not change her name. Following a proper period of mourning, she married his youngest brother, Solomon Sublette, and was not disinherited because she did not lose her name. In 1868, the family graves on the Sublette estate were transferred to Bellefontaine Cemetery. Frances rests beneath a granite obelisk beside both her husbands.

Sublette was a giant among his contemporaries, not only in terms of physical stature but also in his perspicacious business dealings and leadership abilities. He went into the Rockies owning only his weapon and the clothes on his back and came out a man of wealth and influence.

---

1. Margaret Sanborn, *The Grand Teton: The Story of the Men Who Tamed the Western Wilderness* (New York: Putnam, 1978), 74.

PART FIVE

CIVIL WAR
PATRIOTS

 Hailing from Springfield, Illinois, a mere ninety miles from St. Louis, President Abraham Lincoln well understood the peculiar mix of North and South, East and West that was St. Louis. More than that, he understood what a delicate balancing act it would be to keep the city and state in the Union, but it was a balance he considered crucial to his strategy for a Union victory. To give the state direct links to Washington, D.C., he appointed two of his seven cabinet members from St. Louis, Edward Bates (see Part 1) and Montgomery Blair. Historians agree that "whoever dominated Missouri would tend to dominate the entire Trans-Mississippi"[1] because the state served as a strategic base for operations along the vast inland water way. Lincoln needed not only the state's strategic location but also its wealth, industry, transportation, political leverage, and manpower behind his war effort.

Loyalties were divided in Missouri, and allegiances were never clear cut. Missouri hung on to the Union by a hair. Even though only 10 percent of the population owned slaves, Confederate sympathies ran high. At the same time that Hamilton Gamble served as wartime governor of Missouri, the state also had a Confederate government in exile. Even within families, the Edward Bates family included, some sons wore blue and others gray. Before he became a Confederate general, Sterling Price led the state convention that voted against secession. Today, however, many who pledged allegiance to different flags lie side by side in peace at Bellefontaine Cemetery.

Missouri was literally a battleground from the earliest days of the war. On May 10, 1861, not even a month after the fall of Fort Sumter, Rebels attempted to seize the Federal Arsenal at St. Louis, "the largest cache of weapons and ammunition west of the Mississippi."[2] Only decisive action by Frank Blair (see Part 1) and Nathaniel Lyon defeated the Confederates at Camp Jackson that day. This battle initiated a long and bloody struggle for the state.[3] "Missouri faced a military and organizational challenge exceeded by few other states. During the course of the Civil War, Missouri reported a total of 1,162 military events. . . . Only two states, Virginia (2,154) and Tennessee (1,462) . . . "[4] had more. Beyond actual battles, bushwhackers and guerillas brought the war home to civilians.[5]

As befits a state so battle torn, Missouri offered up 100,000 soldiers to the Union army as well as 90,000 to the state militia and 40,000 more to the Confederacy. The state had a distinguished military background since territorial days when it had been the jumping-off point for expeditions to the West. St. Louis was the site of Jefferson Barracks, the country's largest military post during pre-war days,[6] and many of the Civil War's greatest leaders, including Robert E. Lee, Jefferson Davis, Ulysses S. Grant,[7] and William Tecumseh Sherman, had been billeted there before the Civil War.

St. Louis supplied much more than troops to the cause. Just as the city "was the great base for the exploration of the West, so St. Louis became the great base for the war in the West. Armies and supplies went out by river, rail, and wagon road."[8] Early on, St. Louis came to be the war's great humanitarian center as well. In 1861, a citizens' group led by William Greenleaf Eliot proposed an organization to handle the wounded and sick, refugees, and, later, freedmen from the North and South. Ably led by James Yeatman, the Western Sanitary Commission operated similarly to today's Red Cross, with volunteers and donations to provide military hospitals (see Part 1). The commission sent floating hospitals down the Mississippi to all the great battles along the river.

Buried among Bellefontaine's hills are many men and women, military and civilian, of significance to the War between the States. Cemetery gatekeeper Manuel Garcia compiled a list of 124 such individuals. The greatest preponderance are from the military, with as many generals who wore gray as blue, including the commanding Union general of the second battle of Bull Run, John Pope, and the Confederate general who brought the war home to Missouri, Sterling Price, as well as the great politician Frank Blair, who, according to Sherman, "did more than any single man"[9] to hold St. Louis in the Union. Eight of Bellefontaine's soldiers won the Congressional Medal of Honor for bravery on the field of battle. Many of Lincoln's intimates also came from St. Louis and lie in Bellefontaine.

---

1. Albert Castel, "A New View of the Battle of Pea Ridge," *Missouri Historical Review*, Spring 1956, 149.
2. Louis S. Gerteis, *Civil War St. Louis* (Lawrence: University of Kansas, 2001), 1.

3. Primm, *Lion of the Valley*, 237. Interestingly, both Ulysses S. Grant and William Tecumseh Sherman witnessed it as civilians.

4. James A. Hamilton, "The Enrolled Missouri Militia," *Missouri Historical Review*, July 1975, 414.

5. *Missouri in the Civil War*, Manuel Garcia files, Bellefontaine Cemetery, 399. Missouri suffered the most incidents of bushwhacking and guerilla warfare of any state during the war.

6. Stephen Engle, *Don Carlos Buell, Most Promising of All* (Chapel Hill: University of North Carolina, 1992), 23.

7. Ulysses S. Grant's father-in-law, Frederick Dent, was from St. Louis and is buried in Bellefontaine Cemetery. His monument bears the legend "Died in the Executive Mansion" because the White House was known by that name in his day.

8. Ernest Kirschten, *Catfish and Crystal* (Garden City, NY: Doubleday, 1960), 215.

9. William Tecumseh Sherman quoted in William Winter, *The Civil War in St. Louis* (St. Louis: Missouri Historical Society, 1994), 106.

HAMILTON GAMBLE
1798–1864

DURING THE CIVIL WAR, Hamilton Gamble served his state and country well as governor of Missouri. He walked a tightrope of commitment to the Union, balancing over an abyss with Radical Republicans on one side clamoring for the state to abolish slavery and pro-South constituents on the other side desperately clinging to their human property. Gamble biographer Dennis Boman says that "Gamble and Lincoln developed an important relationship forged by their common goal of preserving the Union and returning peace to Missouri and the country."[1] Lincoln not only saw Missouri as the keystone in the arch of the border states, but also was determined to keep the wealth and political importance of St. Louis firmly in place behind the Union.

While Gamble took a stand in the center of the political life of Missouri almost as soon as he arrived from his birthplace of Virginia by way of Tennessee at the age of twenty, he first rose to national prominence in a battle that was fought in the courts. He served as chief justice of the Missouri Supreme Court during the Dred Scott trial. Of the three Missouri jurors, Gamble gave the lone dissenting opinion in 1852 in which he held that Scott should have his freedom from slavery. Five years later, the U.S. Supreme Court would refuse Scott that right on the grounds that, as a slave, he was not a citizen. The case is considered a bellwether for the Civil War.

When Gamble's future brother-in-law Edward Bates (see Part 1) informed him that Caroline Coalter loved Gamble but could not marry him because of his dissipation, Gamble renounced drink, and she married him in 1827. Gamble served as Missouri's secretary of state, then retired from public life for three years due to ill health. In 1861, when a state convention convened to deal with the crisis caused by Governor Claiborne Fox Jackson's casting his lot with the Confederacy, the Jackson administration was deposed, and Gamble was named governor of the new provisional state government. The convention would elect him to that position the following year.

In his inaugural address, Gamble immediately invoked the two most serious problems that would plague his administration—slavery and the maintenance of law and order. A former slave owner himself, Gamble immediately reassured the 10 percent minority of slave owners in the state that he would protect their property rights. Nevertheless, as the war progressed, he came to believe the state must transition from a slave to a free labor system. In 1863, he reconvened the state convention in order to enact a gradual plan of emancipation. During the ensuing four years of war, the state would be torn by its conflicting allegiances to North and South and subjected to more than one thousand military events and, even worse, to frequent attacks on civilians by guerillas and bushwhackers.[2] Since the federal government could not contribute the money or men to the internal defense of Missouri, Gamble raised a state militia for that purpose despite the fact that the state treasury had been emptied by the previous administration's defection to the Confederacy.

When Governor Gamble died in office January 31, 1864, within sight of Union victory, the members of the St. Louis Bar attended his funeral and declared thirty days of mourning in his honor.[3] The crowd watching his funeral procession stretched for a mile to Bellefontaine Cemetery, "the adornment of which he had largely contributed in life."[4] He rests alongside his wife, Caroline, beneath a monument of double broken columns signifying the everlasting unity of the couple as well as life cut short.[5] Without Hamilton Gamble's leadership, Missouri would surely have seceded from the Union. The fate of the United States hung in the balance.

---

1. Dennis K. Boman, *Hamilton Gamble, Lincoln's Resolute Unionist* (Baton Rouge: Louisiana State University, 2006), 122.
2. Hamilton, "The Enrolled Missouri Militia," 414.
3. Marshall D. Hier, "A Hero's Death for a Lawyer: Hamilton Rowan Gamble," *St. Louis Bar Journal*, Winter 1989, 51.
4. Ibid.
5. Manuel Garcia, *Oral History*, tape LXIV, 977.

THE LIFE OF JOHN POPE reads like a Greek tragedy. During the Civil War, he rose very quickly in the U.S. Army only to be brought down by his own hubris. Tall, handsome, and portly, he was the very image of a good soldier and a loyal Republican. But he became one of the Civil War's more controversial figures and one of the most hated Union generals,[1] despised by Confederates and Federals alike.

John Pope was born in 1822 in Louisville, Kentucky, to Nathaniel and Lucretia Pope, the fourth of nine children. His father was a distant cousin of George Washington and a distinguished statesman in his own right. Nathaniel used political connections to secure an acceptance to West Point for his son. There, John was best known for sitting on a horse well and for having set a daring, new fashion. He wore pants with buttons down the center instead of the side. The convenience of the style soon caught on although it scandalized the ladies.

After graduation, John Pope went to work for the army as an engineer posted to Florida, Georgia, and Maine. With the outbreak of the Mexican War, Lieutenant Pope was assigned to the Engineering Corps of General Zachary Taylor's army in 1846. Promoted to captain, he spent the intervening years until the outbreak of the Civil War mapmaking and surveying in Minnesota and the Southwest and planning lighthouses in the Great Lakes—scant preparation for a command of 67,000 in one of the Civil War's crucial conflicts.

In 1859, he married Clara Pomeroy Horton, daughter of Congressman Valentine B. Horton. This family connection along with his father's relationship with Abraham Lincoln powered his rapid rise in the army, starting with his serving as military escort to the new president on his inaugural journey. Lincoln would later promote Pope over more experienced generals based on familiarity and a few rather insignificant victories.

Immediately after the Confederates fired on Fort Sumter on April 12, 1861, Pope resigned his commission in the regular army, left the lighthouses behind, and went to Illinois to organize and command six thousand volunteers gathering at Springfield. At this point, he was thirty-nine years old and had not led so much as a platoon.

At first, Pope's every effort was met with success. Responding to the appeals of Union generals in the neighboring state of Missouri, Pope marched his volunteers across the Mississippi to restore order. At Blackwater River in December 1861, Pope gained a victory over Confederate forces that surrendered after firing only a single volley.

Against a backdrop of Confederate dominance, Pope would next score two victories in two months, which created a sensation in a United States eager for any reversal of fortune. Union general Ulysses S. Grant's successes at Forts Henry and Donelson in Tennessee in February 1862 set the stage for Pope's most noted campaign. Grant had freed the Upper Mississippi, but rebels still held sway over the lower river from a fort at Island No. 10 across from New Madrid, Missouri. Pope took the city of New Madrid, but surrounding swamps prevented him from marching to Island No. 10. Capitalizing upon a colleague's idea, he ordered his engineers to cut a canal to ferry his soldiers over to the fort. Combining his troops' assault with a bombardment by two ironclad gunboats, Pope captured the garrison on April 7, 1862, without sacrificing a single Union life. Newspapers desperate for any Union victory trumpeted the news across the North. Nowhere was it noted that the Confederates had abandoned the fort before Pope's men arrived there. Still, Pope was promoted to major general.

Within weeks, Lincoln would elevate him from commander of a division to commander of an entire army. Yet none of his much-ballyhooed victories had fully tested Pope in the ways of war. On June 19, Secretary of War Edwin Stanton sent Pope a telegram summoning him to Washington, D.C., and presented him with a plan to combine three separate armies into the Army of Virginia. This command was charged with protecting Washington and drawing Confederate general Robert E. Lee away from Richmond so Union general George McClellan could capture the Confederate capital. Recognizing himself as a Westerner taking over an Eastern command that promoted him over three generals superior to himself in rank, Pope turned down Stanton's offer, calling the command a "forlorn hope."[2] The next day, Lincoln convinced him to accept.

A staunch Republican, Pope was lionized in the capital, where he loudly pronounced that slavery should be abolished and McClellan relieved of command. Vain and boastful, Pope blared orders to his new troops, contrasting his success in the West with their defeats and retreats in the Virginia theater. His braggadocio galvanized his enemies and earned him the disrespect of his troops and the enmity of the generals who had served under the previous commander, General McClellan. When Pope issued a series of general orders, it signaled a change in the administration's policy, but the resulting blame fell on his head alone. He commanded his troops to live off the land and to treat civilians as spies. It was a path that would escalate to Union general William Tecumseh Sherman's March to the Sea.

Pope now stood at the pinnacle of his success. Then fortune turned its back on him. On July 19, his only child died. On July 29, he left Washington to join the Army of Virginia to meet his fate at the second battle of Bull Run. He was outgeneraled by Robert E. Lee and Thomas "Stonewall" Jackson. Pope's defeat put General Lee twenty miles from the U.S. capital.

Still, Pope would accept no blame and would go to his grave convinced that McClellan and his coterie had sabotaged his best efforts. While historians differ as to exact figures, Pope lost approximately 14,400 men, and Lee lost about 9,300. Yet Lee did not succeed in his ultimate ambition: total destruction of the Union army. Pope ordered a successful retreat. Outside of Washington, he handed over his army to McClellan, who would soon vanquish Lee at Antietam. When McClellan relieved Pope of command, his former soldiers cheered, mocking the man from Illinois.

Pope was then sidelined to Minnesota to keep Native Americans in check. In the final twenty years of his career, Pope proved a capable administrator and developed compassion for the Indians and insight into their plight. He came to believe that U.S. policy and white settlers' transgressions provoked Native American aggression.

He felt the solution to the Indian question lay in education and civilization at the hands of the missionaries, with the ultimate goal of assimilation.

Pope died of "nervous prostration" while visiting a brother-in-law in Ohio. His body was returned home, where he was hailed as "a distinguished citizen of St. Louis"[3] and buried with full military honors at Bellefontaine Cemetery.

---

1. Manuel Garcia, *Oral History*, tape LXIX, 405.
2. Wallace Schutz and Walter Trenerry, *Abandoned by Lincoln: A Military Biography of General John Pope* (Urbana: University of Illinois Press, 1990), 94.
3. Obituary, *St. Louis Republic*, September 23, 1892.

STERLING PRICE

1809–1867

THE CAREER OF STERLING Price teetered on the line dividing heroism from infamy. While he had served his state nobly as state representative, congressman, and governor, he wreaked havoc and destruction in Missouri in 1863 as a Confederate general. Still, he inspired his men, was mourned as a hero, and, in a final stroke of irony, was carried to Bellefontaine Cemetery in the same hearse that had borne Abraham Lincoln to his final resting place in Springfield, Illinois. This time, a parade of ex-Confederate soldiers accompanied the hearse. Price was buried on a ridge of the cemetery along with his daughter-in-law and her stillborn baby, who had both died the same day he had.

Price lies beneath a thirty-two-foot obelisk of Maine granite that bears a handsome circular insignia reading "Sterling Price, Born in Prince Edward County, Virginia, September 14, 1809. Died September 29, 1867," as well as an inscription that extols him as "Farmer, Legislator, Governor, Brigadier General during the Mexican War, Major General in the Confederate States Army. His purity of character was equaled by his exalted patriotism. This monument is erected by his friends as a tribute to his worth." A group of his friends, with Trusten Polk as president, first met in 1870 to raise $50,000 for the monument by appealing to all ex-Confederates of Missouri.

Price started out as a farmer but then went into politics and the military. He purchased a farm near Keytesville in Chariton County, Missouri, where he lived the aristocratic life of a tobacco planter. He married Martha Head in 1833 and had six surviving children. Price soon aroused the admiration of his neighbors, who elected him to serve in the Missouri General Assembly for three terms, from 1836 to 1838 and again from 1840 to 1844. He so distinguished himself there that he was named Speaker of the House in 1840. In 1844, he was elected to Congress, but in 1846 he resigned before his term was up to serve in the Mexican War. As a colonel of Missouri volunteers, he accompanied General Stephen Watts Kearny (see Part 1) to New Mexico. There, he put down an insurrection of 1,500 New Mexicans and Pueblo Indians with a mere 350 soldiers, earning a promotion to brigadier general.

Price returned to Missouri a hero and was elected governor in 1852, serving from 1852 to 1857. While Missourians struggled between divided allegiances as the Civil War approached, Sterling Price did his best to support both the North and the South. He called himself a "conditional Union man" but he owned slaves. He led the state convention that voted against secession in March 1861, although he was also in the minority who voted for an additional resolution that "the State of Missouri will not hesitate to take her stand in favor of her southern brethren"[1] should conflict come.

An incident of Federal zealotry led Price to accept command of the Missouri State Militia that had declared its hostility to the U.S. government. At Camp Jackson outside St. Louis, Federal troops under the leadership of Frank Blair and Nathaniel Lyon forced the surrender of Missouri State troops, killing civilians including women and children. Nevertheless, a few days later, Price came back into the Union fold by issuing a joint proclamation with General William Harney, commander of U.S. forces in Missouri, saying that they had the common objective of "restoring peace and good order to the people of the State, in subordination to the laws of the General and State governments."[2] On June 11, 1861, he and Governor Claiborne Jackson met with Blair and Lyon, who had recently replaced Harney in command. After hours of fruitless negotiation, Lyon finally declared, "Rather than concede to the State of Missouri one single instant the right to dictate to my government in any matter however unimportant, I would see you, and you, and you, and you, and every man, woman and child in the State, dead and buried. This means war."[3]

Price could straddle the line no longer. He and Lyon met a week later at the battle of Wilson's Creek, outside of Springfield, Missouri. Price emerged the victor; Lyon lay dead on the battlefield. It was at Wilson's Creek and his subsequent outstanding victory in the battle of Lexington, Missouri, that Price earned the reputation as one of the South's most beloved generals. But his victories ceased with the battle of Pea Ridge, Arkansas, March 7–8, 1862. The Confederates were repulsed and driven from Missouri until the last year of the war.

In April 1862, Price took a commission in the Confederate army, officially becoming a rebel against the government he had once served. He led his Missouri regiments in defeats at Iuka and Corinth, Mississippi, in the fall of 1862. On July 4, 1863, he participated in a disastrous Confederate assault on Helena, Arkansas, which was overshadowed by the South's defeats at Vicksburg and Gettysburg the same day. In the spring of 1864, Price assumed command of the District of Arkansas and soon thereafter received the commission that he had been lobbying for since he left the state—permission to undertake the campaign to liberate Missouri.

Price intended to capture the city of St. Louis and all of its wealth and power. Directly in his path stood Fort Davidson, the Union garrison at Pilot Knob, Missouri, commanded by the hated brigadier general Thomas Ewing Jr., brother-in-law of General William Tecumseh Sherman. On September 26, 1864, while General Andrew Jackson Smith's federal troops moved in to protect the city of St. Louis, Price thrust his vastly superior force of 12,000 men against the 1,450 defenders. As the Confederates advanced over the plain surrounding the hexagonal fort, they met with a firestorm that took out over 1,000 soldiers while the Yankees lost only 28. Even so, the Federals knew they could not hold out against such superior forces over the course of another day of battle, so Ewing took his men out of the fort under cover of nightfall beneath the very noses of the Confederate troops.

Because the Union strengthened its defenses in St. Louis and Jefferson City in response to his approach, Price did not attempt to attack these strongholds. Instead, he wended his way westward, raiding and destroying as he went. Perhaps these were his most controversial campaigns, for he brought the notorious guerillas William Quantrill and "Bloody Bill" Anderson into his army. In Westport, Kansas, on the Missouri border, Price met his Waterloo. Utterly vanquished by a Union army that outnumbered his forces 2–1, Price lost more than one thousand men and abandoned his crusade to bring his state into the Confederacy. As a result of alleged blunders in the Missouri campaign, Thomas C. Reynolds, Missouri's Confederate governor in exile, demanded Price be tried in a court of inquiry. The war ended before the trial was completed, but Price considered himself vindicated.

Following the surrender, Price joined a party of Confederate generals immigrating to Mexico to avoid reprisals. There, Emperor Maximilian gave them land. Price was recognized as the leader of the Confederate settlement, which was named Carlota in honor of the emperor's wife. Price set about farming and built a house for his family with his own hands, but he became sick and impoverished.

Defeated in his Mexican endeavor as well, Price returned to St. Louis with his family in January 1867. Though offered a pardon, he refused to accept it. His admirers whose cause he embodied raised $50,000 to set him up in an apartment and a business as a commission merchant. He succumbed to cholera in September soon after opening shop. In 1911, the Missouri legislature allocated the $11,000 in salary that Price refused to take as governor to erect a statue in Keytesville honoring the man of conflicted loyalties, like the state that he served and loved.

1. Ralph Rea, *Sterling Price, the Lee of the West* (Little Rock, AR: Pioneer Press, 1959), 35.

2. Agreement between Harney and Price, May 21, 1861, as quoted in Jefferson Davis, *The Rise and Fall of the Confederate Government* (New York: D. Appleton, 1881), 417.

3. Allen Nevins, *The War for the Union* (New York: Scribner's, 1960), 14.

ANDREW JACKSON SMITH
1815–1897

THE INSCRIPTION ON Union general Andrew Jackson Smith's monument in Bellefontaine Cemetery bears the legend, "a soldier who never met defeat." An undefeated Northern general in the Civil War was extraordinary, for the Union fought losing campaigns until 1864. Ironically, Smith's marker, "erected by his companions in arms," stands a stone's throw away from the grave of Sterling Price, a Confederate general who often met defeat, sometimes at the hands of Smith himself.

By all accounts dictatorial and brusque, Smith was kindly and beloved by his men. His soldiers affectionately called him "Baldy." His dry sense of humor may have contributed to his popularity. Smith was the son of a general who fought in the War of 1812 and the grandson of another general who served under George Washington in the Revolutionary War. His father sealed his fate by naming his youngest son after the hero of the battle of New Orleans. When "A. J." left his Pennsylvania birthplace to attend West Point, he was appointed cadet by the president of the United States, the very hero for whom he was named. While stationed at Jefferson Barracks in the 1840s, he married a native, Ann Mason Simpson, the daughter of a prominent physician. They had six children, but only one survived childhood.

When the Civil War broke out, Smith earned rapid promotions and proved himself a valiant warrior, defeating even the seemingly invincible Nathan Bedford Forrest. In 1861, Union general Henry Halleck hastily summoned Smith to serve as his chief of cavalry in Missouri. He was promoted to general in 1862 and two years later to major general. Over the next three years, Smith served with such distinction in battles at Corinth and Vicksburg, Mississippi and Pleasant Hill, Louisiana, and in the defense of St. Louis from Price's raiders that Union general William Tecumseh

Sherman considered Smith the man to accomplish any crucial task. Sherman needed his railroad supply lines protected from the wily Confederate Forrest. Forrest promised Smith a relentless attack. Nevertheless, when the day of reckoning came on July 14, 1864, Smith dug his troops into trenches at Tupelo, Mississippi, and emerged the victor, in clear possession of the battlefield. Unfortunately, Smith found food and ammunition running low and his men exhausted, so he was forced to retreat.

Four months later, when Confederate general John B. Hood attacked Nashville, Union general George Thomas sent for Smith for the defense. Following success at Nashville, Smith was sent to New Orleans and then to take Mobile, Alabama, in the final days of the war, and was appointed military commandant of the city after the war. He was such a fair administrator that even the conquered people welcomed his command.

After the Civil War was over, in 1866, Smith was assigned to the 7th Cavalry to fight the Native Americans. His most noteworthy action at this post was to court-martial then–lieutenant colonel George Armstrong Custer, later notorious for his tragic defeat at the battle of the Little Bighorn.[1] In 1868, Smith was appointed commander of the Department of the Missouri.

Following his stint in the Indian Wars, Smith resigned from the military in 1869. When President Ulysses S. Grant wanted to honor Smith's service to his country upon his retirement, Grant sent him to St. Louis, awarding him the important position of postmaster. Smith left the post office in 1881 after winning an election for city auditor, a position he kept until his retirement in 1885. He was called back to battle on the streets of St. Louis in 1877. Along with General John Marmaduke, he commanded a citizens' army of one thousand men during a general labor strike that nearly brought the city to its knees. Smith and Marmaduke opposed confronting the strikers, because "they did not think it necessary, and they feared the militia would provoke armed resistance."[2] Thanks in large part to their discerning judgment, the strike ended without bloodshed.

When Smith died in 1897, a military escort marched his casket to Bellefontaine. His funeral services were "without any ostentation as Gen. Smith was very simple in all his tastes."[3]

---

1. Shirley A. Leckie, *Elizabeth Bacon Custer and the Making of a Myth* (Norman: University of Oklahoma, 1993), 106. Smith had Custer court-martialed for "absence without leave from his command" and "conduct to the prejudice of good order and military discipline." Custer had deserted his post to visit his wife at a fort ten miles away after being informed that she was engaged in a flirtation with another officer.

2. Primm, *Lion of the Valley*, 313.

3. Obituary, January 31, 1897, Manuel Garcia files, Bellefontaine Cemetery.

PART SIX

CAPTAINS OF
INDUSTRY

The founders of St. Louis's great manufacturing companies who are interred in Bellefontaine Cemetery came to St. Louis from other places, burning with ambition, determined to make their fortune and change the world. They had the ability to realize what opportunities their time and place offered and to take advantage of them. Many times, the first generation in an industry persisted against great odds to leave a legacy for a son to take the company to new heights. So many entrepreneurs and capitalists made St. Louis their home that by 1890 it was not only fourth in population in the nation, but also fourth in gross value of its manufactured products.[1]

St. Louis drew talent like a magnet. Impressed by the town when he came for a Baptist convention, Alanson D. Brown convinced his brother George Warren Brown to follow him, both brothers becoming shoe manufacturers. Likewise, the Rand and Johnson families settled in St. Louis to manufacture shoes, coming from Mississippi by way of Tennessee. Brewers Adolphus Busch and Adam Lemp joined the German community and stayed to manufacture the drink their countrymen loved (see Parts 1 and 2). Another German American, Edward Mallinckrodt Sr., was born in St. Louis, where his parents had recently settled, fleeing political unrest in their native land (see Part 1).

Often, it took the second generation to build upon the first generation's success and make an industrial company grow to national importance. Edgar Monsanto Queeny and Edward Mallinckrodt Jr. both made their fathers' companies great (see Part 1). Donald Danforth, son of the flamboyant Ralston Purina founder William H. Danforth, took the company from $19 million in annual sales to $850 million over his thirty-one years at the helm.

The city has a diverse manufacturing base, exemplified by the companies of the men buried in Bellefontaine Cemetery. The Busches and Lemps, among many others, represent the brewing industry. Browns, Rands, and Johnsons stand for shoes. Mallinckrodts and Queenys represent commodity chemicals. Because of St. Louis's central location, transportation industries are represented in strength. William K. Bixby made railroad cars (see Part 1). James S. McDonnell Jr. made an entirely logical decision when he selected St. Louis as the site for his new aircraft manufacturing company (see Part 1).

In many ways, business made St. Louis the great city it is, but that is because these captains of industry were so much more than businessmen. First and foremost, they had a vision of what they wanted to accomplish with their lives. The businesses they built were the first step to achieving that vision. Once they had created their wealth, they were able to realize its full implications and leave a legacy for the entire nation.

---

1. Primm, *Lion of the Valley*, 327.

ALANSON D. BROWN

1847–1913

GEORGE WARREN BROWN

1853–1921

ALANSON D. BROWN and George Warren Brown had a lot in common. The two brothers came to St. Louis from New York two years apart to make their fortunes. This was accomplished when each started his own shoe company. The brothers were born in Upstate New York to a family of farmers whose ancestors date to the Revolutionary War. While early members of the Brown family had been quite wealthy and had endowed Brown University, Alanson and George's parents were hardworking, middle-class farmers. Both brothers were eager to escape the farm and establish themselves in business.

Alanson showed an early aptitude for business. An uncle from Columbus, Mississippi, hired him as a clerk for the uncle's general store. Impressed by his industry and intelligence, his uncle made Alanson a partner three years later. Traveling to St. Louis for a Baptist convention, Alanson became convinced that the city was the up-and-coming place with its ambitious people and its central location as a distribution center.

Selling his share in his uncle's store, Alanson moved to St. Louis in 1871 with $13,000 to invest in a new business. He joined with James W. Hamilton to start a wholesale shoe business as jobbers selling shoes imported from East Coast manufacturers. The concern proved an immediate success, earning $225,000 with four salesmen in the first year. Operating on a strictly cash basis enabled the company to survive a financial panic two years later. Within six years of its founding, Hamilton,

Brown and Company earned $1.5 million, which would be close to $30 million in 2006 dollars.

Among the company's star salesmen was Alanson's brother George. After graduating from a business college in Troy, New York, George set out from the farm in 1873 to make his fortune. After a few weeks of looking around in St. Louis, the twenty-year-old took a position as a shipping clerk for his brother Alanson. Ten months later, he was promoted to traveling salesman. In northern Missouri, a new territory for the company, George met a discouraging situation. Not only was the country still recovering from the financial panic of 1873, but the shoes he had to sell were not well suited for the needs of his customers. Figuring out the specific shoes his customers wanted and then explaining these to Hamilton and Brown, George prospered as a salesman. He determined the market would be better served with shoes manufactured in St. Louis. He tried to convince his brother to manufacture shoes, but Alanson refused because several others had failed at the project in St. Louis. Although offered a partnership, in 1878 George left Hamilton, Brown, taking his savings of $7,000 plus an additional $5,000 to start making shoes. His company was first known as Bryan-Brown, later Brown-Desnoyers, then Brown Shoe Company by 1893, and now Brown Group. After five years, the firm was selling $8 million worth of shoes a year. In a scant twenty years, St. Louis became "the greatest shoe market selling direct to the retail trade in the world"[1] thanks to George Brown's initiative.

Among those who prospered was his brother Alanson. Five years after George had demonstrated that shoes could be successfully manufactured in St. Louis, Hamilton, Brown and Company started making shoes as well. The company soon surpassed George's firm and within a few years had the largest shoe manufacturing business in the world.[2] Although he was not the first to do so, Alanson Brown became known as "the father of shoe manufacturing in St. Louis,"[3] no mean boast since the honorary designation for the city was: First in shoes, booze, and news, and last in the American League. By 1913, Hamilton, Brown made 38,000 shoes daily in seven factories.

In addition to serving on many charitable, banking, and business association boards, George Brown was a director of the 1904 Louisiana Purchase Exposition. A cartoonist at the fair gave George the inspiration for one of his most popular lines of shoes: Buster Brown, whose winking face can still be seen in the heel of children's shoes.

Both Brown brothers considered wealth the means of improving life for their fellow man. As a result, the name Brown lives on in St. Louis. When George died, he left extensive legacies to social welfare organizations in the St. Louis area. Because he and his wife, Bettie Bofinger Brown, had only one son who was amply provided for, she used most of her husband's residuary estate to make a $781,000 gift to Washington University in St. Louis, which established the George Warren Brown School of Social Service.

ALANSON D. BROWN

Alanson also made important philanthropic contributions to St. Louis institutions, although Hamilton, Brown did not survive long after his death. Of his six children, only Alanson C. Brown went into the shoe business, succeeding his father at the helm of the company that went out of business in the 1940s.

George and Alanson rest eternally across the street from each other in Bellefontaine Cemetery, Alanson in a domed mausoleum designed by World's Fair architect Isaac Taylor and George in a hexagonal tomb designed by the firm of Mauran, Russell and Crowell. Because the Brown brothers believed their good fortune came with great responsibility, their name lives on in St. Louis today.

---

1. Stevens, *The Fourth City*, 251.
2. Frances Hurd Stadler, *St. Louis Day by Day* (St. Louis: Patrice Press, 1989), 173.
3. Ibid.

WILLIAM S. BURROUGHS

1855–1898

WHEN WILLIAM Seward Burroughs came to St. Louis from Upstate New York in 1881, he dedicated himself to the creation of an adding machine that would be infallibly accurate. He was twenty-six years old with an inventive genius that had already gained him several patents, and he had been supporting himself at a variety of jobs since he was fifteen. The Burroughs adding machine forever changed business and banking.

Burroughs was working in his father's model shop in 1881 when his father, an unsuccessful inventor himself, moved from Auburn, New York, to the manufacturing center of St. Louis. A year after his move to St. Louis, William received his first patent, for a folding chicken coop. Soon, however, his creative energies focused entirely on a problem he had encountered in his days as a bank clerk: the need for a machine to add long columns of figures. He was not the first to come up with the idea of a machine to do the rote work of addition: In seventeenth-century France, adding machines had been developed as mechanical curiosities, but they were unsuitable for practical use. Burroughs was not even the only inventor chasing that dream; in St. Louis alone several inventors were trying to realize a machine that would be not only accurate but also easy to operate. Many, like his own father, also had a genius for invention, but what made William Seward Burroughs different was his single-minded determination.

William worked ceaselessly, undiscouraged by the repeated failures of his invention. He found financial backers who believed in him enough to keep bankrolling him through seven years of failure. In 1884, he was able to convince Thomas Metcalfe and Richard M. Scruggs of the Scruggs-Vandervoort-Barney dry goods company that he was on the scent of a practical solution to the problem. They advanced him $700 to pay his salary and expenses for a year. Two years later, he was close enough to the desktop machine he envisioned to incorporate the American Arithmometer Company to manufacture it with $100,000 in financial support from his backers. In 1888, he applied for its patent, and his investors had enough confidence in him that they raised an additional $100,000 to manufacture the device. In 1891, they began manufacturing and marketing a machine that would not only calculate but also print the figures and sums.

To operate a Burroughs adding machine, clerks pushed digits on a keyboard and pulled a crank to total them. Toothed segments and gears added the digits. A hydraulic regulator caused the pressure to be consistent no matter how hard anyone pulled the handle, because consistency made for accuracy. The Burroughs Registering Accountant, as his successful machine was called, cost $475, a princely sum in 1891; it soon, however, became a necessity for banks and other commercial enterprises.

By 1904, the Burroughs Adding Machine Company, the new name for the American Arithmometer Company, moved to Detroit. The smaller city offered it ten free acres to build its plant, according to investor G. A. Buder.[1] Burroughs Corporation changed its name to Unisys in 1986 when it merged with Sperry Corporation.

Tuberculosis forced Burroughs's retirement in 1897, and he died the next year, leaving a widow, Nina, and four children. He died in Citronelle, Alabama, and his remains were brought to St. Louis to be buried in Bellefontaine Cemetery a year and two months later. He rests beneath a monumental obelisk with the inscription: "Erected by his associates as a tribute to his genius."

His death at the tender age of forty-three prevented Burroughs from reaping the financial rewards of his efforts, but his true reward was the accurate functioning of his machine. Burroughs's arithmometer was the first computer to sit on the desktop. When he died, the company's production was just under one thousand machines. By 1926, the Burroughs Corporation would sell 1 million machines.

---

1. "Adding Machines Were Product of Several St. Louis Inventors," *St. Louis Post-Dispatch,* n.d., Manuel Garcia files, Bellefontaine Cemetery.

DONALD DANFORTH SR.

1898–1973

DONALD DANFORTH SR. was the son of a famous and flamboyant father, William H. Danforth, who founded the Ralston Purina Company and the American Youth Foundation. Donald also was the father of sons who occupied the limelight, William H. Danforth II as chancellor of Washington University in St. Louis and John C. Danforth as senator. Although he sometimes stood in their shadows, Donald led Ralston Purina out of the Depression with bold business moves. He took the company from $19 million in annual sales at the time he assumed its presidency in 1932 to $850 million annually at his retirement in 1963. In addition, he was a philanthropist and a civic leader with a commitment to St. Louis evidenced in his decision to build Ralston's new headquarters in the city when many corporations were deserting it for the suburbs.

In 1894, William Danforth, or "W. H.," a country boy from Charleston, Missouri, invested $4,000 that his father lent him in a feed company. In the era before cars, feed stations for horses served as the filling stations of the day. A great salesman, promoter, and motivator of men, W. H. had built Ralston to national prominence by the time his only son entered the business in 1920. Donald soon proved himself as a businessman, though in a "quiet, considerate and conscientious"[1] style more like his mother's than his father's.

During the Great Depression, sales fell off. The sixty-two-year-old W. H. handed over the reins of power to his son. While there was much speculation as to the reasons that this still young and vigorous entrepreneur relinquished control, Donald modestly stated: "I think Father wanted me to take over when things were at the bottom. There was no place to go but up and he was anxious for me to get credit for a good record."[2]

Indeed, "after 1932, Purina never again [operated] in the red, and by 1939 [elevated] profits to $2.9 million."[3]

While other companies were cutting back or closing, Donald moved boldly and courageously to expand Ralston Purina by opening six new feed mills from 1933 to 1935 and changing the corporate structure to decentralized production centers. Other hallmarks of his forty-three-year tenure include profit sharing, the introduction of Dog and Cat Chow, and the Purina research farm.

In a quiet, dignified manner, Donald Danforth Sr. assumed a leadership role in his company and also became an advocate for St. Louis. He was the first president of the United Fund of St. Louis. Most of all, his accomplishments are measured by the progress of Ralston Purina. Under his aegis, the small, family-owned business became one of the largest corporations in America.[4]

1. Bill Smith, "A Checkered Past," *St. Louis Post-Dispatch*, September 25, 1994, F10.
2. Gordon Philpott, *Daring Venture: The Life Story of William H. Danforth* (New York: Random House, 1960), 107–108.
3. *The Ralston Chronicle* (St. Louis: Ralston Purina Co., 1994), 12.
4. *St. Louis Post-Dispatch*, July 15, 1973.

JAMES MARITZ SR.

1895–1981

JAMES MARITZ JR.

1922–1994

WILLIAM MARITZ

1928–2001

EDOUARD MARITZ, the first member of his family to settle in St. Louis, came to this country in 1850. In 1894, his son Edward started a company in his home, with no capital. It is now worth $1.5 billion.

In 1894, Edward, the son of an Icarian socialist who immigrated from Switzerland, began manufacturing and selling jewelry and watches from his home on Magnolia Avenue. Two of his three sons, James and Lloyd, joined the company as teenagers. By 1918, thanks to Edward's keen business sense, the company employed fifteen traveling salesmen and five full-time employees in addition to the three Maritzes. The business prospered, and in 1921 Maritz Jewelry Manufacturing Company became America's first major importer of Swiss watch movements.[1] The company used these to make wrist- and pocket watches. James became one of the first men in St. Louis to wear a wristwatch.[2] Business boomed in 1925 because of James's idea to allow employees of large companies to purchase watches and jewelry at a discount.

In 1929, adversity struck, but out of it came great opportunity. Founder Edward died, and the company had not yet recovered from his passing when it was hit hard by the Depression. By the end of the year, besides the Maritz brothers, only four employees remained of the original twenty, and business was so poor that several times the company could not meet payroll. Both brothers took loans on their homes to keep the business afloat. Then James, the company's top salesman, known to the employees as "the Boss," came up with a strategy to keep the then-named Maritz Watch and Jewelry Company viable. The company began selling watches and personalized jewelry to companies to reward employees for sales and service, a more emotionally satisfying token than money alone. This simple concept provided the genesis of a new industry, and by November 1930 Maritz Sales Builders was born. The company printed an incentive awards booklet and opened a showroom to display premiums offered to clients' employees as rewards. In 1931, Carradine Hat Company became the first national client, followed by Chevrolet, Shell Oil, and Ralston Purina.

James and Lloyd had disagreements that intensified, and the brothers decided they could no longer work together. They split the original Maritz Company. Lloyd ran the jewelry company until he died; it then closed. James and his son James junior were left with the incentive company. James junior was one of the three children of James and Eugenia Uhri Maritz, along with William and Jean.

By 1950, the postwar economic boom had carried Maritz Sales Builders on its rising tide, and the company had forty-five employees based in St. Louis. Two years later, the number of employees doubled. William started working for the company in 1953 upon his return from the Korean War. Among many other innovations, he helped plan the company's modern headquarters in Fenton, Missouri. After their father died in 1981, brothers James junior and William disagreed on major issues. James junior eventually sold all of his shares back to the company. With his son James III he formed a company that imports and distributes shoes.

Ten years later, William engaged in another struggle for control of the company, this time with his sister, Jean Maritz Hobler. In 1994, the company bought back the Hobler family shares for a reported $60 million paid over five years.

Despite his feuds with his siblings, William presented a face of confidence and optimism to the community as he led his company to ever-greater achievements. Gregarious and personable, he was convinced that his leadership best served the company. The figures proved him right. At the time he joined the company in 1953, Maritz Inc. did close to $5 million a year in sales. When he stepped down in 1998, sales had grown to $2.5 billion.

William also devoted himself to the improvement of the community in which he lived. In the late 1980s, he started a Maritz-incentive-type program for the St. Louis Public Schools, rewarding students for attendance with T-shirts, baseball tickets, and other prizes, and he funded the program with $3 million. He is credited with founding the Laclede's Landing Redevelopment Corporation, which developed St. Louis riverbank warehouses into an entertainment district. In another move to enhance the riverfront, he cofounded the VP Fair, a Fourth of July celebration there.

Unfortunately, William's children fell out with each other just as their father and grandfather did with their siblings. Once again, William put the good of the company ahead of family loyalty. Shortly before he died, William, with his son Stephen, had his other two sons, Peter and Philip, removed from the board. The brothers and their sister sued Stephen, and the siblings did not settle until five years later in 2007.

Choosing not to rest eternally in the family plot in Bellefontaine Cemetery, William purchased a new lot in the same cemetery. According to Bellefontaine Cemetery superintendent Michael Tiemann, William planned everything himself, designing a simple but bold headstone and sketching the monument and stone entryway on a piece of scratch paper.[3] In death as in life, he maintained control.

---

1. Dale Richard Larsen, *Contributions of Edouard Maritz and His Descendants to the City of St. Louis, Missouri* (Sunnyvale, CA: Icarian Society, 1997), 40.
2. Ibid.
3. Michael Tiemann, *Oral History*, tape I, 15.

GUIDO PANTALEONI

1858–1948

GUIDO PANTALEONI transformed the night as "the engineer responsible for the then fabulous electric system of the 1904 St. Louis World's Fair,"[1] a time when people "had never even dreamed of entire buildings illuminated by electricity."[2] More important, as a longtime associate of George Westinghouse, he played an instrumental role in making electricity available for practical applications.

Pantaleoni was born in Macerata, Italy, in 1858. When Westinghouse was visiting Italy in 1882, he became friends with Pantaleoni's father, the first president of the Italian senate. Guido Pantaleoni acted as translator and impressed Westinghouse so much that he took the young engineer back to the United States with him. In the United States, Pantaleoni worked on electric lighting that offered significant advantages to railroad signaling for Westinghouse's company, Union Switch and Signal.

On a visit to Italy after the death of his father, Pantaleoni took a step that became "the starting point of the great development of the alternating-current system,"[3] which is in use throughout the world today. He made the acquaintance of Lucien Gaulard, who had recently patented an alternating-current (AC) electrical system with John Gibbs. Excited by the possibilities this new system offered, Pantaleoni cabled Westinghouse, who then secured an option on the new technology, which allowed electricity to be transmitted safely over long distances, overcoming the limitations of the direct-current system devised by Thomas Edison. Over the next few years, Pantaleoni commuted to Pittsburgh from St. Louis to work on the AC system with other Westinghouse engineers. After working for Westinghouse as general manager, he settled in St. Louis to set up electrical power plants throughout the midwestern United States.

As a founder of Westinghouse Electric Company, Pantaleoni was able to envision the possibilities of alternating current and recognize the forerunner of a system that would provide instantaneous electrical connections among peoples across the globe.

---

1. "Guido Pantaleoni Dies at Age 90," obituary, Manuel Garcia files, Bellefontaine Cemetery.
2. Diane Rademacher, *Still Shining: Lost Treasures from the 1904 World's Fair* (St. Louis: Virginia, 2003), 6.
3. Henry Goslee Prout, *A Life of George Westinghouse* (New York: Scribner's, 1922), 101.

JACKSON JOHNSON
1859–1929

OSCAR JOHNSON
1864–1916

FRANK RAND
1876–1949

THE RANDS AND JOHNSONS were cousins who came to St. Louis from Holly Springs, Mississippi, via Memphis, Tennessee, in 1898 to found what would soon become the world's largest shoe manufacturer. Oscar Johnson, Jackson Johnson, and Edgar Rand along with John C. Roberts founded Roberts, Johnson and Rand Shoe Company. Rand's brother Frank would join them a few months later.[1] Remarkably, in a city with twenty-six shoe companies, Roberts, Johnson and Rand would become the fifth largest within five years of its birth. When the company merged with Peters Shoe Company to found International Shoe Company in 1911, it grew so fast that the company led the world in shoe production by 1923.[2]

All of the cousins took positions of responsibility in their St. Louis shoe companies. Jackson Johnson, who had been the first president of Roberts, Johnson and Rand, became the first president of International Shoe. Oscar Johnson succeeded him at the helm when Jackson became chairman in 1916. Rising from traveling salesman, Frank Rand, the youngest of the cousins, stepped up to the president's desk in 1916 when Oscar Johnson died suddenly, apparently of heatstroke, at age fifty-two.

International Shoe made the Rand and Johnson families very wealthy. By 1929, the company had spawned thirty-eight millionaires.[3] Family members remained cooperative, with in-laws as well as direct descendants working together. By 1960, the shoe company was by far the world's largest with $266 million in sales and 35,500 employees.[4] The company made 50 million pairs of shoes each year in fifty-five shoe factories with thirty-two tanneries and supply plants.[5]

OSCAR JOHNSON

The Johnson family also had a dark side. Oscar Johnson Jr. was kidnapped in 1935 when he was thirty years old. He managed to foil his assailants by breaking the key in the ignition of his Cadillac. "The terrifying experience left him with his already pronounced reclusiveness magnified."[6] His only child, Irene Johnson Barnes, would mirror his attitude until she died a recluse whose body was not discovered for weeks after her death.

The fates of the Rand and Johnson families were intertwined in blood, money, and, especially, the company and philanthropies that were their great legacy to the city of St. Louis. Unfortunately, that company has been drastically modified. By 1966, International Shoe became a division of Interco, a holding company. A 1991 bankruptcy dictated that changes needed to be made. As manufacturing shoes in the United States was no longer profitable, Interco divested itself of the old International Shoe Company in 1994. Today, the corporate descendant of the old Roberts, Johnson and Rand Company no longer makes or sells shoes, and it goes by the name of Furniture Brands.

---

1. Esley Hamilton, application for Theodore Link Historic District, National Register of Historic Places Nomination Form.
2. Ibid.
3. John McGuire, "And Now: A First in Museums," *St. Louis Post-Dispatch*, October 19, 1997.
4. Kirschten, *Catfish and Crystal*, 424.
5. McGuire, "A First in Museums."
6. Florence Shinkle, "Little Princess Lost," *St. Louis Post-Dispatch*, September 3, 1995.

LUYTIES

PART SEVEN

PROFESSIONALS

 Today, St. Louis is one of the country's top medical centers, with Washington University Medical School ranked third among the nation's medical schools.[1] The city's first mayor, elected in 1823, was physician William Carr Lane, who laid the foundation for a public health system. Later, St. Louis was home to the nation's first great medical researcher, William Beaumont (see Part 1), as well as the first woman to receive the Nobel Prize in Medicine, Gerty Cori (see Part 1).

In 1840, when St. Louis had but 36,000 people, the first medical school in the city opened its doors, founded by the brilliant but eccentric Dr. Joseph Nash McDowell. McDowell's medical school, along with that of his rival, Dr. Charles Pope, eventually became part of Washington University Medical School. Absorbing these early medical colleges, the school first achieved eminence under the leadership of Robert S. Brookings (see Part 1). A multimillionaire capitalist who retired from business at age forty-six, Brookings devoted his energies to philanthropy by donating his time and money to the university. Today, patients come from across the country, even the world, seeking treatment at St. Louis's medical center.

Among Bellefontaine Cemetery's hills rest many of the lawyers who laid the legal framework for the state during territorial days. Edward Hempstead served as attorney general for the territory. An attorney general for the state of Missouri, Edward Bates (see Part 1) was considered one of the most eloquent voices in the state constitutional convention during the transition from territory to state.

Crusaders for woman suffrage included Virginia Minor (see Part 1), who studied law to strengthen her case, and Phoebe Couzins, Washington University Law School's first female graduate (see Part 3). James O. Broadhead was among the founders of the American Bar Association in 1878. When he first arrived from Virginia, Broadhead tutored Edward Bates's seventeen children and later read law under Bates.

St. Louis acquired its first newspaper, Joseph Charless's *Missouri Gazette*, just forty-five years after the city was founded. During the nineteenth century, the city of St. Louis had as many as 145 newspapers,[2] for there, as in other Western boomtowns, "new periodicals started off blithely every year."[3] Fervent politicians such as Thomas Hart Benton and Frank Blair Jr. (see Part 1) edited journals as the best means of promulgating their ideas to a wide public. Blair also founded three papers, two of which evolved into the *Globe-Democrat* and the *Post-Dispatch*.

Al Spink (see Part 10) spawned a journalistic dynasty when he founded the *Sporting News* in 1886. For the next ninety-six years, the "bible of baseball" was owned and edited by members of his family, starting with his brother Charles Claude Spink, who came to run the advertising and circulation departments in 1887. Charles took over in 1899 as editor, eventually passing leadership on to his son, Taylor Spink, who turned it over to his son, Johnson Spink.

While most accounts credit Joseph Pulitzer and his rival, William Randolph Hearst, with creating the new journalism, St. Louis's Joseph McCullagh of the *Globe-Democrat* wrote the first interview and developed the poll. Thus, St. Louis became known for journalism, which forms another piece in the city's triad of accomplishments—First in shoes, booze, and news.

So many mayors, senators, congressmen, governors, and cabinet members rest eternally in Bellefontaine Cemetery that the cemetery could practically hold a shadow government. Of St. Louis's forty-two deceased mayors, the graves of twenty-four can be found in Bellefontaine. A twenty-fifth, John Darby, was among the cemetery's founders, but lies elsewhere. This distinguished list includes the first mayor, William Carr Lane, the entrepreneurial David Rowland Francis (see Part 1), and World's Fair mayor Rolla Wells.

The U.S. Congress is amply represented among the hills of Bellefontaine, including both senators representing Missouri in the U.S. Capitol's Statuary Hall: Thomas Hart Benton, Missouri's first senator, and Lincoln's hatchet man Frank Blair. Of Missouri's governors, seven lie in Bellefontaine. Finally, the cemetery boasts six cabinet members.

As a city grows, its merchants and industrialists must be able to borrow capital to finance their expanding businesses. When St. Louis was founded in 1764, the coin of the realm was fur. Wealth was measured in land and animal skins. As the economy diversified, barter became too unwieldy. The city's first bank, the Bank of St. Louis, was founded in 1816 and followed in 1817 by the Bank of Missouri. Both printed their own currency in the form of banknotes and soon met an "inglorious end,"[4] the former due to a dishonest employee in 1819, the latter thanks to a credit collapse in 1821. Burned by those early failures, St. Louis became a center of conservative banking. In 1828, the Bank of the United States established a branch in St. Louis, a sign of the city's growing wealth and commercial power. St. Louis's leading capitalist, John O'Fallon, was named president (see Part 1).

During the nineteenth century, many of St. Louis's leading businessmen went into finance. William Sublette and Robert Campbell first earned money in the fur trade and then went into banking (see Part 4). Merchants and manufacturers such as Robert Barnes, Robert S. Brookings, and William K. Bixby later went into finance and became philanthropists as well (see Parts 1 and 11). When the Federal Reserve System was founded in 1911, St. Louis became home to one of the system's twelve branches (see William McChesney Martin Sr. and Jr., Part 1). In the nineteenth century, movers and shakers built up capital and then used their wealth to lend it to other entrepreneurs. They used their success to help others finance their dreams.

---

1. *U.S. News & World Report*, April 1, 2005.
2. The number of newspapers was figured based upon the author's count of nineteenth-century St. Louis newspapers in *Newspapers in Missouri—A Union List* compiled by the staff of the Missouri Newspaper Project. Some lasted less than a year. Others served special interests, such as *Town and Farm*, *Mining Investor*, and *Stock Yard Daily Journal*. Many were written in German.
3. Max Putzel, *The Man in the Mirror: William Reedy* (Westport, CT: Greenwood Press, 1972), 52.
4. Primm, *Lion of the Valley*, 107.

JAMES O. BROADHEAD
1819–1898

IN A LONG AND distinguished career, crowned by being elected the first president of the American Bar Association, James Overton Broadhead brought his considerable legal talents to the service of his state and country. Though Virginia born, he was an ardent Unionist during the Civil War and helped keep Missouri from joining the Confederacy. Later, he served as congressman, special prosecutor of the Whiskey Ring cases, and ambassador to Switzerland.

Broadhead was a tutor for his neighbor's children. The neighbor was Edward Bates (see Part 1), one of the state's eminent lawyers, who would become attorney general for Abraham Lincoln. They became lifelong friends.[1] Broadhead read law under Bates for three years, earning his license in 1842. In 1878, he was elected the first president of the American Bar Association, which he had helped organize.

In 1882, when he was running for Congress, he aroused the ire of the editor of the *St. Louis Post-Dispatch*, so that his name would be forever linked with a notorious murder. The editor, John A. Cockerill, became incensed over Broadhead's alleged corruption in a case in which Broadhead first represented the city by making an agreement with the gaslight company and then switched teams to represent the gas company against the city. Although his reasons for doing so are not clear, Broadhead remained quiet and did not defend himself against the *Post-Dispatch*'s accusations.[2] Despite Broadhead's restraint, his partner Alonzo Slayback could not exert self-control. When Slayback burst into Cockerill's office, the editor shot and killed him at point-blank range. Although a grand jury dismissed murder charges against Cockerill, who pled self-defense, he was tried and found guilty in the court of public opinion. Crowds stormed the newspaper's offices, and people dropped their subscriptions within weeks. Cockerill left town, but Broadhead was elected to Congress. Votes revealed that the populace did not take the newspaper's accusations seriously.

1. Scharf, *History of St. Louis*, 602.

2. Donald F. Brod, "John A. Cockerill's St. Louis Years: A Study of the Campaign That Brought Them to an End," *Missouri Historical Society Bulletin*, April 1970, 233.

JOSEPH CHARLESS SR.

1772–1834

JOSEPH CHARLESS JR.

1804–1859

CHARLOTTE TAYLOR BLOW CHARLESS

1810–1905

JOSEPH CHARLESS SR. came to St. Louis in 1808 to found the first newspaper west of the Mississippi. Fleeing Ireland after the Irish Rebellion of 1795, he was from then on a proponent of liberty.

Although the population of St. Louis was only 1,100, hardly enough to support a newspaper,[1] and Missouri was not yet a state, territorial governor Meriwether Lewis enticed Joseph senior with a $225 subsidy. In his capacity as printer, Joseph not only founded the *Missouri Gazette* on July 12, 1808, but also that same year printed the territory's first book, *The Laws of the Territory of Louisiana*, an indispensable component of good government. He published the first editions in both French and English because St. Louisans spoke one or the other. A year's subscription to the newspaper cost only $3 and could be paid in produce; nevertheless, subscribers owed him as much as $1,200 by 1810.

He retired from the newspaper in 1820 after Missouri became a state, perhaps because his opposition to slavery caused such an uproar. (After one interim owner, his son Edward bought the paper and changed its name to the *Republican*, which continued to publish until it was bought by the *Globe-Democrat* in 1919.) Joseph senior died in his bed at the age of sixty-two.

Joseph junior and his wife, Charlotte, raised her younger siblings after her parents died. He went into business with her brother Henry Taylor Blow in a prosperous drug and paint concern known as Charless, Blow and Company (see Part 1). Charless was also president of two banks, the Bank of the State of Missouri and the Mechanics Bank, as well as a director of the Pacific Railroad. He helped found Washington University in St. Louis and served on the city's Board of Aldermen as well as on the board of the public schools. Joseph junior was gunned down in the streets of St. Louis. His assailant, who was later hanged, had become embittered at Joseph Junior when the latter testified against him in a jury trial.

JOSEPH CHARLESS JR.

Charlotte Taylor Blow Charless left her own legacy of commitment to social justice. After her retired housekeeper died in the poorhouse, Charlotte resolved to found "a 'home' for the 'respectable poor' who had served their generation, and were bereft of friends and fortune, suffering alone in neglect and poverty."[2] When she brought the concept to her husband's attention, he gave her $500, the first donation of the $20,000 she raised to buy the building in Carondelet that still serves sixty-five residents today. She ran the board until she left St. Louis to live with her daughter in 1859. In tribute to "this remarkable woman who almost singled handedly began a charitable institution that has stood the test of time,"[3] the Home of the Friendless was renamed Charless Home in 1977.

---

1. William H. Lyon, "Joseph Charless, Father of Missouri Journalism," *Missouri Historical Society Bulletin*, January 1961, 133.

2. Gary V. Sluyter, *St. Louis' Hidden Treasure: A History of the Charless Home, 1853–2003* (St. Louis: The Senior Circuit, 2003), 8.

3. Sluyter, *St. Louis' Hidden Treasure*, 15.

KO KUEI CHEN
1898–1988

BORN IN 1898 IN SHANGHAI, Ko Kuei Chen came to the United States to study physiology on a scholarship that the United States awarded Chinese students as part of the reparations for the Boxer Rebellion. After college, Chen's uncle, a Chinese herbalist, suggested that he look into *ma huang*, a shrub that grew in the shadow of the Great Wall that was reputed to have legendary powers to reduce fevers and stimulate circulation. Chen and a colleague isolated the drug ephedrine as its active ingredient and found it effective in treating asthma and heart disease. By 1927, Eli Lilly and Company was manufacturing the drug, and it opened a Shanghai branch a year later. Chen rose to be Lilly's director of research. Eventually, he was awarded the coveted Remington Honor Medal, the highest tribute of the American Pharmaceutical Association. Chen bridged both worlds of China and the United States, bringing many drugs based upon ancient Chinese herbal medicine into the Eli Lilly and Company repertoire.

Chen's daughter, Mei Chen Welland, said that during his entire career, "My father was always very aware of William Beaumont,"[1] the first great American physiological researcher (see Part 1). After Chen died at the age of ninety in San Francisco, the family brought his cremains to rest in the same hallowed ground as his honored predecessor. Bellefontaine Cemetery superintendent Michael Tiemann said, "Beaumont was his hero because of [his] digestive studies. . . . That is why there is a beautiful Chinese monument . . . because Dr. Chen wanted to be buried next to Beaumont one hundred years later."[2] Welland added, "My father was a planner. He was very organized and wanted no loose ends. He loved the thought of being buried next to Beaumont so I researched the city and found Bellefontaine."[3] The Chen family plot lies catercorner from the Beaumont lot.

1. Mei Chen Welland (Ko Kuei Chen's daughter), conversation with the author, 2005.

2. Michael Tiemann, *Oral History*, tape V, 106–107.

3. Mei Chen Welland, conversation.

JOHN COCKERILL
1845–1896

JOHN COCKERILL made Joseph Pulitzer's newspapers sell. When Pulitzer bought the ailing *St. Louis Post* and *St. Louis Dispatch* newspapers, Cockerill started as managing editor. Though his editorial skills had driven the *Post-Dispatch* to success, Cockerill was forced to leave town in 1882 before his personal troubles took the paper down. Later, he moved with Pulitzer to the *New York World*.

When Cockerill got out of the army in 1862, he went directly to work setting type. He rose through the ranks in weekly newspapers in Ohio. He got his first big break in 1869 when he was called to the then struggling *Cincinnati Enquirer* as a reporter. Perhaps because of his friendship with the owner's son, he rose to managing editor the next year. In 1874, Cockerill covered a gruesome murder with a five-column headline and five graphic illustrations—a huge amount at a time when line drawings had to suffice for pictures. Most significantly, a new style of journalism was born. Day after day, the *Enquirer* ran stories of murder and mayhem, and circulation soared. While the *Enquirer* was only reaching around ten thousand subscribers when Cockerill came to the paper, his formula increased the paper's circulation to close to ninety thousand by the time he left it in 1877.

Cockerill and his formula for journalistic success made a big impression on a young, immigrant, Missouri editor named Joseph Pulitzer, who visited Cincinnati in 1872 as a representative of a St. Louis German newspaper. Six years later, Pulitzer bought a tired St. Louis paper known as the *Dispatch* at a sheriff's sale and merged it with another paper known as the *Post* the following year. He sent Cockerill a telegram inviting him to be managing editor. They crusaded against murder, political corruption, boodle, vice, and filthy streets. Circulation and profits soared. In 1881, the formerly failing paper earned $85,000.

Good fortune took a turn for the worse the next year. Cockerill printed an exposé about attorney James O. Broadhead, who was running for Congress. The attorney had been representing the city against the gas company when he changed teams to represent the gas company in the same case. Cockerill printed stinging editorials denouncing Broadhead for learning St. Louis's side of the case and then using it to work for the city's adversary. Broadhead's partner, Alonzo Slayback, was incensed. On the afternoon of October 13, 1882, Cockerill sat in his office talking with the paper's business manager and composing-room foreman. Slayback stormed in, pistol in hand, followed by William Clopton. "The action was confused and fast. No two accounts tell the same story but they all agree that Cockerill . . . remembered the gun in his desk. . . . This was the moment Slayback started to take off his coat. Slayback's friends make much of this detail, contending the lawyer planned only to give the editor a sound thrashing."[1] Slayback pointed his gun at Cockerill. The business manager lunged for Slayback. Cockerill was backed against a window. The window broke, and Cockerill was forced to his knees. Cockerill shot and killed Slayback.[2]

Cockerill had two friendly witnesses testify for him at the hearing; Slayback's side had only Clopton. Cockerill's friends said he shot in self-defense. According to cemetery gatekeeper Manuel Garcia, "Clopton insisted that Slayback was unarmed."[3] An opposing newspaper, the *Republican*, made much of Clopton's assertion. Conveniently, at the inquest, the business manager pulled out a gun that he claimed he had taken out of Slayback's hand. Garcia believes that "the gun, a British bull dog, . . . the same make as the gun used to assassinate President Garfield, . . . was a gun that most people would have remembered. However, no one recalled that Slayback owned any gun."[4] After two weeks, the grand jury failed to indict Cockerill. Officially, his slate was wiped clean, but the public considered him guilty. A drunken mob stormed the *Post-Dispatch* headquarters, threatening to burn it down. More important, Cockerill's disgrace sent subscribers and advertisers elsewhere, and revenues plunged. After the paper lost 1,300 subscribers,[5] Pulitzer's defense of his editor became less enthusiastic. Cockerill resigned in 1883.

Pulitzer then sent Cockerill to edit the *New York World*. Together they crusaded against vice and corruption in a larger city with bigger sins. That failing newspaper soon became the city's biggest seller. By 1886, "the *World* was the most profitable newspaper ever published up to that time."[6] Throughout his career, Cockerill had proven himself adept at spotting and nurturing talent. In 1887, he hired Nellie Bly, one of the first female reporters. She proved an effective muckraker and wrote a sensational series about a trip she made around the world.

Cockerill later went to work for the *New York Herald* as its Far Eastern correspondent. He died of apoplexy in 1896 in Cairo, Egypt. Although he had not lived in St. Louis for thirteen years, his body was interred at Bellefontaine Cemetery in the lot called Elk's Rest. Cockerill had been exalted ruler of the Elks in his St. Louis days and had donated the 1,350-pound bronze statue of an elk to the Elks Club lot. Slayback had also been a member of the Elks, an organization based upon, in Cockerill's words, "charity, justice, brotherly love, and fidelity."[7]

---

1. Homer W. King, *Pulitzer's Prize Editor: A Biography of John A. Cockerill, 1845–1896* (Durham, NC: Duke University, 1965), 108.

2. David Linzee, *St. Louis Crimes & Mysteries* (St. Louis: Palmerston & Reed, 2001), 88.

3. Manuel Garcia, *Mark Twain in St. Louis: A Biographical Tour of Bellefontaine Cemetery* (St. Louis: n.p., 2002), E.

4. Ibid.

5. Donald Brog, "Cockerill's St. Louis Years," *Missouri Historical Society Bulletin*, April 1970, 237.

6. King, *Pulitzer's Prize Editor*, 143.

7. Ibid., 232.

ALBERT GALLATIN EDWARDS
1812–1892

IN 1887, ALBERT GALLATIN EDWARDS founded the securities firm A.G. Edwards and Sons. This firm became the country's largest broker of stocks and bonds that was not headquartered on Wall Street, until 2007 when it merged with Wachovia. Edwards had a lineage as distinguished as his career. His father, Ninian Edwards, served as chief justice of Kentucky as well as senator and governor of Illinois. The town of Edwardsville, Illinois, was named after Ninian. A. G. Edwards's brother, Ninian Wirt Edwards, a lawyer and representative to the Illinois state legislature, was a close friend of Abraham Lincoln and introduced Lincoln to Mary Todd, his wife's sister. Abraham Lincoln and Mary Todd were married in the younger Ninian's parlor, despite family objections to the cultivated lady's union with a homespun lawyer.

In 1834, A. G. Edwards graduated from West Point and was commissioned a second lieutenant, which eventually took him to St. Louis. After fighting in the Black Hawk War against the Native Americans, he was assigned to a cavalry regiment at Jefferson Barracks in St. Louis. There, he served along with Jefferson Davis under the command of Lieutenant Colonel Stephen Watts Kearny (see Part 1). In 1835 in St. Louis, Edwards married his first wife, Louise Cabanne, a descendant of the city's founding Chouteau family. Upon marriage, he resigned from the army and went to work for the William L. Ewing Company, a commission merchant. When Louise and their only child, a son, died six years later, Edwards underwent a religious conversion, becoming a devout Presbyterian. In 1850, he married Mary Ewing Jenckes, the niece and ward of his boss. They had three sons and a daughter whom they raised in the then-rural community of Kirkwood.

Edwards would find his quiet family life shattered by the Civil War. A staunch Unionist, he was led by his convictions to the defense of his state. He was a close friend of Governor Hamilton Gamble (see Part 5) because both served as elders of the Second Presbyterian Church. Gamble appointed him to command the division of the Missouri militia protecting St. Louis and Jefferson counties.

Edwards had a career in finance that paralleled and succeeded his military career. Gamble appointed him Missouri bank examiner as well as brigadier general. Thanks to his "ability as a financier combined with his inflexible business integrity,"[1] he served as U.S. treasurer of the subtreasury at St. Louis during all five administrations subsequent to Lincoln. Upon retirement at age seventy-five, he decided to found a brokerage business with his son Benjamin Franklin Edwards, who would leave the firm for a bank five years later. At that time, another son, George Lane Edwards, joined A.G. Edwards and Sons. George would succeed as president of the brokerage when Albert retired at age eighty. An Edwards family member served as president of A.G. Edwards and Sons continuously for four generations until Benjamin F. Edwards III retired in 2001.

His mind clear to the end, A. G. Edwards died at age eighty after an illness of a few days. His funeral took place at the family home in Kirkwood. His casket then proceeded by train to the city of St. Louis, where it would be borne to Bellefontaine Cemetery. In all of Edwards's many careers—as Indian fighter, wholesale merchant, general, financier, and broker—he brought a knife-sharp intelligence and an inflexible sense of honor and integrity to every task, fine qualities upon which to build a brokerage that would last more than a hundred years.

---

1. Stevens, *The Fourth City*, 975.

WILLIAM CARR LANE
1789–1863

DR. WILLIAM CARR LANE was elected St. Louis's first mayor in 1823, just four years after he had settled in the city. The handsome and gregarious Lane was so popular and his administration so effective that he was re-elected to lead his adopted city eight times.[1] He thus bears a double distinction—the only physician-mayor and the only mayor elected to so many terms. He laid the groundwork for a great urban center. A Liberty ship was named for him during World War II, and St. Louis honors his name with Carr Lane Middle School and Carr Lane Avenue.

Born and educated in Pennsylvania, Lane came west as an army surgeon. Although he had settled in St. Louis only the year before Missouri became a state in 1820, he soon leaped into politics, all the while maintaining a lucrative medical practice.[2] He served as aide-de-camp to the first elected governor, Alexander McNair,[3] in 1821 and as quartermaster general of the state in 1822. The next year, St. Louisans voted to incorporate as a city and elected Lane their first mayor. When he won with 122 votes to Auguste Chouteau's 70, this defeat of St. Louis's first citizen was considered a watershed designating the end of French dominance. Earning a salary of $300 a year, he served five consecutive terms, then took a hiatus from 1829 to 1838, after which he served another three terms. While executing his mayoral duties, he also was elected to and served in the Missouri State House of Representatives in 1826.

Not surprisingly, the physician-mayor put the highest importance on matters of public health. In his first inaugural address, Lane proposed a board of health. Unfortunately, the Board of Public Health did not heed his warnings about poor drainage or his later call for a waterworks. These measures would have prevented in large part the cholera epidemic of 1849, which would claim more than four thousand lives. He also brought health issues to the fore when he promoted the creation of a city wharf and advocated cleaning the riverfront of the "pestilential influence of decomposing animal and vegetable matter."[4] He also founded a city hospital.

Mayor Lane put a priority on the street improvements fundamental to making St. Louis a viable urban center. Main Street was paved. Although the city stretched along the river for less than three miles and to the west only three-quarters of a mile, the mud streets were aligned in a fashion that would promote the population's growth. Lane then changed the old French names of all the city streets to numbers and trees, like the names of Philadelphia's streets.

Identifying the most pressing needs for urban progress, Lane also called for public schools in his first inaugural address. In 1838, during a later Lane administration, the St. Louis public school system was established. At a time when the population stood at close to 36,000, he presented a vision for St. Louis as a major city.

1. *American Biography*, 583. He was elected to nine terms, according to Scharf, *History of St. Louis*, 655.

2. Darby, *Personal Recollections*, 215.

3. Ibid.

4. Scharf, *History of St. Louis*, 656.

EUGENE WILLIAM SLOAN
1893–1986

EUGENE WILLIAM SLOAN graduated from Smith Academy in St. Louis and Princeton University in New Jersey. During World War I, he served as a captain in the same Missouri artillery unit as Harry Truman, according to Bellefontaine superintendent Michael Tiemann.[1]

Sloan was known as "the Father of the Baby Bonds."[2] As assistant to the undersecretary of the U.S. Treasury Department from 1935 to 1941, he was the creator and first administrator of the U.S. savings bond program. During the Depression, bonds were sold to the public to fund the public debt. Sloan, who had been a banker before he entered the public sector, came up with the idea of selling these bonds as a savings vehicle for individuals. Tiemann said, "This gentleman was responsible for me giving up half my allowance when I was a little kid. Because I got a $1.00 allowance in the early 1950s, $.50 had to go to buy two $.025 savings stamps to buy savings bonds. When you got $18.75 worth of stamps, you put it in a book and then you could buy a bond valued at $25."[3]

During World War II, he became executive director of the War Savings Staff. In 1943, Treasury Secretary Henry J. Morgenthau Jr. appointed him deputy commissioner of the public debt. After the war, Sloan returned to private banking in Chicago. When he retired from banking, he moved to a ranch near Arcadia, Missouri, where he raised cattle. When Sloan died at age ninety-one in 1986, his body was brought to Bellefontaine Cemetery for burial.

---

1. Michael Tiemann, *Oral History*, tape XII, 191.
2. Obituary, White Funeral Home, Manuel Garcia files, Bellefontaine Cemetery.
3. Michael Tiemann, *Oral History*, tape VII, 115.

ERASTUS WELLS

1822–1893

ROLLA WELLS

1856–1944

ERASTUS WELLS showed enterprise, thrift, and aggressiveness from an early age. He was born the son of a farmer in Upstate New York in 1822.[1] After moving to St. Louis in 1843, he started the Case and Wells omnibus line. By 1850, the company operated six lines with four stables and one hundred employees.

In 1859, Erastus started the first street railway company west of the Mississippi. When he drove the first horsecar over the track at Fourth and Olive, his ceremonial role was met with great fanfare. He also established a narrow-gauge railroad that ran to Florissant, Missouri, convenient to his country estate. In addition, he served as president and vice president of two banks and as president of the Laclede Gas-Light Company.

In 1847, Erastus began a career of public service dedicated to progress and the best interests of his adopted hometown. Serving on the city council for fifteen years culminating in 1869, he started the metropolitan police system and pushed for improved sanitary measures. Moreover, as congressman, he was instrumental in having the first black man appointed to represent the United States as an ambassador to a foreign country.

At his death, Erastus left an estate of $1.5 million, "the largest ever administered upon in St. Louis County"[2] according to his obituary. Rolla Wells, one of Erastus's four children by his first wife, Isabella Henry Wells, served as executor.

Rolla proved a worthy successor to his father. In 1901, Rolla ran for and was elected mayor, serving eight years, a term that encompassed the

ERASTUS WELLS

ROLLA WELLS

Louisiana Purchase Exposition. He ran the city on a sound, business-like footing and emerged untarnished from the many investigations of government corruption in the era. He arranged for the construction of city hall in 1903 and for the paving of the city streets. His most impressive achievement was the clarification of the city's drinking supply. With the plan for the World's Fair grounds calling for fountains and cascades to spew as much as 20 million gallons of water a day, Rolla thought it imperative to turn the brown, muddy Missouri water crystalline. After investing $10,000 in a new waterworks, St. Louis's taps ran clear for the first time on March 21, 1904, just weeks before the fair commenced.

Rolla became a friend of President Woodrow Wilson when they were classmates at Princeton University. He served as treasurer of the National Democratic Committee from 1912 to 1916, starting during the first Wilson campaign. He also served as governor of the Federal Reserve Bank of St. Louis from its institution in 1914 until 1919. The suburb of Wellston is named after the Wells family country estate.

---

1. Sources differ as to his birthdate. His obituary calls it 1823 but his monument at Bellefontaine reads 1822.
2. *Erastus Wells Estate*, Manual Garcia files, Bellefontaine Cemetery.

PART EIGHT

TITANS OF
TRANSPORTATION

 Perhaps because its location generated much of its growth, the economy of St. Louis has depended in ample measure upon transportation. Settlers first reached the city or left it by flatboat and wagon, or even on foot. With the steamboat age, the big paddle wheelers and the romance of the river dominated the town. Although the river initially barred rail traffic from crossing, James Buchanan Eads's bridge spanning the Mississippi turned St. Louis into the country's most trafficked railroad terminus, second only to Chicago (see Part 1).

The first train west of the Mississippi left St. Louis for the outlying city of Cheltenham (today's Hill neighborhood) in December 1852, and tracks would reach Kirkwood by the following May. Early railroading in Missouri was fraught with corruption and disaster, yet the railway progressed. Samuel Fordyce was personally responsible for laying ten thousand miles of rail through the southwest United States (see Part 1). William Bixby created a company that owned all aspects of railroad car production, from mining the ore to milling the lumber to building the cars (see Part 1).

When passenger service died out in the second half of the twentieth century, heavy freight traffic maintained the city as a railroad hub. St. Louis's barge and trucking trade flourished due to the confluence of a Mississippi River port with both rail and interstate highway hubs. Missouri became the first state to construct interstate highways.[1] While the city's central location had advantages for aircraft manufacturers, it was the creative energy and vision of individual St. Louisans that created aviation headquarters there.

St. Louis's strategic location led French fur traders Pierre Laclede and Auguste Chouteau to found the city so that they would be able to trade with what would become the western United States. The implications of that location at the confluence of the Mississippi and Missouri rivers have dominated the city ever since.

---

1. When the Federal-Aid Highway Act was signed into law June 29, 1956, Missouri was the first state to award a construction contract on what was then known as Highway 66, now a part of Interstate 44, and the first to complete a section of the Interstate 70 at St. Charles, November 9, 1956. (*The Interstate Highway System of Missouri: Saving Lives, Time and Money,* http://www. tripnet.org/MissouriInterstateStudy060806.pdf.)

SAMUEL GATY

1811–1887

ALTHOUGH SAMUEL GATY was orphaned at seven and had only seven months of schooling, he made his way in the world by means of luck, pluck, and mechanical genius. He ran away from a farm at the age of eleven to be an apprentice at a foundry. After several false starts, he became the owner and director of St. Louis's largest foundry, which manufactured the first steamboat engine west of the Mississippi. Engaging in a variety of businesses, he rose to great wealth and became a stalwart of city government in St. Louis.

Samuel Gaty was born in Jefferson County, Kentucky, in 1811. The misfortunes of his childhood started with the untimely death of his mother when he was four and then of his father when he was seven. He was so alone in the world that he did not even learn his true name until he researched it as a grown man. Although his real name was Getty (his ancestors had founded Gettysburg, Pennsylvania), a misguided teacher taught him to spell it Gaty, and Gaty it remained. According to his obituary, he was "bound out to a farmer just before his father's death," but "he tired of that, and, running away, indentured himself to . . . machinists and founders"[1] in Louisville. He proved so talented and resourceful that he was named foreman of the foundry at the age of fourteen.

Hearing that St. Louis offered opportunity for the ambitious, Gaty headed west to start a foundry there with his life savings of $250. His plan failed, but luck entered Gaty's life in the form of a broken shaft on the steamboat *Jubilee*. Because no machine existed that could turn a shaft in the city, Gaty ingeniously solved the problem and manufactured the first steamboat shaft west of the Mississippi with a lathe and two cogwheels. Having earned a reputation for ingenuity, he established his own foundry in 1831.

Through the twenty-five years of his foundry's operation, Gaty had many partners, including Gerard B. Allen, an original board member of Bellefontaine Cemetery, and John McCune, a steamboat captain. The business grew until it occupied an entire block and employed two hundred men, quite a contrast from its humble beginnings as a small frame building with six employees.[2] Not only did this shop repair steamboats, but it built engines and whole boats as well, including the first engine and the first steamboat west of the Mississippi. According to cemetery gatekeeper Manuel Garcia, ""No other person contributed more in iron work for railroads and steamboat construction than [Samuel Gaty]."[3]

As his wealth increased, Gaty invested in other ventures. Luck struck again when he won $40,000 in the Havana lottery. He put his winnings into a steamboat, which he later sold. He also put money into railroads and became president of the western division of the Ohio and Mississippi Railroad, as well as the Hope Mining Company and the St. Louis Transfer Company.[4] His reputation only increased when an East St. Louis street was named for him.

Gaty was not only a business leader, but also, in a quiet and unassuming way, a civic leader. He served for ten years on the Board of Aldermen and the City Council, assisting in laying out streets and establishing waterworks. He was one of several to pledge his own funds to help St. Louis banks weather the financial crisis of 1857.

But steamboats were his true love, and Gaty would sit on his porch in his declining years and watch them pass on the Mississippi.[5] He rests eternally in one of Bellefontaine's more unusual lots. A circle of twenty-eight marble bollards (low rectangular posts) surrounds an obelisk topped by a shrouded urn. Each side of the obelisk bears an image of the seasons of nature. Two bollards topped with urns, one shrouded and the other uncovered (representing life and death, according to cemetery superintendent Michael Tiemann), flank the entrance to the surrounding circle.[6]Alternating with plain faces, thirteen of the remaining stones are carved with bas-relief images of the stages of human life. Unfortunately, the detail of the marble relief has worn away. The images that are left appear primitive; nevertheless, they have great charm. They reflect the life of Samuel Gaty, a dramatic cycle from poverty to wealth, from obscurity to prominence.

1. Obituary, *Globe Democrat,* Manuel Garcia files, Bellefontaine Cemetery, June 9 or 10, 1887.

2. Jacob N. Taylor and M. O. Crooks, *Sketch Book of Saint Louis* (St. Louis: G. Knapp, 1858), 214.

3. Manuel Garcia files, Bellefontaine Cemetery.

4. James V. Swift, "Up the Hill to Fame and Fortune: The Career of Samuel Gaty," *Missouri Historical Society Bulletin,* October 1972.

5. "From Show Place to Truck Place, 110-Year-Old North Side Mansion to Be Razed," *St. Louis Star-Times,* January 30, 1951.

6. Michael Tiemann, *Oral History,* tape XII, 184.

ALBERT BOND LAMBERT
1875–1946

MAJOR ALBERT BOND LAMBERT, the president of Lambert Pharmacal Company, is the man for whom St. Louis's Lambert Air Field was named. When Charles Lindbergh conceived of his 1927 flight across the Atlantic, Lambert was the first of eight St. Louisans of vision and courage that Lindbergh approached to back his dream. Lambert raised no questions about the dangers involved; he pledged $1,000 on the spot. Lindbergh called Lambert "among the most active leaders in Midwestern aviation."[1]

Lambert was born with a silver spoon in his mouth, and he used it to feed his city with good works. His father, Jordan W. Lambert, founded the Lambert Pharmacal Company in 1881 when Albert was six. Jordan bought the rights to an antiseptic developed by Joseph Lawrence and marketed it primarily to physicians. In 1876, Lawrence had watched Joseph Lister demonstrate carbolic acid's ability to prevent infection. Three years later, Lawrence came up with a milder antiseptic, which he named Listerine. Just eight years after he had started manufacturing and selling Listerine, Jordan died at age thirty-seven, in 1889, and his wife died four months afterward, leaving six orphans with Albert the oldest at age twelve. The company was held in trust for the young brood until 1896, when twenty-one-year-old Albert assumed the presidency.

By the time Albert Lambert retired at age fifty from Lambert Pharmacal in 1925, he had already begun a second and even more successful career in public service. His efforts ensured that St. Louis became a center for aviation. A great athlete—he won silver medals in golf in both the 1900 and 1904 Olympics—flying was his favorite sport. He first went aloft in a balloon while setting up the Parisian branch of Lambert Pharmacal. When he returned to the United States, he took lessons in 1909 in a heavier-than-air flying machine from one of its inventors, Orville Wright.

Thanks to Lambert, St. Louis hosted many balloon and airplane shows that promoted the commercial and military advantages of flying. At the first free aviation meet in America at St. Louis's Fairgrounds Park in 1910, President Theodore Roosevelt "showed his confidence in aviation by taking an airplane ride."[2] During this meet, the far-sighted Lambert showed the public that airplanes—then considered a slightly foolish way for daredevils to risk their lives—had great potential in warfare. He had aviators bomb painted canvas battleships with tomatoes. In 1913, he predicted the U.S. Navy's need for a strong aviation wing, and Secretary of the Navy Josephus Daniels requested Lambert form a naval air reserve.[3] When World War I broke out, he immediately enlisted in the army and earned the rank of major by training balloonists. He also established the Missouri Aeronautical Reserve Corps during the war.

For these reasons, as well as his role backing Lindbergh, St. Louis would be justified in honoring this father of flight by naming its airport after him. The present airfield owes its very existence to Lambert. Always farsighted, he realized the city need a bigger airfield than those available in the public parks. In 1920, he purchased 169 acres northwest of St. Louis and cleared, graded, and drained the land while building hangars. In 1927, when the city passed a bond issue, Lambert sold the city his airfield for $68,000, the 1920 price of the property alone, declining payment for appreciation of the land and throwing in his improvements for free. When the city needed an additional 300 acres, he magnanimously advanced the airport $230,000 for its immediate purchase and allowed the city to reimburse him at cost. According to James J. Horgan in *City of Flight*, because of Lambert's generosity, St. Louis paid $650 an acre, while Chicago had to spend $12,000 per acre for that city's airfield.[4] Upon his death, American Airlines adopted a resolution extending sympathy to his family and city, calling him, "a distinguished citizen of St. Louis and a pioneer in the development of aviation,"[5] who "conceived and fostered the development of Lambert Field, thereby contributing to aviation in St. Louis and in this nation."[6]

1. Charles Lindbergh, *The Spirit of St. Louis* (New York: Ballantine Books, 1953), 36.

2. "Maj. Lambert Gave City Start in Aviation," *St. Louis Globe-Democrat,* March 11, 1956.

3. "Maj. A. B. Lambert Dies in His Sleep; Pioneer St. Louis Aviation Backer," *St. Louis Post-Dispatch,* November 12, 1946.

4. James J. Horgan, *City of Flight* (St. Louis: Patrice Press, 1984), 13.

5. "Civic Leaders at Rites for Maj. Lambert," November 15, 1946, Michael Tiemann files, Bellefontaine Cemetery.

6. Ibid.

WILLIAM MASSIE
1831–1910

ALTHOUGH WILLIAM MASSIE was a legendary steamboat captain, he is best remembered for the bullet he took to his grave in Bellefontaine Cemetery. It was the bullet that killed Wild Bill Hickok, flying straight through Hickok's skull and lodging in Massie's wrist. Although the shooting took place on dry land, most of the other great moments in Massie's life happened on the water, where he had encounters with many of the West's most notorious characters and narrow escapes from such desperadoes as the James gang. He commanded salaries as high as $1,000 a day[1] at a time when a skilled laborer earned $4 daily.[2] He claimed, "No other man knows the Missouri River as I do."[3]

Massie was born alongside the Missouri River near Hermann, Missouri, in 1831. His parents came as pioneers with Daniel Boone and settled in the area in 1799. They witnessed the passage of the Lewis and Clark expedition,[4] and Indians killed Massie's uncle. Shortly after the first steamboat traveled up the Missouri in 1819, his father started a wood yard to provide fuel for the passing river traffic.

Massie made and lost several fortunes on the river.[5] It never fazed him because he knew he could always make more money with his great skill as a pilot. Unfortunately, he was a terrible poker player. Massie once lost in one sitting his entire $7,500 salary for a round trip between St. Louis and Fort Benton, Montana.[6]

It was during another poker game that Massie met the bullet that killed Wild Bill Hickok. Massie and Hickok were in the second day of a poker game in Deadwood, South Dakota. Massie sat in front of Hickok, and Hickok had his back to the door. The last words Hickok ever spoke were addressed to Massie, who was beating him at the game: "The old duffer—he broke me on the hand."[7] One shot killed Hickok instantly. It traveled through the back of his head, out his cheek, and into Massie's left wrist. Hickok fell off his stool with his cards still in hand. The cards he held—a pair of aces and a pair of eights with an unknown fifth card—have been known ever after as the dead man's hand.

Hickok was not the only historical character Massie knew. On many occasions Massie carried Buffalo Bill Cody on his boat to the Upper Missouri, and they became friends. In 1862, during the Civil War, guerillas attacked one of Massie's boats. The James gang along with the Younger Brothers and Quantrill's Raiders ran along the bank firing at his steamboat for two or three miles. More often it was Indians who fired at the boats. Massie's steamboat was ambushed by Sitting Bull's warriors in 1875 while he was carrying soldiers and preachers to the Indian territories. When the Mormons left Nauvoo, Illinois, Massie piloted the ship that took them to Council Bluffs, Iowa, on their way to Salt Lake City.[8]

Massie could read the ways of the river beyond charting the course of a boat. His words of 1909 seem prescient now in light of the 2005 flooding of New Orleans:

> I've seen the river before they "improved" it and afterward, and I say: Give me the river the way nature made it before them cadets from Boston [the Corps of Engineers] . . . begin foolin' with it. . . . Look at the delta! When the French held New Orleans it was within twelve miles of the gulf; now it's 120 miles. It's the levees that's done that; the mud that'd have spread out all over these lowlands and built them up if they had let it alone has been carried out into the gulf.[9]

Massie spent sixty-seven years on the river, starting as a cabin boy at age twelve[10] and becoming a pilot by eighteen. Although he owned many steamboats and served as captain of many more, it was as a pilot that he made his mark. He continued to pilot riverboats until four months before he died at the age of seventy-nine in January 1910, and he had plans at the time to get back on the river in the spring.

---

1. "Capt. W. R. Massie Dies," *St. Louis Post-Dispatch*, January 30, 1910.
2. Scott Derks, *The Value of a Dollar* (New York: Grey House, 2004), 10.

3. "Old Missouri River Pilot Makes Record from Kansas City," *St. Louis Post-Dispatch,* March 20, 1907, 18.

4. Paul W. Brown, "Old Day on the Missouri," *The Saturday Evening (Burlington, Iowa) Post*, April 1909.

5. "Mrs. Massie to Be Buried Here Today," *St. Louis Globe-Democrat,* August 26, 1924.

6. Dr. E. B. Trail, "William R. Massie, 'Mountain' Steamboat Pilot," *Bulletin of the South Dakota Historical Society*, July 1970, 3.

7. *They Called Him Wild Bill,* Manuel Garcia files, Bellefontaine Cemetery, 298.

8. Brown, "Old Day."

9. Ibid.

10. Eugene Stephens, *Genealogical Sketch of Captain William Rodney Massie,* Manuel Garcia files, Bellefontaine Cemetery, March 7, 1945.

PART NINE

ARTISTS
AND
ARCHITECTS

 The authors, painters, musicians, architects, and landscapers interred in Bellefontaine Cemetery only hint at the variety and richness of artists from St. Louis. They include the great poet Sara Teasdale, the novelist William S. Burroughs II, the architect William Eames, portrait painters, a history painter, a musician, and a founder of the Missouri Botanical Garden.

Burroughs and Teasdale predominate as literary figures significant to the country as a whole. Both were born and raised in St. Louis but left to live in New York City. Burroughs eventually migrated to Lawrence, Kansas, for the final years of his life. Despite the literary fame he achieved, he maintained, "All I ever wanted to be was sewer commissioner of St. Louis County."[1] He is famed for *Naked Lunch*, a witty, obscene novel that cast a long shadow over the succeeding generation of writers. Sara Teasdale was born to an upper-middle-class St. Louis family who spoiled and overprotected her. Winner of the first Pulitzer Prize in poetry, she wrote sensitive and strange poems that seem deceptively simple at first.

Artist Carl Wimar, patron Henry Taylor Blow (see Part 1), and portrait artists Manuel de Franca and Alban Jasper Conant, among others, founded the Western Academy of Art. The first arts organization west of the Mississippi, the academy had an art school, its own collection, and an annual exhibition. Wimar decorated the dome of St. Louis's Old Courthouse and left a legacy of paintings portraying the American Indian tribes of the Old West.

A German immigrant who added greatly to the beauty of the St. Louis area was George Engelmann. One of Engelmann's strengths as a botanist was his ability to render fine drawings of flowers and plants. Engelmann's interest in botany led him to collaborate with Henry Shaw on establishing the Missouri Botanical Garden.

In the nineteenth century, St. Louis, the third largest city in the United States by 1870,[2] expressed its civic pride in the quality of its public buildings. Likewise, the town's wealthy exhibited their success to the world in the form of mansions set apart from the hustle and bustle of the city. Aware of the city's phenomenal growth, architects moved to St. Louis to take advantage of the building explosion. Perhaps because Almerin Hotchkiss had laid out Bellefontaine Cemetery with the highest standards of design, many of the city's architects, engineers, and patrons chose it for their final resting place. Five architectural monuments that evoke St. Louis—the Arch, the Old Courthouse, Union Station, Eads Bridge, and the Wainwright Building—were either designed by an architect, commissioned by a patron, or envisioned by a city father buried in Bellefontaine. The chief architect and landscape architect of the 1904 World's Fair also lies in Bellefontaine, as do many who designed the city's finest residences.

Although French settlers founded the city in 1764, the earliest examples of French colonial architecture were all wiped out in the name of progress. The Great Fire of 1849 destroyed 440 buildings in fifteen blocks, most of the existing downtown, and inspired a boom in St. Louis architecture. As the gateway to the West, the center of the fur trade, a steamboat port, and a railroad hub, St. Louis drew the ambitious seeking to make their fortunes. The population increased almost five-hundred-fold between 1820 and 1890, as the Mississippi River town swelled from 10,000 to 450,000.

Building slowed after the turn of the twentieth century, but in 1923, St. Louis passed an $86 million bond, the largest for any city to that time, which resulted in Memorial Plaza. The resulting east-west parkway and its public buildings give the city orientation and breathing space. During the 1960s, the population of St. Louis County surpassed that of the city for the first time, and urban renewal produced many controversial housing projects as well as the Jefferson National Expansion Memorial and the Arch, the emblem of the city. Starting in the late twentieth century, the population again shifted with a migration from the suburbs back into the city. These urban pioneers have taken advantage of St. Louis's fine nineteenth century architecture to renovate homes and transform warehouses into lofts.

Five of St. Louis's major architectural monuments have strong ties to the cemetery. William Rumbold designed the dome of the Old Courthouse, which is now framed by Eero Saarinen's Gateway Arch. The Arch would not have existed without Luther Ely Smith (see Part 1). Smith envisioned turning the city's blighted riverfront into a park and shepherded the project to completion for the last eighteen years of his life. The top of the Arch affords a view of Eads Bridge, James Buchanan Eads's masterpiece that brought the railroad across the Mississippi to St. Louis (see Part 1). As the city became the second largest railroad hub in the nation, it required a station appropriate to its position. Theodore Link won the design competition for Union Station, which was completed in 1891. One year earlier Ellis Wainwright had hired Louis Sullivan to design the Wainwright Building, now known as the world's first skyscraper and considered an architectural masterpiece (see Part 2).

Wainwright also commissioned Sullivan to build a tomb for his bride and himself, and it is Bellefontaine's finest monument. Among many other remarkable markers are the Pierce tomb and the Hotchkiss Chapel by Eames and Young, the Busch tomb by Thomas Barnett, the Ames monument by Rumbold, the Brock mausoleum by George Ingham Barnett, and the A.D. Brown mausoleum by Isaac Taylor, the chief architect of the 1904 World's Fair.

When nineteenth-century world traveler Burton Holmes, who spent fifty years writing about far corners of the globe, visited St. Louis, he remarked, "St. Louis has more beautiful homes than any other city in the world."[3] It is very likely he was referring to the private places all developed with one exception by German engineer Julius Pitzman, who was influenced by the landscape design of Bellefontaine's Almerin Hotchkiss (see Part 12). Bellefontaine offers the opportunity to pay homage to these master builders who have given the city so much of its architectural character.

---

1. Harper Barnes, "William Burroughs Comes Home," *St. Louis Post-Dispatch*, n.d.

2. George McCue, *The Architecture of St. Louis* (St. Louis: City Art Museum, 1971), 8.

3. Burton Holmes quoted in Charles Savage, *Architecture of the Private Streets of St. Louis* (Columbia: University of Missouri Press, 1987), vii.

WILLIAM SEWARD BURROUGHS II was raised in a conventional St. Louis family. Always the picture of irony, he dressed in a gray suit and a fedora while making drugs and dissipation the purpose of his life. After accidentally murdering his second wife, he found his calling as a writer. His shockingly obscene novel *Naked Lunch*, considered a classic, made Burroughs the standard-bearer of the Beat generation and a cultural icon who was featured on the cover of the Beatles album *Sergeant Pepper's Lonely Hearts Club Band* and in his own Nike commercial.

Despite heroin addiction, heavy drinking, and a fascination with fire-arms, Burroughs died of a heart attack at the ripe old age of eighty-three. He is buried at Bellefontaine Cemetery in the same lot as his grandfather, William Seward Burroughs, who invented the adding machine. According to cemetery gatekeeper Manuel Garcia, Burroughs's burial was attended by "a Volkswagen bus load of hippies. They threw whatever they had in their pockets into the grave as a remembrance. The people at the burial asked two burly looking guys to go stand by the grave. They did, cross-ing their arms over their chests, holding guns."[1] Burroughs's publicist and son James Grauerholz, adopted when Burroughs was seventy-one and Grauerholz thirty-seven, arranged the burial. Grauerholz made plans for a monument for his father's grave, but they were not realized until August 5, 2007. On that day, a simple headstone and a bench were placed on the lot. Instead of flowers, Grauerholz brought a basket of heirloom tomatoes, Burroughs's favorite food.

Burroughs was born at 4664 Pershing Avenue, a Central West End mansion, and the family was attended by a maid, a nanny, a cook, and a gardener. They sold their stock in the Burroughs Adding Machine Com-pany (see Part 6) in 1929 for $200,000, a sum that enabled them to make it through the Depression. His parents, Mortimer and Laura Lee Burroughs, supported him throughout his life to the tune of $200 a month until *Naked Lunch* earned him an income. To the Beat generation, that was a fortune.

Because Burroughs's parents sent their two sons to John Burroughs High School (no relation), they built a house across the street on Price Road in the tony suburb of Ladue when Burroughs was twelve. Never feeling as if he fit in, he was sent to the Los Alamos Ranch School in New Mexico at age fifteen. He hated it, but he did enjoy the opportunity to become an expert marksman. He developed his first documented homosexual crush there, and he had his first drug overdose when he gave his visiting mother the slip and bought knockout drops at a drugstore. The U.S. government later bought the Los Alamos school and developed the atomic bomb there. "It seemed so right, somehow," said Burroughs.[2]

The writer-to-be did not find college at Harvard University any more favorable. He did not socialize with his peers. For graduation, his parents gave him his allowance and a trip to Europe. Spending a semester in medical school at the University of Vienna, he met Ilse Klapper, a German Jew fleeing the Nazis. Although he married her to save her from the Nazis by securing her passport into the United States, they never lived together.

Burroughs spent the next several years bouncing around between New York, St. Louis, and Chicago, after another brief stint at Harvard. He studied philosophy, worked as a delivery boy for his parents' gift shop, worked at an ad agency, took one job as a detective and another job—that he relished—as an exterminator. In Chicago, he met up with two John Burroughs School alumni, David Kammerer and Lucien Carr, who were to have a fateful impact upon his life. Carr was a student at the University of Chicago. Kammerer had been Carr's high school teacher and developed a fixation upon him. In 1943, when Carr transferred to Columbia University to get away from him, Kammerer followed, and Burroughs went along. Kammerer and Burroughs developed a bond.

In New York, Carr introduced Burroughs to Columbia classmates Jack Kerouac and Allen Ginsberg. The three of them became the literary lights of the Beat generation. They lived together, collaborated, and used each other as models for characters in their books. In Kerouac's classic *On the Road*, Bull Lee represents Burroughs. Although Ginsberg and Burroughs would become lovers for a time, Ginsberg and Kerouac introduced Burroughs to his second wife, Joan Vollmer. According to biographer Barry Miles, "It was his first and only serious relationship with a woman."[3]

Disaster struck on August 13, 1944, when Kammerer and Carr were out drinking. Jealous of Carr's girlfriend, Kammerer made a pass at Carr in New York's Riverside Park. Carr fought back, stabbing Kammerer to death with a Boy Scout knife. He panicked and rolled the body into the Hudson River. He ran to Burroughs and confessed. Burroughs urged Carr to get a lawyer and claim self-defense. Carr then spent two days drinking with Kerouac before he could summon the courage to confess to the police. Both Burroughs and Kerouac were arrested for failure to report a homicide. Burroughs's father flew to New York to bail out his son, but Kerouac's father refused to do so. Kerouac languished in prison until his girlfriend's parents posted his bond with the stipulation that they marry. Prejudice against homosexuality led to a light sentence for Carr—only two years in the penitentiary.

Around this time, Burroughs developed a morphine habit. Ginsberg, Kerouac, and Vollmer joined him in experimenting with narcotics. Vollmer became addicted to Benzedrine to the degree that she hallucinated and spent ten days in detox in a psychiatric hospital. At the same time, Burroughs had been remanded to the custody of his parents for possession of narcotics. He decided it was time to get out of New York before their fast-paced life killed them. An old friend from St. Louis had started a cotton and citrus farm in Texas. Burroughs sold the idea to his parents to bankroll him for a Texas cotton farm as well. Vollmer was pregnant. Burroughs farmed in his habitual suit and tie and soon planted marijuana among the cotton. On July 21, 1947, their son William S. Burroughs III was born addicted to speed. Vollmer bottle-fed him because her milk was laced with amphetamines.

After trouble with the police, Burroughs took his lawyer's advice and left the country in 1949 for Mexico and its lax drug laws. There, on September 6, 1951, his life changed forever. Burroughs and Vollmer had been drinking all day when they went to a friend's party to sell a handgun. Burroughs tells of what happened next: "I was very drunk. I suddenly said, 'It's time for our William Tell act. Put a glass on your head.'"[4] She put a glass of gin on her head; Burroughs aimed and missed the glass, shooting her through the temple and killing her instantly. He told the police that story as well as another version about dropping the gun and yet another about accidentally discharging it while showing someone how to load it. His Mexican lawyer got him out of jail in thirteen days, and Burroughs's son was sent to live with his parents.

Vollmer's death haunted him his whole life, but in a stroke of tragic irony it drove him to become a writer. That lifelong struggle bore fruit six years later in Tangier, Morocco, with what would become *Naked Lunch*. Kerouac came up with the title after he heard Ginsberg misread Burroughs's scrawl for "naked lust." Burroughs explains in the introduction to the 1990 edition: "The title means exactly what the words say: NAKED Lunch—a frozen moment when everyone sees what is on the end of every fork."[5] The free and easy life of Morocco released his creativity but sent him on a downward spiral into drug addiction. In 1956, he borrowed $500 from his parents to take a cure, the drug apomorphine, in London. When he returned, he wrote furiously. Kerouac and Ginsberg came to Morocco to type up the manuscript and organize it. Fed up with Tangier, Burroughs followed Ginsberg to Paris in 1958. There, the next year, Ginsberg sold the idea of *Naked Lunch* to the Olympia Press.

In 1962, a Boston bookseller was arrested on obscenity charges for selling *Naked Lunch*, and the case went to trial four years later. The Supreme Court of Massachusetts handed down a verdict that stated the novel was not obscene. Along with Ginsberg, Norman Mailer testified for the defense, calling it "a book of great beauty . . . Burroughs is the only American novelist living today who may conceivably be possessed by genius."[6] The poet Dame Edith Sitwell, however, termed it "psychological filth."[7]

Over the course of his lifetime, Burroughs was to publish some sixty-odd books, many of them unreadable due to techniques he invented known as the "cut-up" and the "fold-in."[8] These entailed cutting and reassembling the narrative or folding in bits of other literary works. His tales of drugs and depravity inspired punk and rock musicians with terms such as "Steely Dan" and "heavy metal"[9] taken from *Naked Lunch*. He also played bit parts in movies, most notably the junkie priest in the 1989 film *Drugstore Cowboy*. He even ended up a rich man, thanks to the publicity efforts of his adopted son and sometime lover, Grauerholz.

Burroughs's obscene books and debauched lifestyle took him far from Ladue, Missouri. He lived in Paris, New York, Mexico City, and Tangier yet returned to St. Louis again and again, perhaps seeking out the approval he never gained as a youth. Even though he did everything in his power to escape his roots, Burroughs specified that his remains come home to rest beside his ancestors in the Valley of the Mississippi.

---

1. Manuel Garcia, *Oral History*, tape III, 45.

2. Barry Miles, *William Burroughs, El Hombre Invisible* (New York: Hyperion, 1993), 28.

3. Ibid., 41.

4. Ibid., 53.

5. William Burroughs, *Naked Lunch* (New York: Castle Books, 1959), v.

6. William S. Burroughs Jr., James Grauerholz, and Barry Miles, *Naked Lunch: The Restored Text* (New York: Grove Press, 2001), iv.

7. Roger Kimball, "The Death of Decency," *Wall Street Journal*, August 8, 1997.

8. Richard Byrne, "William Burroughs (1914–1997)," *The Riverfront Times*, August 6, 1997.

9. Lorin Cuoco and William H. Gass, *Literary St. Louis: A Guide* (St. Louis: Missouri Historical Society, 1997), 184.

WILLIAM S. EAMES
1857–1915

A RENAISSANCE MAN, William Eames was an architect, art critic, painter, and student of literature, as well as a hunter and fisherman. He designed a plethora of prominent office buildings and residences in St. Louis and around the country. He was the first St. Louisan elected president of the American Institute of Architects,[1] serving two terms. According to architectural historian Charles Savage, the work of Eames and his partner Thomas Crane Young "earned distinction for bringing the architecture of St. Louis to a level comparable with the best in the nation."[2] And according to preservation historian Esley Hamilton, "Eames was one of the finest designers St. Louis ever produced."[3]

Born in 1857 in Clinton, Michigan, Eames moved to St. Louis at the age of six. Except for European sojourns, he lived in St. Louis until the penultimate months of his life. According to obituaries, he suffered a "nervous breakdown"[4] and sought rest in travel, living in Seattle for several months,[5] but returned to his hometown to die at age fifty-eight.

Eames's talent won early recognition. After earning his B.A. at Washington University in St. Louis, Eames completed his education studying European architecture on a Grand Tour. Upon returning to St. Louis that same year, Eames was appointed the city's deputy commissioner of public buildings, an important position for a young man. Among the buildings he designed in this capacity was the Red Water Tower, a designated city landmark still standing in Hyde Park.

Resigning from the city staff in 1885, Eames went into private practice with Thomas Young, a Wisconsin native who had studied at the Washington University School of Architecture. Among their first commissions was a house for the director of the St. Louis Museum of Fine Arts, Halsey Cooley Ives. This commission led to many more designs for mansions, including eight in the city's premier extant enclave, Westmoreland-Portland Place. Among the firm's residential commissions was an 1888 house on Lucas Place designed for Robert S. Brookings (see Part 1).

Brookings must have been well satisfied with his home, for six years later he and Samuel Cupples gave Eames & Young the firm's largest commission: the eighteen warehouses of Cupples Station. In its day Cupples Station was critical to the economic life of the city because the warehouses served almost all of the city's wholesale dealers.[6] In 1900, Cupples Station became a cornerstone of the Washington University endowment, for that year Brookings and Cupples donated the $3 million complex to the university.

Cupples Station provided St. Louis a uniquely efficient means of receiving and shipping goods. To build the complex, Eames & Young served not only as architects but also as "technologists, engineers and traffic expediters—specialties that today would be divided among teams of experts."[7] Located close to the Eads Bridge tunnel, tracks brought trains directly into the buildings, where they were unloaded and the goods were warehoused until sold and shipped out again. Eames & Young relied heavily on a new technology to lift heavy freight up to the upper floors: elevators, forty-five hydraulic and ten electric, that continued to function through the 1970s. An 1897 article in the *Architectural Review* said, "In all other cities, merchandise is carted twice, and often more times; in St. Louis it can be said it is not carted at all. Goods are billed to Cupples Station and they are shipped from the same spot."[8]

While some fell to the wrecking ball to make way for Busch Stadium, and others burned in 1965, ten Cupples Station buildings remain. They are massive red brick structures, plain and straightforward, yet well proportioned and handsome in an understated manner appropriate to their function. Their arches and the red brick used throughout unify the complex.

Eames & Young designed residences for many prominent St. Louisans, including David R. Francis, Christine and Benjamin Blair Graham, and two for Brookings. Westmoreland Place, Portland Place, and Washington Terrace pay tribute to their talents. They were also involved in the development of Westmoreland. The houses represent many different historical styles.

While Cupples Station represented technological excellence, there was an imaginative and aesthetic side to Eames's work as well. This aspect of his work can be seen in St. Louis in such landmarks as his mansions in the Central West End, the lion gates of University City, the Lammerts Building, the Ely Walker Building on Washington, and the Grand Avenue University Club Tower, as well as the Hotchkiss Chapel at Bellefontaine Cemetery. Today, Eames's body of work has made him known by architects if not by the general public. While his Cupples Station warehouses reveal straightforward, functional buildings, his mansions and commercial buildings are decorated with restrained sculptural detail. While his buildings exhibit different vocabularies of style, all have a massive presence among St. Louis's architectural treasures.

---

1. Charles Savage, *Architecture of the Private Streets of St. Louis* (Columbia: University of Missouri, 1987), 136. He served 1904–1905 and 1916–1917.
2. Ibid.

3. Esley Hamilton in Julius Hunter, *Westmoreland and Portland Places* (Columbia: University of Missouri Press, 1988), 186.

4. "Funeral of Eames Set for Tomorrow," *St. Louis Republic,* March 6, 1915.

5. "William S. Eames, 58, Dies after Long Illness," *St. Louis Globe-Democrat,* March 6, 1915.

6. Toni Flannery, "The Cupples Warehouse Block," *Missouri Historical Society Bulletin,* January 1972, 88.

7. Ibid.

8. Charles Jenkins, "Eames and Young," *Architectural Reviewer,* June 30, 1897, 67.

GEORGE ENGELMANN
1809–1884

THANKS TO GEORGE ENGELMANN'S efforts, the Missouri Botanical Garden is considered one of the best in the world in research and conservation.[1] Today his name endures in the Engelmann Professorship at Washington University in St. Louis, the Engelmann Woods near Labadie, Missouri, and the Engelmann spruce. His portrait bust can be seen at Shaw's Garden in the Strassenfest German Garden. Believing that climate influenced disease, Engelmann made accurate measurements of the temperature three times a day, noting wind, rain, and humidity. According to a 1984 article in the *St. Louis Post-Dispatch*, "The records of Dr. Engelmann are still referred to whenever studies are made of long-term weather patterns in St. Louis."[2]

George Engelmann was born in Frankfurt, Germany, the eldest of thirteen children. The artist would aid the scholar in him, for his voluminous writings on plants are illustrated with accurate drawings. He attended medical school because that was the best place at the time to pursue scientific studies. Student uprisings sent Engelmann from the University of Heidelberg to Berlin to Würzburg. Ironically, to receive his medical degree there in 1831, he wrote his final paper on plant monstrosities. Reading this, German poet and naturalist Johann Goethe praised his abilities as an observer of the natural world.[3] The next year, Engelmann studied in Paris, where he met up with other prominent naturalists such as Louis Agassiz. Engelmann said he "led a glorious life in scientific union"[4] with his friends there.

Nevertheless, when an opportunity beckoned him to America, the twenty-three-year-old Engelmann jumped at the chance to explore all the scientific richness there. In 1832, an uncle offered to pay his expenses to travel to the United States if Engelmann would invest his money there. The aspiring naturalist's first stop was a German community near Belleville, Illinois. He collected prairie plants and seeds and sent them back to Frankfurt, where they were eagerly received.

Still holding to his commitment to scientific research, Engelmann next moved to St. Louis to work as a physician in the winter of 1834–1835. Spring inspired explorations into the Arkansas frontier, where he collected botanical specimens and observed geological formations. Upon his return to the city in 1836, he set up his practice in earnest and within six months was elected to the Medical Society of Missouri. By 1840, he had become one of the busiest doctors in the city, successful enough to return to Frankfurt to marry his fiancee, Dorothea Horstmann, who had waited patiently for eight years. Engelmann was the first to use forceps for difficult obstetrical deliveries, a controversial practice at the time. The rest of his life, Engelmann would maintain a flourishing medical practice while pursuing his botanical and meteorological studies at night.

Engelmann became a mainstay of the St. Louis German community, even introducing the city to the German custom of the Christmas tree.[5] He helped publish the first German-language paper the *Anzieger* and another paper, *Das Westland*, to draw pioneers together and inform potential immigrants in the Old Country about St. Louis. He hoped to make the city a center of learning with his Academy of Science.

Although his writings fill sixty volumes, Engelmann's greatest legacy to the world stems from his collaboration with Henry Shaw. Shaw had come to St. Louis at the age of nineteen with little besides a set of cutlery, and he retired at thirty-nine a wealthy man. Following ten years of foreign travel, he returned to St. Louis determined to establish a botanical garden. Shaw sought guidance from the most eminent man in the field, Sir William Hooker of Kew Gardens, England, who advised him to consult with Engelmann. At first, Shaw and Engelmann had a somewhat uneasy relationship. Fearing Shaw would create just a pretty garden, Engelmann urged him to make his garden a center of research as well. Shaw sent him to Europe several times to buy books and specimens, which would become the nucleus of a great library and collection, today considered one of the world's top botanical libraries.[6] (Upon Engelmann's death, his only child, George Julius Engelmann, a renowned physician, donated his father's library and collections to the garden.) Engelmann even named the garden. Shaw would have given it a Latin moniker but took Engelmann's advice to put the name in simple English. Shaw offered Engelmann the first directorship of the garden, but Engelmann turned him down because he did not want to "live so far away from St. Louis"[7] (today the garden sits well within the city limits). Trusting no one else, Shaw then served as the director until his death. To honor his mentor, Shaw endowed a chair of botany at Washington University, calling it the Engelmann Chair.

Engelmann's devotion to scientific study brought about his death. While clearing a path through the snow to his meteorology instruments in February 1884, he fell, caught a cold, and died a few days later. More than fifty carriages followed his casket to Bellefontaine Cemetery, where it was laid to rest covered with "an immense mass of plants and greenery which Henry Shaw esteemed it his privilege to supply for the occasion."[8]

---

1. "Plant Science," Missouri Botanical Garden, www.mobot.org/plantscience; "St. Louis," Frommer's, www.frommers.com/destinations/stlouis.

2. John J. Archibald, "The Godfather of the Garden," *St. Louis Post-Dispatch*, August 20, 1984.

3. Michael Long, "George Engelmann and the Lure of Frontier Science," *Missouri Historical Review*, April 1995, 255.

4. Ibid., 253.

5. Dorothy J. Caldwell, "Christmas in Early Missouri," *Missouri Historical Review*, January 1971, 127.

6. Library, Missouri Botanical Garden, www.mobot.org/MOBOT/molib.

7. Edgar Anderson, *Henry Shaw: A Pictorial Biography* (St. Louis: Missouri Botanical Garden, 1977), 9.

8. "The Engelmann Interment," Manuel Garcia files, Bellefontaine Cemetery.

THEODORE LINK
1850–1923

UNTIL EERO SAARINEN'S Gateway Arch was completed in 1965, Theodore Link's Union Station had symbolized the city of St. Louis. Opened in 1894, the railroad station Link designed was commensurate with the city fathers' vision for St. Louis. When the Eads Bridge connected St. Louis to the whole eastern United States in 1874, the city stood poised to become a great railroad center, but its old railway station could serve a mere fourteen passenger trains a day.[1] When Union Station welcomed its first travelers, it was the largest railroad station in the world.[2] By the 1940s, Union Station handled 100,000 passengers a day on 290 trains.[3] The 1899 *Encyclopedia of the History of St. Louis* calls it "the pride of the city, and, in many respects, the finest railway station in the world, a proud monument to [Link's] artistic skill."[4] Today St. Louis remains dotted with Link's monumental workplaces, churches, and residences in architectural styles so eclectic they hardly seem the work of the same hand.

Born near Heidelberg, Germany, in 1850, Link studied engineering and architecture in Germany, London, and Paris all before he was twenty, for at that age he immigrated to America in search of his fortune. After practicing in several cities, he settled in St. Louis in 1883 and was celebrated as a top architect throughout his forty-year career in the city. Today he is honored not only as the architect of Union Station, a National Historic Monument, but also by the Theodore Link Historic District, consisting of three mansions on Delmar Boulevard in University City, each a completely different style. Despite all of the architectural flourishes he employed, the Link monument in Bellefontaine Cemetery is plain and forthright, ornamented only by the family name in block letters.

Railroads brought Link to St. Louis in the first place. Three years after he arrived in the United States, he came to the city as a draftsman for the bridges and building department of the Atlantic and Pacific Railroad Company. A year later, in 1874, he left the railroad to draw plans for the new Forest Park. The park's developer, Julius Pitzman, soon recognized the architect's talent and recommended he be promoted to superintendent of parks, a post he held from 1876 to 1877. He prospered in St. Louis and called it home for the rest of his life except for a brief sojourn back east from 1877 to 1883.

While Link designed over a hundred buildings in and around St. Louis, the competition for the new Union Station made him a superstar. In 1891, the city's Terminal Railroad Association (TRA), an association of six railroads, invited ten architectural firms around the country to compete. The contest Link won called for a modern, utilitarian building with special attention to "convenience . . . lighting, heat, ventilation and drainage . . . water closets, lavatories, elevators."[5] Yet the building Link gave the TRA looks like a fantasy castle from the Middle Ages. It still stands out like Disneyland on Market Street. Made of rusticated stone, Union

Station sports a clock tower and turrets, arched doorways, and gables. Ironically, in 1891, this evocation of medieval European architecture was the most modern style, known as Richardsonian Romanesque after the Boston architect H. H. Richardson.[6] It represents the standards of the age, but inside the medieval castle everything was also up to date.

Inspired by the walled city of Carcassonne, France, Link wanted Union Station to express the idea that "in this day the railway station is as much the means of entrance and exit to a city as was the bastioned gate of medieval times."[7] The overwhelming size of the Great Hall showcases a wealth of decorative detail in green and gilt, marble, and stained glass. Remarkable among these is an allegorical stained glass window designed by the architect himself. It represents three maidens named San Francisco, St. Louis, and New York, who tell all travelers that the rail has connected the country coast to coast. The whole room is ablaze in electric lighting, a new technology at the time it was built.

While the space on the inside of the station is simple and easy to navigate, the building's exterior appears complex. The "head house" of Union Station is two blocks, or 781 feet, long but relatively shallow at 80 feet wide. Link made artful use of setbacks to give the impression of great depth and variety to the facade. The turrets, for example, look massive but they project only eighteen feet in front of the building.

A crowd of twenty thousand turned out September 1, 1894, to dedicate the station and to honor Link and Dr. William Taussig, president of the Terminal Railroad Association. Union Station captured the imagination of the entire country and continued to hold it even eighty years after its dedication, when few travelers used the rundown station. At that time, the *Baltimore Sun* compared it to the Parthenon, saying "Air pollution threatens the Parthenon, and a paucity of railroad trains threatens Union Station in St. Louis, the Western Hemisphere's only comparable structure."[8] Indeed, it proved too good a building to die under the wrecking ball. In 1985, Oppenheimer Properties and the Rouse Corporation rescued it from oblivion with a $135 million renovation that turned it into the hotel/shopping/entertainment center it is today. When Oppenheimer bought the property for $5 million, it paid $1.5 million less than the station cost to build.

Though several of Link's buildings, like Union Station, have been put to uses other than those for which they were intended, and some, such as Barnes Hospital, have changed so much that Link's design is no longer recognizable, others endure. The International Shoe Company building (1910), a tribute to Sullivan's Wainwright Building, has been imaginatively adapted into the City Museum. The three homes of the Link Historic District, on the other hand, have been refurbished and are being lived in as their designer intended. Books can still be checked out at Link's Barr Branch Library, and worship is still conducted at Second Presbyterian Church, Grace Methodist Church, and St. John's United Methodist Church.

The dapper German architect immersed himself so totally in styles of different periods and countries that his own characteristic style vanishes into the details of his buildings. Link once said he was seeking "the promise of immortality,"[9] and Union Station fulfilled that promise.

---

1. M. Patricia Holmes, "The St. Louis Union Station," *Missouri Historical Society Bulletin*, 1971, 251.

2. Sue Ann Wood, "Union Station Steams into Its Second Century," *St. Louis Post-Dispatch Magazine*, May 22, 1994, 10.

3. John McGuire, "A Monument to Its Own Past," *St. Louis Post-Dispatch*, August 29, 1985, 6F.

4. Hyde and Conard, *Encyclopedia of St. Louis*.

5, Frank Peters, "Design: In Spite of Interior Overhaul, Architecture Endures as Art," *St. Louis Post-Dispatch*, August 29, 1985, 6F.

6. When Richardson died in 1886 at age forty-seven, he passed his firm to three associates. One of these, George Shepley, was from St. Louis and had married Richardson's daughter Julia. The firm is today called Shepley, Rutan and Coolidge (Bryan, *Missouri's Contribution to Architecture*).

7. Hyde and Conard, *Encyclopedia of St. Louis*, 2334.

8. McGuire, *Monument*.

9. Candace O'Connor, "Theodore Link, Beyond Union Station," *St. Louis Post-Dispatch Sunday Magazine*, July 13, 1986, 15.

JULIUS PITZMAN
1837–1923

JULIUS PITZMAN, surveyor and engineer, refined the concept of the private place—a residential street that is owned and maintained by the homeowners rather than the city—in America. The grace and privacy of St. Louis's forty such neighborhoods were copied nationally,[1] especially their central green parkways, cul-de-sacs and massive entrance gates as well as their restrictive covenants. While he did not design the houses, he wrote deed restrictions for the neighborhoods that would set an elite tone for St. Louis. He was an advocate for integrating nature and beauty as well as a quiet pace to life within the city, a goal he further served as engineer for Forest Park.

Coming to this country from Germany at seventeen in 1854, Pitzman followed his brother-in-law Charles E. Solomon to St. Louis. In 1856, when Solomon, a former engineer in the Prussian army, was elected St. Louis county surveyor (a position serving both city and county),[2] Solomon must have had great faith in the abilities of his nineteen-year-old brother-in-law, for he put Pitzman in charge of the surveyor's office, superintending drafting and calculations. Four years later when Solomon joined the Union army, Pitzman became acting county surveyor.

A lifelong patriot and staunch Republican, three months later Pitzman considered it his duty to support the Union as well. Rising to major, he served Generals William T. Sherman and Ulysses S. Grant as a topographical engineer, making detailed military maps, four hundred square miles at a time. During General Sterling Price's assault on Missouri (see Part 1), he supervised the building of defensive fortifications until the Confederate threat passed.

Elected county surveyor in 1863, the precise Pitzman, true to his Prussian origins, found many original government surveys inaccurate.

"Finding no map in existence that showed the farms and roads of St. Louis County [and city], Pitzman sent out surveying parties at his own expense. . . . The outcome was the map he published in 1868, which is unquestionably one of the most accurate and complete maps ever produced by private enterprise."[3] Though it cost him $7,000 (approximately $766,000 in 2006 dollars), the survey was well worth the cash outlay, for it made Pitzman's reputation.

All the while Pitzman served in the army and held public office, he carried on a private business, Pitzman's Company of Surveyors and Engineers, founded in 1859. Though he was only twenty-two, he soon built up a lucrative practice. The fact that Pitzman's Company still flourishes is due in large part to its founder.[4] Drawing upon his experience with European private places, Pitzman began developing private places in St. Louis after the Civil War and refined the concept to the extent that the Pitzman private places became a model for residential development for the whole United States.[5] The one St. Louis precedent, Lucas Place, had been laid out by George Ingham Barnett in 1851[6] (see Part 1) as a private street owned and maintained by the homeowners, but it had neither common green space nor gates and was not a cul-de-sac (a security feature because this type of street did not allow through traffic). These innovations would characterize the private places Pitzman developed. Architectural historian Charles Savage believes Pitzman may have been influenced by the "park-like setting"[7] of Bellefontaine Cemetery when he incorporated parkways in his plats. Pitzman's planning went far beyond setting the boundaries of lots. The deed restrictions he wrote would provide covenants for self-governance, setting standards of beauty and utility. In many cases, he served as the only non-resident trustee of the homeowners' associations[8] to ensure his high standards were met.

The forty private places Pitzman platted mark St. Louis with residential beauty. The first was Benton Place off Lafayette Square, developed in 1866 for former postmaster general Montgomery Blair, brother of Union general and Missouri politician Frank Blair. Four years later Pitzman developed Vandeventer Place, which reigned as the most exclusive address in St. Louis until the turn of the century, meeting its demise to the wrecking ball in 1947. He laid out Vandeventer Place with gates at either end, one of which was always locked to prevent through traffic. All homes faced a parkway. All lots were the same size, and houses were set back a consistent thirty feet from the street, giving a certain uniformity and measured pace. Houses had to cost a minimum of $10,000 and the eighty-six residents had to each contribute 1/86th of every common expense.[9] The Vandeventer Place covenants set regulations so strict as to require steps to be scrubbed twice a week and every window to have three layers of lace curtains.[10] Learning from his mistakes at Vandeventer Place—no more step or curtain requirements—Pitzman put his efforts in 1887 to Westmoreland and Portland Places, called "America's premier private places" by author Julius Hunter.[11] His last private place was the 1905 enclave of Parkview Place.

To his private places Pitzman brought a love of landscape that came to fruition in the plans for Forest Park. In the spring of 1874, Pitzman took a trip to Europe to study the finest parks and leading landscape architecture.[12] Upon his return, he joined Hiram Leffingwell in successfully lobbying the state legislature to acquire a great park for St. Louis. The legislature decried the fact that the terrain was so rugged that it would require millions of dollars to improve. "This was Pitzman's opportunity. . . . he showed that the broken and rugged character of the ground was just what was required; that at Forest Park, nature herself had already performed the greater part of the heavy work"[13] Pitzman was appointed chief engineer, working until 1876 with landscape architect Max Kern and architect Theodore Link to lay out the park much as it looks today.

The many private places in St. Louis pay tribute to the surveyor-engineer's sense of pace and gracious lifestyle. Pitzman's life's work also survives to this day in Forest Park and the Pitzman Company. He left the city a legacy of serenity, security, and beauty.

---

1. George McCue, "Private Places: Stately Heritage of Old St. Louis," *St. Louis Post-Dispatch*, December 6, 1987.

2. Solomon defeated Ulysses S. Grant in the election. Ironically, Grant would later be Pitzman's commander.

3. Hyde and Conard, *Encyclopedia of St. Louis*, 1740.

4. Julius Hunter, *Kingsbury Place: The First 200 Years* (St. Louis: Mosby, 1982), 14.

5. Coyle, *Portrait of a River City*, 90.

6. Savage, *Architecture of the Private Places*, 7.

7. Ibid., 10.

8. Ibid.

9. Ibid., 22.

10. Julius Hunter, *Westmoreland and Portland Places* (Columbia: University of Missouri, 1988), 22.

11. Ibid, title page.

12. Hyde and Conard, *Encyclopedia of St. Louis,* 1741.

13. Ibid.

WILLIAM RUMBOLD
1824–1867

ARCHITECT WILLIAM RUMBOLD designed the Old Courthouse dome that was erected as a symbol of the city's power and devotion to justice. Today it stands as a landmark on the St. Louis riverfront within the imposing frame of Eero Saarinen's Gateway Arch.[1]

Born in Scotland in 1824, Rumbold first settled in Cincinnati when he immigrated to this country. Eager to advance himself, Rumbold recognized opportunity in St. Louis's Great Fire of 1849. In the hopes of being chosen to participate in the rebuilding that followed the devastation of downtown, he moved his family to the city in 1851. Within three years he had established himself as one of the city's top architects.[2]

It is most likely that Rumbold received his architectural training in his native land.[3] Certainly his designs reflect a familiarity with the classical vocabulary of architecture, and with such buildings as St. Peter's in Rome and St. Paul's in London. He won his first significant commission in a competition in 1854. As a result, his Tudor design became the St. Louis Public High School at Fifteenth and Olive streets, a building distinguished as the first public high school west of the Mississippi. The handsome building with its five towers made a big impression and set the style for so much St. Louis school architecture.

In 1859, high regard for the high school and victory in another design competition earned Rumbold the position that gave him the opportunity to realize his ambitions. He was appointed county architect when the St. Louis County Court, the three-man administrative board that ran St. Louis,[4] sought an architect to carry out its ambitious plans. First on the agenda was the St. Louis County Courthouse (now known as the Old Courthouse), which had been under construction on and off since 1826 under the direction of a series of architects. Just a few days after becoming county architect, Rumbold denounced the existing dome saying, "He would resign his office rather than continue to work on this terrible dead-fall . . . [S]omeday this dome will crash in and slide into the rotunda like a sheathed telescope."[5] Thanks to the support of the county commission, Rumbold almost immediately started to work designing a dome so innovative that he patented it in 1862. Using a cast-iron skeleton that was both light and strong, Rumbold's dome was constructed simultaneously with the U.S. Capitol Building.

Aside from its innovations, the greatness of the green copper dome resides in the beauty of its proportions and the impression it gives, inside and out, of both solidity and a soaring spirit. Rather than a hemisphere (based upon a concentric circle), which would have seemed too low and squat atop the massive courthouse building, the sides of Rumbold's dome represent circles with two different centers, conceived in a similar manner as a pointed High Gothic arch. A lantern topped by a flagpole covers the point where the curves meet. Inspired by Michelangelo's Baroque dome of St. Peter's in Rome and Sir Christopher Wren's St. Paul's Cathedral in London, the St. Louis Courthouse dome is also set on a drum that exalts it even higher over the building it crowns.

Inside, Rumbold dramatically accentuates the height of the dome's ceiling using a trick inspired by vanishing point perspective. Four rows of balconies rise to encircle the 190-foot rotunda from the floor to the eye of the dome. On each floor, the balcony railing is shorter than the railing on the floor below, increasing the effect of foreshortening to make the distance from floor to ceiling seem greater. In this series of balconies, Rumbold reveals his classical training, for the columns on each floor use a different order, rising from the simplest, Doric, to the more elaborate Ionic, to the most complex, Corinthian. Rumbold hired the city's finest painter, Carl Wimar, to paint frescoes inside the ribs on the dome's ceiling and in the lunettes upon which it rests (see page 315). Designing these along with the architect, Wimar raced to complete them during his last bout with consumption but succumbed to the disease before they were finished. Unfortunately, much of his work has since been painted over.

Although the construction of the dome added $160,000 to the total $1 million (as much as $150 million in 2006 dollars) cost for the Courthouse when it was completed in 1862, the county commission felt Rumbold's work was not extravagant, but appropriate for the growing city. Along with the Arch it is an enduring symbol of St. Louis.

Rumbold, however, considered the Arsenal Street Mental Asylum his best work.[6] It was his last commission, and he did not live to see completed. During the Civil War, Dr. William Taussig of the county court gathered up homeless mental patients after Confederate marauder "Bloody Bill" Anderson burned the Fulton Mental Asylum, releasing its inmates. After Taussig brought them to St. Louis by train, a judge petitioned the county court to build a new asylum because the city lacked a good public institution to serve this population during a time when "the deprivations of war had increased the ranks of the mentally ill in this area."[7] Rumbold came up with a plan "to create a monument to the glory of the county court, of himself, and of those individuals which it would serve."[8] The resulting Arsenal Street Mental Asylum still stands as the St. Louis Psychiatric Rehabilitation Center. Following the simple, rectilinear lines of the Italianate style, it is made of red brick with white limestone trim and a heavy, carved, white cornice. The small dome perched atop the main building has elliptical sides like the Courthouse dome, but its red and white drum seems relatively tall and thin, and its cupola has a jaunty outline. To protect patients from fire, Rumbold located the facilities for cooking, laundry, and heating in a separate service building. This he joined to the main building with an innovative underground delivery system. By the time the asylum was completed in 1869, it cost $850,000 (about $93 million in 2006 dollars) and was "the most expensive mental institution ever erected in this county up to this time,"[9] a tribute to the progressive attitude of the county court.

Unfortunately, Rumbold died two years before the realization of his final project. By the time he died suddenly at age forty-three in 1869, he had risen to such prominence that the "grief-stricken county court adjourned their session on the day of his burial and attended Rumbold's funeral procession to Bellefontaine Cemetery as a group."[10] There he rests beneath a monument of his own design, a marble obelisk of striking proportions, decorated with an upside down torch in low relief.

1. Today both the Arch and the Old Courthouse belong to the National Park Service's Jefferson National Expansion Memorial. The Old Courthouse is as renowned for its architecture as for the Dred Scott freedom suit that was tried there in 1847 and 1850.

2. David J. Simmons, "William Rumbold," *Society of Architectural Historians Missouri Valley Chapter Newsletter* VI, no. 1B (Spring 2000).

3. Ibid.

4. St. Louis City did not separate from St. Louis County until 1876.

5. *St. Louis Evening News,* October 7, 1859.

6. Simmons, *William Rumbold.*

7. Ibid., winter 2000.

8. Ibid.

9. Simmons, *William Rumbold,* winter 2000.

10. Ibid.

SARA TEASDALE
1884–1933

PAMPERED AND COSSETED, the late-life child of wealthy, adoring parents, Sara Teasdale achieved prominence as a poet. Shy and frequently ill, she preferred to remain within the confines of her own apartments, enjoying only the company of a few intimate friends, most of them poets and artists. Although her life was largely uneventful, she conquered literary circles of New York and London and won the coveted Columbia University Prize, the forerunner of the Pulitzer Prize in poetry.

Sara Teasdale was born in 1884. She spent much of her life as an invalid and did not enter school until she was nine. As an adolescent, Teasdale attended Hosmer Hall. The year after graduation, she joined a group of young women who called themselves "the Potters." A classmate from Hosmer Hall and girls from Visitation Academy and Central High School came together to publish a monthly magazine called *The Potter's Wheel*. Each member contributed a piece of writing, a photograph, or a drawing that they bound together by hand.

The Potter's Wheel came to the attention of William Marion Reedy, the St. Louis publisher of the world-renowned magazine *The Mirror*. (Reedy was the first to publish not only Teasdale but also Zoe Akins, Stephen Crane, Vachel Lindsay, Amy Lowell, and Ezra Pound.) In 1907, Reedy published Teasdale's blank verse poem "Guenevere," which was widely reprinted. Her biographer said, "This was followed by other poems, and her reputation as a poet of achievement and promise began to be established."[1]

Teasdale's parents paid to have her first book of poetry printed in 1907, but all of her books thereafter were published commercially and successfully. Teasdale dwelt upon the theme of death in her poetry. "I Shall Not Care" from 1911 imagines herself as looking up from her grave. Probably the best of her books were *Love Songs* (1917) and *Flame and Shadow* (1920). *Strange Victory* was published posthumously. Her poetry was the central fact of her life, and everything else was merely subservient to it.

The editor and a staff member of *Poetry* magazine, a Chicago publication, introduced her to the two loves of her life, one of whom she would marry. Editor Harriet Monroe introduced her to poet Vachel Lindsay in 1913. The two had already been corresponding, and he soon wrote her love letters both rapturous and poetic. That same year, Monroe's assistant, Eunice Tietjens, brought Ernst Filsinger and Teasdale together when she was visiting St. Louis. Filsinger was a reserved and handsome businessman who had loved Teasdale from afar and memorized all of her poems. Soon the two suitors, almost the antithesis of each other, were competing for her affections. One week in May 1914, Teasdale invited Lindsay to visit her at a farm outside St. Louis from Wednesday to Friday and then had Filsinger out for the weekend, perhaps to make a direct comparison. Teasdale settled on Filsinger.

In 1914, Teasdale and Filsinger were married and settled in St. Louis—much to her dismay, for she had set her sights on New York. Unfortunately, his shoe business failed. They lived their entire married life in hotels because she would not set up housekeeping. While they seemed happy to their friends, she confided to John Hall Wheelock, a poet she had once loved, that their honeymoon had been "a fiasco."[2]

The couple moved to New York in 1916, where Filsinger took a new position. His job required extensive travel in Europe, Africa, and South America, and Teasdale could not accompany him due to her ill health. She complained frequently that he worked too hard. Even in New York, he was out many nights studying foreign languages or giving talks on foreign trade, a subject on which he had published two books.

After much thought, Teasdale decided to divorce Filsinger, to his surprise. Waiting until 1929 when he was en route to Cape Town, South Africa, she secretly left New York with a nurse for Reno, Nevada. There she wrote him of the divorce. He was horrified and cabled her to stop the proceedings, but she persevered and refused to see him again, except for a few brief visits.

Writing only a few poems in her remaining years, Teasdale was depressed and reclusive. Her main social contact was a young lady, Margaret Conklin, whom Teasdale had met after Conklin had written her a fan letter. Teasdale came to think of Conklin as a daughter or as her own lost youth. Conklin not only provided her companionship but also helped with all the details of her life, eventually becoming her literary executor.

In 1931, Teasdale traveled to England to work on a new type of project, a biography of Christina Rosetti, the poet whose work she had first loved as a child. She made two trips to England to work on the book and returned to New York in 1933 despondent and with pneumonia. Poet Louis Untermeyer, who was a friend of both Teasdale and her first love Lindsay, attributes her despair in part to Lindsay's suicide a year and a half earlier.[3] Lonely, she took her life with an overdose of sleeping pills. Found dead in her bath at age forty-eight, perhaps Teasdale had been expecting to be rescued but, tragically, her nurse checked on her later than usual. The bath water was still warm.

Although she had made explicit her desire to have her ashes cast over the sea "so that there may be neither trace nor remembrance,"[4] her older sister Mamie would not comply with the request. Following a memorial service in Manhattan, Teasdale's ashes were brought back to Bellefontaine Cemetery and covered with a headstone that reads "Sara Teasdale Filsinger"; Mamie included the name of the husband Sara had divorced. Ernst Filsinger had his ashes laid to rest in his family plot a mere thirty yards away. Perhaps her prophetic imagining of her own death in her poem "I Shall Not Care" had come true, for she predicted "I shall be more silent and cold-hearted than you are now."[5]

---

1. Margaret Haley Carpenter, *Sara Teasdale: A Biography* (New York: Schulte, 1960), 90.

2. William Drake, *Poems of Sara Teasdale: Mirror of the Heart* (New York: MacMillan, 1984), XXX.

3. Louis Untermeyer, *A Treasury of Great Poems* (New York: Simon and Schuster, 1964), 1118.

4. William Drake, *Sara Teasdale, Woman & Poet* (San Francisco: Harper and Row, 1979), 294.

5. Sara Teasdale quoted in Drake, *Poems of Sara Teasdale*, 5.

CARL WIMAR

1828–1862

BORN IN GERMANY, Carl Wimar came to St. Louis as a teenager and showed early promise as an artist. Living with his family on the outskirts of the city, he became acquainted with Indians coming to St. Louis to trade. Knowing that their style of life was threatened by the encroachment of civilization, at an early age he determined to portray their vanishing ways. He clearly presented a romantic attitude in his own life as well. In a photograph by Enoch Long, Wimar poses in the leather leggings worn by Indians and mountain men alike and jauntily clasps a feathered Tyrolean hat, a symbol of his native land.[1] He portrays himself as a hunter—not an artist—by brandishing a long rifle. With his long black hair, high cheekbones, and tanned skin, Wimar often was taken for one of the Indians he idealized.

He was born in 1828 in Siegburg, Germany, a small town near Bonn. His father died soon afterward and his mother remarried. His stepfather, Mathias Becker, immigrated to St. Louis in 1839 and sent for his wife and children four years later when he had established himself as a tavern keeper. The family lived near what is today the site of the St. Louis Public Library but was then the outer edge of the city near Indian camping grounds. The fifteen-year-old Carl already showed precocious talent and was soon apprenticed to sign painter and muralist Leon Pomarede, who had decorated the Old Cathedral.

Legend has it that the family took in an ailing Polish man who recognized Carl's talent. Years later, in 1852, Carl was surprised to receive an inheritance from the Pole that enabled him to travel to Düsseldorf to attend art school. He studied under Emanuel Leutze, the much-admired artist of *Washington Crossing the Delaware*. While engaged in European studies, he continued to paint the reality he had known on the banks of the Mississippi and Missouri, even sending home for Indian buckskins and beadwork to ensure accuracy. Works from the Düsseldorf years include *The Abduction of Daniel Boone's Daughter by the Indians*, 1855, a Western theme whose composition is based upon a classic of the European avant-garde style of its time, *The Raft of the Medusa*, 1819, by Theodore Géricault. Another of his paintings done in Germany, the dramatic *Attack on the Emigrant Train*, 1856, was the earliest depiction of pioneers fighting to fend off an Indian attack on their wagon train. It is the prototype for this image in Western movies. A third painting from this period hangs today in the Saint Louis Art Museum. Titled *The Captive Charger*, 1854, it shows the same clash of civilizations as the previous work, but this time the Indians have triumphed. A band of four Indians warily leads a riderless horse that bears a U.S. Calvary saddle.

Wimar returned to St. Louis in 1856. Because he did not achieve great success as a portrait painter, he was able to devote himself to his ambition of recording the passing ways of the West. To this end, he attempted but failed to get a government commission to visit the western territories. Though his means were limited, in 1858 he managed to scrape up enough to book passage on a six-month fur trading expedition up the Missouri and the Yellowstone rivers. Again in 1859, he spent two months traveling up the Missouri on the first steamboat to reach the headwaters. In his meticulous fashion, he sketched the landscapes and its people in pencil, pastel, and oil. He took along a primitive camera that took ambrotypes, but most of these have been lost. He brought back so many examples of Indian clothing and weapons that his studio would become a kind of museum.

When he returned to St. Louis, he used his sketches as the basis for creating monumental paintings. His meticulous research created images of great accuracy that were widely respected by ethnologists. *Buffalo Hunt* was commissioned by Henry Taylor Blow for his library. Blow, a civic leader who underwrote Dred Scott's lawsuit (see Part 1), founded the Western Academy of Art in 1860. Wimar was among the nine other founding members along with engineer James Buchanan Eads and painters Ferdinand Boyle and Alban Jasper Conant. The Prince of Wales and the British ambassador to the United States, Lord Lyons, attended the opening exhibit, and Lyons commissioned a copy of *Buffalo Hunt*. For the first time in his life, Wimar felt financially secure, and in March 1861 he was able to marry Anna von Senden.

Because of his growing reputation, Wimar was commissioned to decorate the interior of the St. Louis Old Courthouse dome designed by William Rumbold. Wimar felt so honored that he offered to paint the murals for $500, a figure so paltry that the city commissioners doubled his fee. Knowing that he was being eaten up by consumption, he raced to finish four allegorical figures of Law, Commerce, Liberty, and Justice, and four lunettes with an oval portrait beneath each, representing Edward Bates (see Part 1), Thomas Hart Benton (see Part 1), and George and Martha Washington. He was so weakened by tuberculosis that he was sometimes carried into the building and up the scaffolding on a cot, where he lay painting. The four allegories were unfortunately painted over. When the other frescoes began to flake away, they were restored by Wimar's half-brother, August Becker, to the point where they exhibit Wimar's composition but not the effect of the painter's hand. He completed the Old Courthouse decorations four months before his death. The last work he painted portrayed Chief Bear Rib, a favorite character.

Carl Wimar died at the early age of thirty-four. On November 30, 1862, Wimar was buried in his in-laws' plot in Bellefontaine Cemetery. A week later, he would be moved to his half-sister's lot for reasons unknown. Two years later, his only child, Winona, would share this grave. So closely did he identify with the Indians that he had given her a Dakota name meaning "first-born child." They lie together beneath a worn, marble obelisk that reads "Chas. Wimar," the anglicized name he took when he became a citizen.

---

1. Rick Stewart, Joseph D. Ketner II, and Angela L. Miller, frontispiece in *Carl Wimar: Chronicler of the Missouri Frontier* (Fort Worth, TX: Amon Carter Museum, 1991).

PART TEN

MEN OF SPORTS

St. Louis, named the "Best Sports City" in 2002 by the *Sporting News*,[1] boasts residents who have been enamored of sports since the 1880s. Bellefontaine Cemetery touts many fans and a few sports figures. Interred there are two colorful owners of baseball teams as well as the owners of the *Sporting News* itself. Professional athletes include two baseball players and a bare-knuckle boxer.

Although both baseball magnates owned the St. Louis Browns, they actually owned completely different teams. From 1881 to 1898, the team named for its brown stockings belonged to Chris Von der Ahe, a canny German-born saloon keeper. The Browns would first make Von der Ahe very wealthy and then take him into bankruptcy. After the team was sold, the new owners changed the color of the stockings to cardinal red: Hence, their new name was born.

Recording the glories and indignities of sport, St. Louis was home to the *Sporting News* from its founding until 2008. Three generations of the Spink family, Charles, Taylor, and Johnson Spink, edited and published the paper for ninety-six years. Founded in 1886, the paper dedicated its pages to in-depth coverage of baseball until Johnson Spink took his seat in the editor's chair in 1962. With keen insight into the public's expanding fascination with professional athletics, Johnson expanded the paper's coverage to other sports.

---

1. Wachovia Securities advertisement, *St. Louis Post-Dispatch*, March 5, 2008, C6.

CHARLES C. SPINK

1862–1914

MARIE TAYLOR SPINK

1868–1944

J. G. TAYLOR SPINK

1888–1962

C. C. JOHNSON SPINK

1916–1992

FOR NINETY-SIX YEARS, the Spink family published and edited the *Sporting News* (*TSN*), the colorful tabloid newspaper known as the "Bible of Baseball." Alfred Henry Spink, the first sportswriter of the *St. Louis Post-Dispatch*,[1] listened to the advice of his publisher, Joseph Pulitzer, who said, "Given a good business manager and an editor who can really write, any newspaper should fast become a good paying institution."[2] Spink founded the *Sporting News* in 1886. Editing the paper, balancing the books, and selling all advertisements proved too much for Al, so he called on his younger brother Charles C. Spink, who had been seeking his fortune as a homesteader in the Dakotas. Al Spink offered his brother $50 a week to join him in St. Louis. In Charles, Al found "the type of sound businessman that Pulitzer had spoken of."[3] Not only Charles but also his wife, Marie Taylor Spink, committed body and soul to the success of the *Sporting News*. Their son, John George "J. G." Taylor Spink, who had dropped out of high school after his sophomore year to work for the family paper, cut short his honeymoon to take over as publisher of *TSN* when Charles died. J. G. Taylor Spink ran the paper for almost fifty years until his death in 1962 at which time his son, Charles Claude Johnson Spink, took his seat at the publisher's desk.

The first edition of the paper rolled off the presses in March 1886, and Al Spink touted the *Sporting News* as having "the largest circulation of any sporting paper published west of Philadelphia."[4] (A Philadelphia sports newspaper had been founded three years earlier.) The paper's early success was fueled by fierce local pride in Chris Von der Ahe's St. Louis Browns. The Browns' World Series triumph gave the paper a huge boost that first year of publication. When the Browns defeated their National League rivals, *TSN* blared out the victory in big headlines such as "We Gave 'Em the Goose" or "The World's Championship Now the Property of this Town."[5]

After he joined the staff in 1887, Al's younger brother Charles quickly expanded the paper's circulation and advertising. Even though he knew little about baseball, he understood business. Giving out sample copies, Charles took circulation from 40,000 in October 1887 to 56,500 by the next February.[6] In 1888, the size of the paper expanded from eight to twelve pages to accommodate the increased advertising Charles had solicited. In 1899, Charles became publisher, hiring a string of editors. The multitalented Al left to produce a play he had written soon after Charles had joined the paper. When the production failed, Al returned to work for his hard-driving brother for a few years before taking off permanently by 1899. Under Al's lead, the *Sporting News* had also covered his other interests: boxing, shooting, billiards, cycling, and theater. When Al left for good, Charles gradually phased out Al's other interests, and baseball reigned supreme in the pages of the newspaper for more than fifty years. The short-story writer Ring Lardner edited the *Sporting News* for seven issues from December 1910 to February 1911. As *TSN* legend goes, Lardner went out for lunch one day and never came back.[7]

After Charles died, his wife, Marie Spink, stayed on at the *Sporting News* as vice president and treasurer and was a tremendous influence on her son, who succeeded her husband. Never forgetting the days when the paper operated on a prayer, she continued to practice strict economies, turning off reporters' lamps when they left their desks for a few minutes.

She was said to have a great eye for talent on the ball field, and her obituary in *TSN* said that she "had exerted a greater influence on baseball and baseball journalism than any other woman in the history of the game."[8]

Taylor Spink was only twenty-six years old in 1914 when his father Charles died, catapulting him to the rank of publisher. He was such a fine newsman that a biographer said, "If Taylor Spink had not been born, baseball would have had to invent him."[9] Hiring correspondents wherever baseball was played, Taylor brought vivid reporting to the pages of the *Sporting News*. During his lifetime, he received many awards honoring his dedication to the sport. In 1962, the Baseball Writers' Association of America designated the J. G. Taylor Spink Award, an award for outstanding baseball writing, and named him the first winner. As such, his name is displayed in the Baseball Hall of Fame at Cooperstown, New York. He died a few months later.

Taylor's son, who succeeded him, not only grew up with baseball and the *Sporting News* but was also named after a baseball great, Ban Johnson, his father's close friend and founder of the American League. Groomed since birth to take over the paper, Johnson Spink became president and treasurer of the firm in October 1962, just two months before his father died. In his twenty years at the top, he more than doubled the circulation, from 178,000 to 470,000. Johnson modernized the Bible of Baseball by further extending coverage to other sports. He replaced the cartoons on the covers with full-size photographs, first black and white and then color in 1967. Having no heir, Johnson sold the *Sporting News* to the Times-Mirror Corporation in 1977 for $18 million. After he sold the paper, he turned to collecting art and serving on the boards of cultural institutions. When Johnson died in 1992, he left his collections to the St. Louis cultural institutions that he had supported so actively in life.

---

1. Julian Rammelkamp, *Pulitzer's Post-Dispatch, 1878–1883* (Princeton, NJ: Princeton University, 1967), 49.
2. *Spink Biographies*, Manuel Garcia files, Bellefontaine Cemetery, introduction.
3. Ibid.
4. Ibid., 14.
5. Ibid., 16.

6. "The Sporting News: A History of the Bible of Baseball," http://www.magazines.things-and-other-stuff.com/sporting-nes.html.

7. Ibid.

8. Ibid.

9. *Spink Biographies*, 56.

CHRIS VON DER AHE
1851–1913

WHEN CHRIS VON DER AHE bought the original St. Louis Browns baseball frranchise in 1881, he did not do it for the love of the game but rather to sell more beer at his saloon. The high-living baseball magnate was portrayed by the newspapers as a clown, with his prominent proboscis, portly build, and heavy German accent, but anyone who observed the way he ran the team realized Von der Ahe was a shrewd operator and "an innovative marketer of baseball."[1] With player and later manager Charles Comiskey of Comiskey Park and Chicago White Sox fame, Von der Ahe took the Browns to four pennants and two World Championships from 1885 to 1888. (No team would match this four-year sweep until the New York Giants in the 1920s.) As a result, the "Lucky Dutchman" saw his original $1,800 investment in the team balloon to $500,000.[2] While today's ballparks feature statues of great ballplayers, Von der Ahe put a larger-than-life statue of himself outside the gates of Sportsman's Park. He had the same statue later moved to his burial plot at Bellefontaine Cemetery.[3] According to cemetery legend, he had the year of his death carved into his monument long before he died. The year, 1913, proved correct.[4]

After arriving in St. Louis from Prussia as a teenager in 1867,[5] Von der Ahe soon built up wealth, starting with a grocery store, then a bar, and then real estate investments. When forming the Sportsman's Park and Club Association to set up a ballpark in 1880, Alfred Spink, founder of the *Sporting News*, asked the prosperous saloonkeeper to participate. Von der Ahe said that he didn't understand baseball, but "if it sells beer, then I am all for it."[6] His intuition about a good investment turned him into a wealthy man.

Spink assumed the position of secretary, and Von der Ahe became "Boss President," or "Poss Bresident," as he mangled the pronunciation. By the next year, at age twenty-nine, Von der Ahe had made enough money to purchase the team. Because the new owner was a novice to the sport, Spink helped him assemble his talent, including the star first baseman Charles Comiskey, who would later lead the team to four successive pennants.

While Comiskey provided knowledge of the game and the ability to inspire players, Von der Ahe brought business sense to the team. In their first year in the American Association League, the Browns finished fifth, but they improved steadily until they took first place in 1885. The World Championship of baseball had been born the year before when the winner of the American Association played the victor of the older National League for the title. In 1885, the Browns played the Chicago White Stockings in a nine-game series with a winner-take-all purse put up by the two owners.

The score after the fifth game stood: St. Louis two victories, Chicago two and a forfeit. The teams agreed to drop the forfeit. When St. Louis prevailed, they declared themselves world champions, but the Chicago owner protested. The series went down in history as a tie. The Browns came back to beat Chicago in 1886. In 1887, the Detroit Wolverines bested the Browns for eight out of fifteen games. In the Browns' last World Series, the New York Giants took them down in six of ten games.

The Lucky Dutchman's fortunes began to change in 1892. While the Browns did not finish in first place again, they still played well until the 1892 season. That year, Von der Ahe refused to match the $7,500 salary Cincinnati offered Comiskey, so his star manager left. That same year, the American Association League folded, and the Browns joined the National League. The next six seasons proved disastrous. Twice the Browns finished twelfth out of twelve teams. In 1892 after Comiskey departed, Von der Ahe managed the team himself to an eleventh-place finish. In an effort to draw people who would not support a losing team, he turned Sportsman's Park into "Coney Island West" with merry-go-rounds, beer gardens, a shoot-the-chute boat, a racetrack, and an all-girl band. To pay off his debts, including monthly payments to an ex-wife and a former mistress,[7] Von der Ahe sold expensive players to other clubs and replaced them with less costly talents.

After Al Spink relinquished control of the newspaper to his brother Charles Spink in the 1890s, the *Sporting News* became Von der Ahe's biggest critic,[8] at one point calling him "a baseball corpse."[9] The final blow came in 1898 when the recently renovated grandstand caught fire during a game. The bank that had financed Sportsman's Park foreclosed on him, and the Browns were sold on the courthouse steps to G. A. Gruner for $33,000. Gruner immediately sold the club for a $7,000 profit to Frank and Stanley Robison. In an effort to distance the club from Von der Ahe's losing Browns, the new owners changed the color of the team's socks from brown to red. Since Cincinnati had already taken the name Red Sox, the new club became known as the Cardinals.

Von der Ahe, who had once proclaimed himself "the smartest fellow in baseball,"[10] struggled to survive financially. When he found himself bankrupt in 1908, his old team played the new St. Louis Browns of the American League in a benefit exhibition game. In publicity for the event, the *St. Louis Globe-Democrat* touted him as "the man who did much to make baseball the national game."[11] Afterward, his friends were able to hand him a check for $4,294, which included a $500 donation from Comiskey. Still, Von der Ahe was completely impoverished when he died of cirrhosis of the liver five years later.

Von der Ahe's funeral was orchestrated like one of his baseball events. The *Sporting News* reported that "hundreds of old-time ballplayers" attended. They "crowded the streets for blocks and stood with bowed heads."[12] Comiskey joined Al Spink and former players and umpires as pallbearers for Von der Ahe. The city paid tribute to its baseball magnate who always bragged, "Nothing is too goot for my poys."[13]

---

1. Larry G. Bowman, "Christian Von der Ahe, the St. Louis Browns, and the World's Championship Playoffs, 1885–1888," *Missouri Historical Review*, vol. 91, 385.

2. "Von der Ahe, Once Baseball Magnate, Near Death; Physician Gives Up Hope," *Missouri Republican*, January 19, 1913.

3. *St. Louis Baseball*, Manuel Garcia files, Bellefontaine Cemetery, 247.

4. Landmarks Association, *Tombstone Talks*, 15.

5. Jim Rygelski, "Baseball's 'Boss President,' Chris von der Ahe and the Nineteenth Century St. Louis Browns," *Gateway Heritage*, Summer 1992, 43.

6. George Lipsitz, *Sidewalks of St. Louis* (Columbia: University of Missouri, 1991), 58.

7. "Baseball," Manuel Garcia files, Bellefontaine Cemetery.

8. Rygelski, "Baseball's Boss President," 50.

9. Ibid.

10. "Saga of the Browns—Born 1882, Died 1953, From Von der Ahe to Veeck," *St. Louis Globe-Democrat*, September 30, 1953.

11. Rygelski, "Baseball's Boss President," 51.

12. Ibid.

13. Jim Rygelski, "1885 Browns Were First St. Louis Team to Win in Post-Season," *St. Louis Globe-Democrat*, September 1985.

PART ELEVEN

PHILANTHROPISTS

All of St. Louis's captains of industry became philanthropists. Although many of the businesses they built have faded away, their names endure because of the hospitals, schools, programs, and places of worship they have endowed.

James Yeatman, Robert S. Brookings, and William K. Bixby all retired from business pursuits to careers in philanthropy (see Part 1). Yeatman gave away all of his money during his lifetime. Retiring at age forty-nine, Bixby spent the rest of his life donating his time and funds to causes he believed in.

Siblings Henry Taylor Blow (see Part 1) and Charlotte Blow Charless (see Part 7) both used their wealth to improve life for others. After building a fortune in paint manufacturing, Henry Blow became a civic activist who funded slave Dred Scott in his freedom suit, built a school, and endowed an art academy and a Presbyterian church. Charlotte used her money and energy to advance social justice in St. Louis.

Fleeing anti-Semitism in Germany, Isidor Bush settled in St. Louis. There he came to be respected for his intelligence and wealth, both of which he dedicated to advance tolerance and alleviate poverty.

Robert Barnes had a vision of a non-sectarian hospital for the city. Today that dream has become one of the top medical centers in the world. Isidor Bush's Jewish Hospital is part of the Barnes-Jewish-Children's Hospital (BJC) Group. Barnes wanted none of his benefactions known during his lifetime, but today his greatest gift keeps his name alive.

AT HIS DEATH IN 1892, Robert Barnes endowed the hospital that still bears his name. Today, Barnes Hospital, the largest in the state and the biggest employer in St. Louis, is consistently ranked among the country's top medical centers.[1] From humble beginnings, Barnes rose to eminence as a merchant and banker, leaving almost $1 million to create his vision of a non-sectarian hospital. Surviving his children, he used almost the whole of his fortune to leave a great legacy for the city that had made possible his success.

Barnes had a difficult start in life. Born in Maryland in 1808, he was sent to live with an uncle in Louisville, Kentucky, after his father died when Robert was thirteen. As a young man in his twenties, he spent the first $1,000 he was able to set aside to pay off a loan of his father's and free his mother from debt. In old age, he said that this gift gave him more satisfaction than any other in his entire life.[2] Schooled in the ways of business by his merchant uncle, Barnes moved to St. Louis in 1830. His first position upon arriving in St. Louis was as a clerk earning $25 a month with "the privilege of sleeping in the store."[3]

Alone in the world, Barnes relied on common sense, thrift, industry, and an original way of looking at the world to make his mark. His first year working, he eked savings out of his $25-a-month salary, put it into an interest-bearing account, and "felt [himself] a capitalist."[4] After a year on the job, he was in the position to begin buying and selling in a small way on his own.

Barnes started in the wholesale grocery business and later went into banking. In 1836, he began clerking for a grocer and was made a partner the next year. In 1840, he was named a director of the Bank of the State of Missouri and became president eighteen years later. When Adolphus

Busch first attempted to expand his father-in-law's brewery business, every banker in town turned him down for a loan except Barnes, who advanced Busch $50,000, "the cornerstone on which Mr. Busch began to build his business success."[5] Nearly fifty years later Busch donated many times that amount to Barnes's hospital.[6]

In 1845, Barnes married Louise De Mun Barnes, a great-granddaughter of Therese Chouteau, one of the founders of St. Louis. They had two children, both of whom died in infancy. Although his wife was a Catholic and he had no particular religious affiliation, she readily agreed with his decision to place their benevolent giving in the hands of the Methodist Church. Treating charitable giving as if it were a business, Barnes investigated and determined that the Methodists would do the best job of administering his bequests, saying, "A person ought to invest his money for doing good as he invests it in his business, where it will bring the most returns."[7] The Barnes gave significant sums during their lifetime to a Methodist orphans' home and college. Their most enduring legacy, Barnes Hospital, was also administered by the Methodists.

Barnes willed $940,000 to build and endow a hospital "for sick and injured persons, without distinctions of creed."[8] Predeceasing her husband, Louise Barnes also left the hospital her considerable wealth. Twenty-two years later, in 1914, when ground was broken on Kingshighway, their original gift had grown to $2 million—despite the efforts of three of Barnes's nephews and heirs. In 1909 they unsuccessfully sued Barnes's estate to recover the money, saying seventeen years had elapsed and the hospital had not yet been built.[9]

Barnes could at times seem eccentric in his generosity.[10] He was not always forthcoming and did not mince words. When a collection was taken to bury a former friend who had squandered his wealth in "high living" including giving an actress a $1,000 broach, Barnes refused. He said, "If a man wants to live like a fool and die like a dog, he ought not to be buried like a gentleman."[11] During his lifetime he kept his charitable donations secret. Only after his death was his "business of benevolence"[12] made known.

---

1. *U.S. News & World Report* has consistently placed Barnes near the top of the list of the country's best hospitals since it began the ranking in 1990.
2. Hyde and Conard, *Encyclopedia of St. Louis*, 97.
3. Stevens, *Centennial History*, 737.
4. Hyde and Conard, *Encyclopedia of St. Louis*, 96.
5. Stevens, *Centennial History*, 737.
6. Ibid.
7. Hyde and Conard, *Encyclopedia of St. Louis*, 97.
8. Ibid.
9. "Barnes Heirs Lose Suit to Obtain $1,700,000 Fund," *St. Louis Globe-Democrat,* January 1, 1910.
10. Hyde and Conard, *Encyclopedia*, 96.
11. Ibid.
12. Ibid.

ISIDOR BUSH
1822–1898

FLEEING EUROPEAN anti-Semitism after the Revolutions of 1848, Isidor Bush immigrated to America where he advocated against political oppression, poverty, and ignorance throughout his life. At the behest of his wife, Theresa Taussig Bush, he settled in St. Louis, where he built wealth in the wholesale grocery business, banking, railroads, real estate, vineyards, and liquor distribution. There he became "the most prominent Jew in nineteenth century St. Louis"[1] and founded and led many Jewish and non-sectarian charities and civic groups. A fierce opponent of slavery, he played an important role in state government during and after the Civil War.

Bush was born in 1822 in Prague to a wealthy and cultivated family. Educated by tutors, he was fluent in German, English, French, and Italian and read Hebrew, Greek, and Latin. In 1837, his father moved the family to Vienna, where Bush senior bought a firm that became the largest Hebrew publishing house in the world. As a young man of twenty in Vienna, Isidor published radical newspapers that made him a target for retribution after the Revolutions of 1848. He therefore fled the next year to New York, where he published the first Jewish weekly in the United States.

Following the failure of this paper, Bush moved to St. Louis, where he prospered, first entering the wholesale grocery business with his brother-in-law Charles Taussig. In 1857, he was elected president of a bank, an office he held until 1861, when he joined the army as aide-de-camp to General John C. Frémont, commander of the Department of the West during the Civil War. When Frémont was relieved of duty, Bush, "a mathematician of no ordinary degree,"[2] resigned his commission to work for the U.S. Treasury. He left the government in 1862 for railroads and real estate.

Bush bought land along the railroad right of way south of the city on the Mississippi with the intention of starting a vineyard. "Bush always believed in the pursuit of agriculture by the Jews, and [desired] to spare his only son Ralph from the accidents and vicissitudes of commercial life."[3] Managed by his son and by his foreman and future partner Gustave Meissner, the farms of Bushberg prospered to the point that their catalogs shipped grapevines around the United States and to France, Austria, Australia, Serbia, and Brazil when insects threatened domestic stock there. Most likely written by Isidor Bush, the catalog with its information on cultivation was called "at once the BEST CATALOGUE and the BEST MANUAL on American Grapes that has yet been published."[4] Noted botanist George Engelmann of the Missouri Botanical Garden contributed articles (see Part 9). In 1869, Bush organized a wholesale liquor company that distributed spirits to all parts of the country.

Bush used the proceeds of his many businesses to improve the lives of others. He contributed to the merger of two congregations to form B'nai El, which built one of Missouri's first synagogues in 1855. The same year, Bush established two B'nai Brith lodges, the first Missouri chapter of this Jewish advocacy and service organization. He later served as chairman of the Independent Order of B'nai Brith[5] and its widows' and orphans' funds. He was a founder of the Jewish Orphan Asylum in Cleveland, Ohio, and among the founders of St. Louis's Jewish Hospital. He also served twelve years as president of the German Immigrants' Aid Society of St. Louis. Moreover, his generosity extended beyond organizations to individuals, for he frequently gave financial assistance to young people starting out in life.

Bush served St. Louis in a leadership role during the Civil War. He was elected to the nine-man governing board of the Convention that preserved Missouri for the Union by turning out its Confederate governor and naming Hamilton Gamble provisional governor of the state (see Part 5). Postwar, he served on the state constitutional convention, where he spoke out against harsh Reconstruction policies against Confederates.

Devoted to his adopted city, Bush served in later years on the city council and the public school board, as well on the state board of immigration. In 1882 he was chosen vice president of the Missouri Historical Society.

A modest man who was respected by many, he was mourned by thousands.[6] Following a funeral in the Jewish faith at Temple Shaare Emeth, his remains were interred at Bellefontaine Cemetery with Masonic ceremonies. For all of his business success, civic leadership, and philanthropic generosity, Bush was perhaps best loved for his kind and affable nature.[7] The ditty he wrote about his feelings for wines—"To all their faults a little blind, to all their virtues very kind"[8]—reflects his attitude toward his fellow man.

1. "Isidor Bush and Company," www.historyhappenedhere.org.

2. Jacob Furth, "Sketch of Isidor Bush," *Missouri Historical Society Collections* 4 (1912–1923): 306.

3. Siegmar Muehl, "Isidor Bush and the Bushberg Vineyards of Jefferson County," *Missouri Historical Review*, October 1999, 44.

4. Ibid, 50.

5. Hyde and Conard, *Encyclopedia of St. Louis.*

6. Furth, "Sketch of Isidor Bush," 303.

7. Ibid., 307.

8. Ibid.

PART TWELVE

CEMETERY LORE

 Over the century and a half of its existence, Bellefontaine Cemetery has developed its own rich lore beyond the histories of the individuals buried there. Surprisingly, no ghosts but rather founders, caretakers, and quirky individuals figure in the cemetery tales. Bellefontaine has hosted a wedding, a birthday party, many lawn parties, a death by tombstone, and at least two suicides, among other remarkable events.

THE FOUNDERS

When a group of St. Louis's leading citizens founded Bellefontaine Cemetery in 1849, they sought to establish a burial ground suitable for a city of such importance. When St. Louis became the fourteenth U.S. city, and the first west of the Mississippi, to open a nonsectarian rural cemetery, the city was a boomtown. The 1820 population of 10,000 increased to 14,000 in 1830, and that figure nearly tripled to 36,000 by 1840. Nine years later when the cemetery was founded, St. Louis had close to 100,000 people. In 1870, the city population would reach 350,000, and it would be the fourth largest in the country.[1] Clearly, St. Louis was seen as the land of opportunity. When city fathers situated Bellefontaine in a park-like setting outside of the center of St. Louis, the idea was not to banish death but to put it in the appropriate place, a spot where relatives and friends could visit their departed in a landscape so beautiful that it would give them relief from the overcrowded city.

The founders drew their inspiration from the rural cemetery movement that was born in Paris in 1804 with Père-Lachaise Cemetery. Starting in the Middle Ages through 1804, the Western world buried its dead in churchyards or on family land. With increasing urbanization churchyards filled, and graves had to be dug three or four deep. In 1780 in Paris the thousand-year-old Cemetery of the Holy Innocents broke through the basement wall of an adjoining apartment, causing more than one thousand bodies to crash through.[2] Such disasters inspired the idea of placing a final resting place outside the city proper. Rural cemeteries provided a place for people to stroll while visiting honored dead. The landscape and architectural design combined eighteenth-century Enlightenment ideas of rationality and order with nineteenth-century Romantic concepts of the picturesque and the sublime.

According to *The Yellowstone Story: A History of Our First National Park,* modern cemeteries served as the country's first parks. "Being [areas] of great natural beauty, [they] drew numerous 'parties of pleasure' and couples seeking a trysting place, leading to the suggestion that cemeteries ought to be planned 'with reference to the living as well as the dead, and therefore should be convenient and pleasant to visitors.'"[3]

People in the nineteenth century attached great importance to their burial places because they were close to their dead. The nineteenth-century man lived face to face with death. Until the advent of antibiotics and better sanitary conditions in the early 1900s, life expectancy was only forty-seven years,[4] infant mortality was high, and many families lost most or all of their offspring in early childhood. William Greenleaf Eliot and his wife, for example, had fourteen children, but only five survived them. St. Louisans of that era visited their dead often and erected great monuments and mausoleums to their memory. It was not uncommon for a family to picnic at the cemetery on a Sunday afternoon.

It was this concept of the rural cemetery that led banker William McPherson and former St. Louis mayor John Darby[5] to gather a group of business and social leaders on March 7, 1849, to incorporate what would become the Bellefontaine Cemetery Association. The nonprofit board made up of fifteen trustees from lot-holding families continues to this day. This was the second private nonprofit association in the city, after the Mercantile Library. The Bellefontaine Cemetery Association became the model for all other nonprofits that followed. Shortly after the association's founding, the need for a new cemetery proved urgent when a cholera epidemic and the Great Fire took many lives.

The cemetery association bought the 334[6] acres of land in four acquisitions. In 1849, Almerin Hotchkiss's design of meandering roads and picturesque vistas was sufficient for a dedication ceremony to take place. At the dedication on May 15, 1850, congregational minister and renowned classical scholar Truman Marcellus Post gave the address, saying that Bellefontaine was "the shadow, the counterpart"[7] of the city and that it would exist until "marble after marble crumbles."[8] His words are inscribed on his own marble tombstone, and they have indeed nearly worn away. With the help of the Missouri Botanical Garden's Henry Shaw, Hotchkiss took a wild setting and planted it with hundreds of varieties of trees and shrubs. The plantings were so rich and varied that the cemetery had a finer collection of trees than the Botanical Garden through the 1960s.[9] Hotchkiss's trails follow no straight lines or logical paths. Many visitors have found themselves driving round and round, lost until Hotchkiss's scheme comes to seem a metaphor for the infinite.

SCOUNDRELS, PARTYGOERS, AND SUICIDES

Board member and future mayor Luther Kennett caused a scandal right from the start. Kennett knew that the association had designs on an in-law's estate, so he bought the Edward Hempstead farm for a mere $27 an acre and then sold the same land six months later for $203 an acre. While Kennett proved himself a scoundrel by making such a tidy profit off his own family to build Bellefontaine, others have met tragic ends at the cemetery. Perhaps the saddest story is the death of four-year-old Maggie Davitt on July 1, 1862. Her family was visiting the grave of her brother who had died the year before, when a tombstone fell over and killed her. Others have become despondent and taken their own lives at Bellefontaine. James Dodds killed himself on his wife's grave December 9, 1931, and Joseph Widen took poison in November 1912 next to the tombstone of his mother-in-law, Mary Graham.

Two of the more unusual tales revolve around people who did not want to be separated from those they loved. One man shot his sweetheart and then shot and killed himself on October 27, 1875. Although she lived, with a bullet lodged in her shoulder, David Robert Fagg's sweetheart insisted he be buried in her family plot, the Plochman lot, because "he loved her so much."[10] Perhaps the quirkiest tale yet is the story of Oma Vaughan, who had her leg amputated on July 23, 1908. She wanted to be reunited with her lost limb in death, so she had it buried in Bellefontaine Cemetery[11] twenty days later. However, when the time came, she was buried elsewhere.

Bellefontaine has seen happy times as well. A 1913 article appeared in the *St. Louis Post-Dispatch* describing lawn parties held at the cemetery with paper lanterns, music, and games. Irma Burgess, wife of Frank Burgess, the assistant superintendent who would later be Bellefontaine's third superintendent, hosted the parties. She had grown up on the grounds with her father, Walter Graydon, who worked at the cemetery, so she saw nothing unusual in giving a party there. Burgess said, "We never realized that we were living in an unusual place." She went on to say that she saw no reason to be afraid of ghosts in the cemetery because "if people did arise from the grave, they would haunt their old homes, not the graveyard."[12] On October 22, 2000, Holly and Kevin Bremerkamp held their nuptials at the Receiving Tomb Chapel, now known as Hotchkiss Chapel. (The Receiving Tomb was originally built to hold bodies of people who died when the ground was frozen. Power diggers have obliterated the need to receive the bodies until the spring thaw.) When the Bremerkamps were courting, they considered the cemetery a romantic setting and had picnics there. Their elegant wedding service, which took place on a misty day, was lit with tea lights hung from the ceiling by ribbons because the chapel had no electricity. The formal photographs were taken inside the columns of the Anne Farrar monument. Holly Bremerkamp said, "Bellefontaine is our special place because it is so beautiful and historical."[13] Lynn Parriott also is "fascinated by the cemetery."[14] On June 23, 2007, Lynn held her fifty-third birthday party there with a motor coach taking fifty friends for a tour and lecture. Her invitations read "Mojitos and Mausoleums." Only one friend declined, saying it made her uncomfortable being in the cemetery because it was her birthday too.[15]

While these revelers have loved the cemetery, superintendent Michael Tiemann and gatekeeper Manuel Garcia loved it more. Both researched the cemetery and its people for thirty years. Their tales became the foundation of this book.

---

1. "Population of St. Louis & Missouri, 1820–2000," www.geneologybranches.com/St.louispopulation.html

2. Douglas Keister, *Going Out in Style* (New York: Facts on File, 1997), 14.

3. Aubrey L. Haines, *The Yellowstone Story: A History of Our First National Park,* vol. 1 (Yellowstone National Park, WY: Yellowstone Library and Museum Association in association with the Colorado Associated University Press, 1977), 161.

4. Stephen S. Hall, "Wisdom," *The New York Times Magazine,* May 6, 2007, 60. Hall says, "Americans born in 1960 can expect to live nearly to 70."

5. Darby was one of only two of the founders to be buried elsewhere. He was first interred at Bellefontaine but a family feud caused his remains to be removed to Calvary Cemetery. The other founders are Henry Kayser, Wayman

Crow, James Yeatman, James Harrison, Gerard B. Allen, Philander Salisbury, William Bennett, Augustus Brewster, and William McPherson. Their names are inscribed on a cornerstone of the cemetery wall at the intersection of West Florissant and Calvary avenues.

6. The cemetery later sold seven acres to the State of Missouri for Interstate 70 and gave thirteen acres to Busch Park.

7. Katherine Corbett, "Bellefontaine Cemetery: St. Louis City of the Dead," *Gateway Heritage*, Fall 1991, 62.

8. Manuel Garcia files, Bellefontaine Cemetery.

9. Elinor Coyle, *St. Louis, Portrait of a River City* (St. Louis: Folkestone, 1966), 50.

10. Manuel Garcia, *Oral History*, tape IX, 145.

11. Manuel Garcia, *Oral History*, tape XXX, 707.

12. "Lawn Parties in Cemetery Newest North End Thrill," *St. Louis Post-Dispatch*, July 29, 1913, 2.

13. Holly Bremerkamp, conversation with the author, 2007.

14. Lynn Parriott, conversation with the author, 2008.

15. Ibid.

ALMERIN HOTCHKISS
1816–1903

ALMERIN HOTCHKISS designed Bellefontaine Cemetery and served as its first superintendent for forty-six years. When St. Louis city fathers decided to establish a cemetery, board chairman James Yeatman traveled to New York to bring back the best landscape architect he could find. At Brooklyn's Green-Wood Cemetery, he discovered Hotchkiss, then a young man of thirty years. Hotchkiss was a civil engineer acquainted with the great landscape architect Frederick Law Olmsted,[1] who designed New York's Central Park as well as Washington University in St. Louis.

According to Hotchkiss's obituary, "The tract of land which is now the cemetery was then a wild, rugged woodland. Hotchkiss began improvements at once in a small way and it was not until he had passed the allotted age of three score and ten that he was in a measure satisfied with his work. He lived on the grounds and often used to wander about the place inspecting everything as a farmer might inspect his [domain]."[2]

Hotchkiss laid out a tangle of fourteen miles of roads that traverse the Mississippi bluffs to create inspiring vistas and picturesque resting places. When he arrived in September 1849, he immediately began grading, filling, and building roads.[3] He soon planted more than one hundred species of trees and shrubs that would one day rival the Missouri Botanical Garden in variety and beauty, and he surrounded the 334-acre park with a wrought-iron fence punctuated by four stone gates. In fact, he and Henry Shaw, founder of the Botanical Garden, worked together on both the garden and the cemetery. Hotchkiss had such respect for horticulture that he left the roads in Bellefontaine curvy rather than cut down trees. He also designed the original gatehouse[4] that stood on Broadway, one of St. Louis's main north-south thoroughfares. A bell hanging in the bell tower at the Broadway entrance tolled for every funeral procession. Patterning

Bellefontaine's manual on Green-Wood's, the superintendent advised lot owners about the choice of monuments and the care of plots. Hotchkiss looked after every detail of his necropolis with such devotion that he attended nearly every interment. [5]

Upon arrival in St. Louis, Hotchkiss became friends with two gentlemen of like minds: Henry Shaw, benefactor of the Missouri Botanical Garden, and George Ingham Barnett, the most prominent architect of the day. He and Shaw worked together to bring non-native trees to St. Louis and exchanged notes on experiments on China's ginkgo.[6] Together they discovered that the bald cypress, a tree native to the swamps of the southeastern part of the state, could thrive in the city's smoky atmosphere and hard winters. Many species of magnolia were planted simultaneously at Shaw's Garden and Bellefontaine.[7] They also found a Missouri red granite to be the most durable in this part of the country and used it in many buildings and monuments in Bellefontaine.[8]

Architectural historian Charles C. Savage believes that the beauty of Bellefontaine influenced urban design in St. Louis. He called Hotchkiss's "romantic landscapes" an inspiration for the "parklike character" of St. Louis's private places, the many residential enclaves owned and maintained by homeowners.[9]

Hotchkiss also served as the landscape architect for the town of Lake Forest, Illinois, outside Chicago, and for two cemeteries other than Bellefontaine. The town of Lake Forest and its college also feature winding roads that follow the lay of the land; it was the first community in the Chicago area to have a landscape design.[10] In 1848, the year before Hotchkiss arrived in St. Louis, he designed the Forest Hill Cemetery of Utica, New York, "with rare artistic sense."[11] While employed at Bellefontaine, he traveled to Rock Island, Illinois, to design that city's cemetery, as Chippiannock, in 1855.

By the time of Hotchkiss's death at age eighty-seven in 1903, he had become such a prominent citizen of St. Louis that George Caleb Bingham painted a portrait of his wife, Marianne Moore Hotchkiss. His son Frank Hotchkiss officially succeeded him as superintendent of Bellefontaine, a position he held until 1926.

Although Hotchkiss designed a mausoleum for himself near the Bellefontaine Receiving Tomb, according to superintendent Michael Tiemann,

"He sold the tomb to another family and erected his own monument across the valley on the other side of the hill. His family lot is just a regular lot."[12] In a larger sense, Almerin Hotchkiss's monument is the whole cemetery for he dedicated the better part of his life to "beautifying the spot where he . . . rest[s]."[13]

---

1. *Wainwright Tomb*, Manuel Garcia files, Bellefontaine Cemetery, 122.

2. Hotchkiss obituary, *St. Louis Post-Dispatch,* January 1903, Michael Tiemann files, Bellefontaine Cemetery.

3. Corbett, "Bellefontaine Cemetery," 62.

4. Savage, *Architecture of the Private Streets*, 5.

5. Hotchkiss obituary.

6. Carolyn Hewes Toft and Jane Molloy Porter, *Compton Heights: A History and Architectural Guide* (St. Louis: Landmarks Association, 1984), 8.

7. *George Ingham Barnett and Henry Shaw*, Manuel Garcia files, Bellefontaine Cemetery.

8. Ibid.

9. Savage, *Architecture of the Private Streets*, 6.

10. "Lake Forest, IL," http://www.encyclopedia.chicagohistory.org/pages/709.html.

11. "Forest Hill Cemetery," www.foresthillcemetery.org.

12. Michael Tiemann, *Oral History,* tape XII, 177.

13. Hotchkiss obituary.

MANUEL GARCIA
1929–2006

LOOKING FOR THE GRAVE of poet Sara Teasdale, Manuel Garcia first came to Bellefontaine Cemetery in 1951 at age twenty-two. What he found led him to spend the next thirty-five years researching the people buried there. His studies resulted in a respectable library, many drawers full of articles, and a book titled *Mark Twain in St. Louis: A Biographical Tour through Bellefontaine Cemetery*, published in 2002. When he retired from the *St. Louis Post-Dispatch*, where he had worked as a proofreader for thirty-one years, the staff cartoonist called Garcia the "world's greatest cemetery sleuth" on a caricature of Garcia as Don Quixote. After his retirement from the newspaper, he worked as gatekeeper at the cemetery on weekends and holidays until his death. He said it was "the best job" he ever had, quipping, "Everybody who was Somebody is interred here, and many nobodies are interred here. However, nobodies are Somebodies to someone."[1] He loved everything about the cemetery, from the foibles of the noble people buried there to the peace of the grounds to the wild animals who roam among the graves to the very stones themselves.

Garcia was born in Illinois to Spanish-immigrant parents and attended high school in East St. Louis and Fairmont City. He became such an avid reader that he took a book along on dates when he was courting his wife, Edith. Eventually his love of literature and history led him to delve into the stories of the people of Bellefontaine. During his days at the *Post-Dispatch*, he would "stop at Bellefontaine for twenty or thirty minutes [to do some research]. Then I would go into work. I would stop at the Missouri Historical Society Library . . . I went through from A to Z in the obituaries. Every time I would find a mention of Bellefontaine, I would copy the obituary."[2] He also copied articles and chapters from books until he had amassed eight file drawers of information that he later donated to the cemetery. He put so much into studying the people of Bellefontaine that he said, "There will never be another me. That's not even bragging. Get a life, Garcia."[3] Of all those he researched, without hesitation, his favorite was Frank Blair, the fiery politician and general whose efforts kept Missouri in the Union during the Civil War. With a twinkle in his eye, Garcia said, "That is what I tell everybody, the cemetery has more ex-in-laws of Ernest Hemingway and secretaries of the interior than any cemetery in the world."[4]

Manuel Garcia's vast knowledge of the history of the people who made St. Louis famous and infamous was sought by historians, teachers, genealogists, families, and even television's History Channel, which interviewed him for a television program on Missouri cemeteries. In 2004, so that their knowledge would not be lost, the Bellefontaine Cemetery Association commissioned interviews with Garcia and superintendent Michael Tiemann, who also studied the history of the cemetery during his thirty-year stint there. Over the span of three and a half years Garcia talked about the illustrious lives of Bellefontaine that he knew so well. Garcia's and Tiemann's oral histories have inspired this book.

Today, Manuel Garcia rests beneath a granite marker in Bellefontaine Cemetery that bears a picture of a family of deer and lines from John Donne which read, translated from the Spanish inscription, "Ask not for whom the bell tolls, it tolls for thee."

---

1. Handwritten note found in Bellefontaine Cemetery file.
2. Manuel Garcia, *Oral History,* tape LXVII, 984.
3. Ibid.
4. Manuel Garcia, *Oral History,* tape XXXXII, 749.

PART THIRTEEN

ART AND ARCHITECTURE OF NOTE

 Walking the hills of Bellefontaine Cemetery reveals vistas of beautiful art and architecture. Because the cemetery's original superintendent, Almerin Hotchkiss, planted a wealth of trees and shrubs and laid out the plots with sensitivity to the natural terrain, the natural setting is a fitting location for fine monuments. Because many of St. Louis's wealthiest and most prominent citizens chose to be buried there, they built mausoleums and monuments of great quality.

Among the mausoleums, the Wainwright Tomb by Louis Sullivan is considered "unmatched in quality" by art historians.[1] Its proportions are perfect, its ornamentation superb. Many, if not most, of the mausoleums represent noteworthy architecture. The Beaux Arts tomb designed by Eames & Young for Henry Clay Pierce features five Tiffany windows. Henry Bacon, the architect who designed the Lincoln Memorial in Washington, D.C., designed the neoclassical Mallinckrodt tomb. Prospect Avenue, also known as Millionaires' Row, is lined with impressive mausoleums.

The David R. Francis monument is one of the highlights of Prospect Avenue. Its bronze figure personifies grief. Another beautiful female figure, on the other hand, is depicted with an uplifting attitude, despite its sad story. The Maude Sheble Judge monument pays tribute to a young bride who died in childbirth. The beautiful female figure that Herman Luyties placed upon his grave is neither grieving nor triumphant. "The girl in the glass box," as she is known, seems almost saucy. The Brooks family chose to depict on their grave a dachshund sleeping on a bench; the dog remains their faithful friend in death as in life.[2] On the Elks Club lot, a magnificent bronze elk roams through the graves in solitary splendor.

Some of the most poignant stones honor children whose lives were cut short. On the Eva Whipple monument, a sweet baby sleeps inside a sea shell, its marble so worn that the dates cannot be read. Beside the monumental tomb of brewer Anton Griesedieck resides a small, sad stone marking the lives of three of his children. Twins Walter and Edna, aged three years and six months, and their ten-year-old brother Hugo all perished in 1888.

Bellefontaine Cemetery offers a wealth of art and architecture among its stones. They need only be discovered.

1. Hugh Morrison, *Louis Sullivan: Prophet of Modern Architecture* (New York: W. W. Norton, 1935), Bellefontaine Cemetery, Manuel Garcia files.

2. George Brooks served as director of the Missouri Historical Society.

ANN C. T. FARRAR

1798–1878

ANN C. T. FARRAR rests in an underground burial chamber beneath the small Greek temple bearing her name and the date 1868, ten years before she was buried. She is joined in eternal rest on the lot by forty-two relatives. Many of her relations played formative roles in St. Louis history. Ann Farrar was the niece of explorer William Clark; the sister of one of St. Louis's wealthiest men, John O'Fallon; the wife of St. Louis's first American-born doctor, Bernard G. Farrar; and the mother of Civil War general Bernard G. Farrar Jr. Esteemed for his generosity, Dr. Farrar died of cholera while ministering to the victims of the cholera epidemic of 1849. Although his medical services were often donated, he built up wealth in St. Louis real estate.

The temple is remarkable for its strength, simplicity, and elegance of proportion. Eight columns support a pediment bearing Ann's name in bold letters. The columns belong to the Doric order, the most forthright of the three classical orders of Greek architecture. The temple's colors add a lively twist to its classical perfection with the weathered green of the copper roof contrasting with the temple's warm yellow limestone, a stone that can only be found in Joliet, Illinois.[1]

---

1. Manuel Garcia, *Oral History,* tape IV, 81.

HERMAN LUYTIES

1871–1921

"THE GIRL IN THE GLASS BOX" who guards Herman Luyties' grave is considered one of the most beautiful monuments in Bellefontaine Cemetery. Her figure is voluptuous, her glance coquettish. Whether she represents Luyties' mistress or a more prosaic model is a question that has never been answered.

The twelve-foot-tall marble is a copy of an angel by Italian sculptor Giulio Monteverde. The original graces the monument of a wealthy Genoese merchant named Francisco Oneto. Many copies of this angel have made their way to American cemeteries, but the Luyties copy differs from most because she lacks wings. She also has an attitude. The Genoese statue expresses purity even though she looks up from under her curls very directly at the viewer. That direct glance has turned flirtatious, however, in the Luyties monument, as has her entire posture: Her leg is cocked, her hips sway, and her arms are crossed in casual disdain. Her swelling belly beneath billowing drapery can only represent fecundity. The fact that she is protected in a granite niche behind a glass front only adds to her allure.

Herman Luyties was the son of Dr. Herman C. G. Luyties, who founded Luyties Homeopathic Pharmacy Company in 1853 after moving to St. Louis from Germany three years earlier. "During the 1800s, Luyties supplied most of the pharmacies in the West. We still have an I.O.U. from the Confederate States of America,"[1] said Forrest Murphy in 1994. At the time, he was company president and the sixth generation of the family to run the company.[2] Today Luyties Pharmacal continues to sell homeopathic pharmaceuticals—medicines made from natural plants, animals, and some minerals."[3] Herman Luyties started out working in his father's company. While retaining his position as vice president there, Luyties went on to serve simultaneously as president of both the Walker Pharmaceutical and Sanitol Chemical companies.

Despite his scientific background, Luyties must have had an artistic bent, perhaps because his mother was a French musician. When he took the grand tour of Europe, he brought back the marble statue now marking his grave. Legend has it that Luyties fell in love with Monteverde's model, proposed to her, and was rejected. Superintendent Michael Tiemann asserted, "He had this likeness of her made in Italy and . . . put in the foyer of his townhouse over near Forest Park until the floor started to buckle. . . So then he bought the lot out here. . . . He brought the monument out and put up the granite case and the glass front to protect it. He is buried at the foot of the monument. . . . His wife is buried up the street on her family's lot with his children because she was not about to be buried on this lot with that sculpture."[4] Gatekeeper Manuel Garcia, however, doubts that the story is true because the sculpture is not unique. "If it was my sweetheart, I would make one of her and only one."[5]

Whether a lost love or simply a pretty girl, the Luyties statue looks up at the viewer as if to say, "Don't blame me."

---

1. William Flannery, "Family Business: Luyties Pharmacal Started in 1853," *St. Louis Post-Dispatch,* September 5, 1994, 3.
2. Luyties Pharmacal still exists though it has not been headquartered in St. Louis since 1999.
3. Flannery, "Family Business."
4. Michael Tiemann, *Oral History,* tape I, 16.
5. Manuel Garcia, *Oral History,* tape XXV, 401.

BORN IN VIRGINIA, General Richard Barnes Mason was the great-grandson of George Mason, father of the Bill of Rights of the U.S. Constitution. Richard Mason took over from Stephen Watts Kearny as military governor of California in 1847. After the establishment of peace, during the difficult transition from Mexican to U.S. government, he became the first civil governor of the territory as well. As a result, California honors his name in two locations: Fort Mason and Mason Street in San Francisco.

Under the military regime of Mason's predecessor Kearny, John C. Frémont was court-martialed over an attempt to usurp power. Mason would figure in the trial because Frémont had challenged Mason to a duel, but Kearny refused to let them fight. Mason was also involved in another court-martial. In a prescient move, he had had Jefferson Davis, the future president of the Confederacy, tried by court-martial in 1835 on charges of being "highly disrespectful and insubordinate."[1]

In California, Mason struggled with a kind of interregnum because it was not appropriate for the army to retain control, but no civil laws existed. The U.S. Congress had not yet developed a code of law for the new territory. When gold was discovered at John Sutter's mill in January 1848, the legal situation grew dire. The California Gold Rush of 1849 occurred without the benefit of property, criminal, or customs laws. Wage inequities caused by the Gold Rush led to mass desertions by Mason's troops. Mason's August 17, 1848, report of the discovery of gold and its effect on the new territory " . . . remains today the most authentic and descriptive story of the discovery of the gold deposits in California, especially at Sutter's Fort. It was copied in all parts of the world, published everywhere in the newspapers and distributed in thousands of pamphlets."[2]

Relieved from military and civil governorship in the spring of 1849, Mason returned with his wife, Margaret Hunter Mason, and daughters, Emma and Nanny, to take command at Jefferson Barracks, where the cholera epidemic was raging. Sadly, Mason fell victim and died in 1850. He was buried in Bellefontaine Cemetery next to his wife's plot. She would rest between him and her second husband, Civil War general Don Carlos Buell.

Mason's wife and daughters erected one of the cemetery's most noteworthy monuments to his memory. John Struthers, a Philadelphia artist who had also made George Washington's gravestone, carved it of dark brown freestone. A cannon, cannonballs, kegs, and ropes are piled, rising powerfully from one end to the other. A shroud covers them as if they are dead and in mourning. It is a simple but eloquent tribute to a consummate soldier.

1. *The Man*, Manuel Garcia Mason-Buell file, Bellefontaine Cemetery, 62.
2. *American Biography*.

WILLIAM CONRAD SEVERSON
1924–1999

NINE YEARS BEFORE HE DIED, sculptor William Conrad Severson erected his eighteen-foot-tall burial monument of carved pink granite at Bellefontaine Cemetery. After looking at many cemeteries over decades, he and his wife selected Bellefontaine as their final resting place. Once the artist had established the site for his grave, he designed the monument as a simple spire that incorporated slits aligned with the sun. When the sun shines through them, these slits cast a shining cross within the shadow of the marker on summer and winter solstices and vernal and autumnal equinoxes. Thus it becomes a monument to his faith and the passage of time as revealed in this specific place.

Severson was born in Madison, Wisconsin, in 1924. While he began making art and won national scholastic awards for his sculpture in middle school, his education was interrupted by military service during World War II. Upon his return to civilian life, he earned his B.S. in applied art at the University of Wisconsin–Madison and his M.F.A. at Syracuse University. In 1951, he was a summer fellow at the McDowell Colony, a prestigious artists' colony in New Hampshire. From 1953 to 1955, he taught art at St. Louis Country Day School. For the rest of his life, he devoted himself solely to making sculpture.

Severson primarily made art for public places. For the most part, his works were created specifically for their site. He had commissions all over the United States and in Saudi Arabia and Russia. Prominent monuments in St. Louis include works at Oak Knoll Park and in front of the Mercantile Tower on the Gateway Mall. Among other important works is a statue of Danish philosopher-theologian Sören Kierkegaard for the National Cathedral in Washington, D.C. Winning an international competition, he created a sculpture for a building in Jeddah, Saudi Arabia, that pays homage to the Arabic heritage in mathematics. Working with two physicists, the sculptor made a piece incorporating tiny computers within stainless steel tetrahedrons attached to golden spheres. When a telescope senses cosmic rays, it fires commands that cause neon tubes to flash.

In contrast to many of his works, *Continuum*, Severson's name for his sculptural monument at Bellefontaine Cemetery, appears quite simple. The four-sided stone shaft appears to have a diagonal cut to form a diamond-shaped top. *Continuum* is actually made of two pieces representing two partners in a love relationship, like the sculptor and his wife, Grace Seipp Severson, who stand united but separate. In a 1991 article, Severson said of this sculpture, "I understand the yearning for closeness, caring, nurturing, but I also know that there is an inner me and an inner Grace; a chasm we cannot cross that separates us. We reach across in love as friends, sexual partners and parents, but we are still our own islands."[1]

The Seversons started visiting cemeteries because of their interest in genealogy. The artist came to love them as "magical stone forests."[2] His family monument, which appears deceptively simple but is actually quite complex, has added to the magic of Bellefontaine Cemetery.

---

1. *Stone in America*, June 1991, Manuel Garcia files, Bellefontaine Cemetery.
2. Ibid.

COLOR PHOTOGRAPH LIST

PAGE 1

Top: Ellis Wainwright, detail
Bottom: Ellis Wainwright

PAGE 2

Top: Adolphus and Lilly Anheuser Busch
Bottom left: Henry Pierce
Bottom right: Edward Mallinckrodt

PAGE 3

Herman Luyties

PAGE 4

David R. Francis

PAGE 5

James Yeatman

PAGE 6

Top: Ringen family
Bottom: Ann C. T. Farrar

PAGE 7

Samuel Gaty

PAGE 8

Top: Bagnell brothers
Middle: Dr. D. S. Brock
Bottom: William Russell

PORTRAIT PHOTOGRAPH LIST

All photographs are from the collections of the Missouri History Museum, except for that on page 327. In many cases, the photographer and the date of creation are unknown. Only the photographs with identifying information are listed here.

REFERENCE LIST

BOOKS

Ambrose, Stephen. *Undaunted Courage*. New York: Simon & Schuster, 1996.

Baird, John D. *Hawken Rifles: The Mountain Man's Choice*. Big Timber, MT: The Buckskin Press, 1976.

Barnes, Harper. *Standing on a Volcano: The Life and Times of David Rowland Francis*. St. Louis: Missouri Historical Society Press, 2001.

Barry, John. *Rising Tide*. New York: Simon and Schuster, 1997.

Beaumont, William. *Experiments and Observations on the Gastric Juice and the Physiology of Digestion*. Birmingham, AL: The Classics of Medicine Library, 1980.

Boman, Dennis K. *Hamilton Gamble, Lincoln's Resolute Unionist*. Baton Rouge: Louisiana University Press, 2006.

Bremner, Robert P. *Chairman of the Fed: William McChesney Martin Jr. and the Creation of the American Financial System*. New Haven, CT: Yale University Press, 2004.

Bryan, John Albury. *Missouri's Contribution to American Architecture*. St. Louis: St. Louis Architectural Club, 1928.

Buckley, Jay. *William Clark: Indian Diplomat*. Norman: University of Oklahoma Press, 2008.

Cain, Marvin. *Lincoln's Attorney General: Edward Bates of Missouri*. Columbia: University of Missouri Press, 1965.

Carpenter, Margaret Haley. *Sara Teasdale*. New York: Schulte, 1960.

Caveny, Graham. *Gentleman Junkie: The Life and Legacy of William S. Burroughs*. Boston: Little, Brown, 1998.

Chittenden, Hiram Martin. *The American Fur Trade of the Far West*. New York: The Press of the Pioneers, 1933.

Churchill, Winston. *The Crisis*. New York: MacMillan, 1921.

Clarke, Dwight. *Stephen Watts Kearny, Soldier of the West*. Norman: University of Oklahoma Press, 1961.

Colvin, Howard. *Architecture and the Afterlife*. New Haven, CT: Yale University Press, 1984.

Corbett, Katherine T. *In Her Place: A Guide to St. Louis Women's History*. St. Louis: Missouri Historical Society Press, 1999.

Coyle, Elinor M. *Saint Louis: Portrait of a River City*. St. Louis: Folkestone Press, 1966.

Cuoco, Lorin, and William Gass. *Literary St. Louis*. St. Louis: Missouri Historical Society Press, 2000.

Curl, James Stevens. *The Victorian Celebration of Death*. Detroit: Partridge, 1972.

Dains, Mary, ed. *Show Me Missouri Women*. Kirksville, MO: Thomas Jefferson University Press, 1989.

Darby, John. *Personal Recollections of People I Have Known*. St. Louis: G. I. Jones, 1880.

Dictionary of American Biography. The. New York: Charles Scribner's Sons, 1937–1994.

Dorsey, Florence. *The Story of James B. Eads: The Road to the Sea and the Mississippi River*. New York: Rinehart, 1947.

Drake, William. *Sara Teasdale, Woman and Poet*. San Francisco: Harper & Row, 1979.

Eads Bridge, The. Princeton, NJ: The Art Museum of Princeton University, 1974.

Eliot, Charlotte C. *William Greenleaf Eliot: Minister, Educator, Philanthropist*. Boston: Houghton, Mifflin, 1904.

Etlin, Richard. *The Architecture of Death*. Cambridge, MA: MIT Press, 1984.

Ferguson, George. *Signs and Symbols in Christian Art*. London: Oxford University Press, 1971.

Foley, William. *Wilderness Journey: The Life of William Clark*. Columbia: University of Missouri Press, 2004.

Forrestal, Dan J. *Faith, Hope and $5,000*. New York: Simon and Schuster, 1977.

Frankel, Catherine Schaefer. "Mohican Cottage on Lake George." Master's thesis, University of Pennsylvania, 1990.

Garcia, Manuel. *Mark Twain in St. Louis: A Biographical Tour through Bellefontaine Cemetery*. St. Louis: n.p., 2002.

Gerteis, Louis S. *Civil War St. Louis*. Lawrence: University of Kansas Press, 2001.

Goodwin, Doris Kearns. *Team of Rivals*. New York: Simon & Schuster. 2005.

Gould, Emerson. *Fifty Years on the Mississippi: Or, Gould's History of River Navigation*. St. Louis: Nixon-Jones, 1899.

Hafen, LeRoy R. *The Mountain Men and the Fur Trade of the Far West*. Glendale, CA: Arthur H. Clark, 1968.

Hall, Kermit. *The Oxford Companion to the Supreme Court of the United States*. New York: Oxford University Press, 1992.

Havighurst, Walter. *Voices on the River: The Story of the Mississippi Waterways*. New York: Macmillan, 1964.

Hernon, Peter, and Terry Ganey. *Under the Influence: The Unauthorized Story of the Anheuser-Busch Dynasty*. New York: Simon & Schuster, 1991.

Holt, Earl K. *William Greenleaf Eliot: Conservative Radical*. St. Louis: First Unitarian Church, 1985.

Horgan, James J. *City of Flight: The History of Aviation in St. Louis*. Gerald, MO: Patrice Press, 1984.

Horsman, Reginald. *Frontier Doctor: William Beaumont, America's First Great Medical Scientist*. Columbia: University of Missouri Press, 1996.

Hunter, Julius. *Westmoreland and Portland Places*. Columbia: University of Missouri Press, 1988.

Hyde, William, and Howard Conard. *Encyclopedia of the History of Saint Louis*. New York: Southern History Co., 1899.

Irving, Washington. *The Adventures of Captain Bonneville, U.S.A., in the Rocky Mountains and the Far West*. Norman: University of Oklahoma Press, 1986.

Jackson, Robert W. *Rails across the Mississippi: A History of the St. Louis Bridge*. Urbana: University of Illinois Press, 2001.

Jones, Landon. *William Clark and the Shaping of the American West*. New York: Hill & Wang, 2004.

Keister, Douglas. *Going Out in Style*. New York: Facts on File, 1997.

Kennedy, John F. *Profiles in Courage*. New York: Harper Brothers, 1961.

King, Homer W. *Pulitzer's Prize Editor: A Biography of John A. Cockerill, 1845–1896*. Durham, NC: Duke University Press, 1965.

Kirschten, Ernest. *Catfish and Crystal*. Garden City, NY: Doubleday, 1960.

Landmarks Association. *Tombstone Talks*. St. Louis: Author, 1975.

Marion, John Francis. *Famous and Curious Cemeteries*. New York: Crown, 1977.

McCall, Edith. *Mississippi Steamboatman: The Story of Henry Miller Shreve*. New York: Walker, 1966.

McDonnell, Sanford. *This Is Old Mac Calling All the Team*. St. Louis: Author, 1999.

Meigs, William M. *The Life of Thomas Hart Benton*. New York. Da Capo Press, 1904.

Mendelson, Anne. *Stand Facing the Stove*. New York: Henry Holt, 1996.

Meyer, Dr. Jesse S. *Life and Letters of Dr. William Beaumont*. Saint Louis: C. V. Mosby, 1912.

Miles, Barry. *William Burroughs/El Hombre Invisible/A Portrait*. New York: Hyperion, 1993.

Morrison, Hugh. *Louis Sullivan: Prophet of Modern Architecture*. New York: W. W. Norton, 1935.

Nevins, Allen. *The War for the Union*. New York: Scribner's, 1963.

Oglesby, Richard Edward. *Manuel Lisa and the Opening of the Missouri Fur Trade*. Norman: University of Oklahoma Press, 1984.

Parrish, William E. *Frank Blair: Lincoln's Conservative*. Columbia: University of Missouri Press, 1998.

Primm, James Neal. *Lion of the Valley: St. Louis, Missouri, 1764–1980*. St. Louis: Missouri Historical Society Press, 1998.

Rammelkamp, Julian. *Pulitzer's Post-Dispatch, 1878–1883*. Princeton, NJ: Princeton University, 1967.

Roosevelt, Theodore. *Thomas Hart Benton, Gouverneur Morris*. New York: Charles Scribner's Sons, 1926.

Sandweiss, Lee Ann. *Seeking St. Louis: Voices from a River City, 1670–2000*. St. Louis: Missouri Historical Society Press, 2000.

Savage, Charles. *Architecture of the Private Streets of St. Louis*. Columbia: University of Missouri Press, 1987.

Scharf, J. Thomas. *History of St. Louis City and County*. St. Louis: L. H. Everts, 1883.

Shepley, John Rutledge. *Our Family*. Venice, FL: Sunshine, n.d.

Shoemaker, Floyd C. *Missouri, Day by Day*. Columbia: State Historical Society of Missouri, 1942.

Sluyter, Gary V. *St. Louis' Hidden Treasure: A History of the Charless Home, 1853–2003*. St. Louis: The Senior Circuit, 2003.

Smith, Elbert B. *Magnificent Missourian: The Life of Thomas Hart Benton*. New York: J. B. Lippincott, 1958.

Stadler, Frances Hurd. *St. Louis Day by Day*. St. Louis: Patrice Press, 1989.

Steffens, Lincoln. *The Shame of the Cities*. New York: Hill & Wang, 1957.

Stevens, Walter B. *Centennial History of Missouri*. St. Louis: Clarke, 1921.

———. *St. Louis: The Fourth City*. Chicago: Clarke, 1909.

Stewart, Rick, Joseph D. Ketner II, and Angela Miller. *Carl Wimar: Chronicler of the Missouri River Frontier*. Fort Worth, TX: Amon Carter Museum, 1991.

Teasdale, Sara. *Mirror of the Heart*. New York: MacMillan, 1984.

Walker, Stephen P. *Lemp: The Haunting History*. St. Louis: Lemp Preservation Society, 1988.

Winter, William. *The Civil War in St. Louis*. St. Louis: Missouri Historical Society Press, 1997.

NEWSPAPERS AND JOURNALS

Daily Democrat

Gateway Heritage

"How Much Is That?," Economic History Net, http://eh.net/hmit/.

Missouri Historical Review

Missouri Historical Society Bulletin

Missouri Republican

St. Louis Globe-Democrat

St. Louis Post-Dispatch